1. *Actor's Image: "Earth and Heaven Spin in Wild Discord"*

THE DIRECTORIAL IMAGE:

The Play and the Director

FRANK McMULLAN

Associate Professor of Play Production

School of Drama, Yale University

THE SHOE STRING PRESS   Hamden, Connecticut

To
Alexander Dean
Late great teacher and director

CONTENTS

ILLUSTRATIONS

ACKNOWLEDGMENTS

First of all, I acknowledge my incalculable debt to my students, who have taught me more than I can ever teach them. To those who were once my teachers and are now colleagues I express my thanks for their instruction, cooperation, and collaboration—and friendship. I am especially indebted to John Gassner and Alois Nagler, who read this book in manuscript and gave me much-needed advice and encouragement. I appreciate very much, too, the comments and suggestions made by Mrs. Frank P. Bevan.

I thank the following for their permission to quote from the sources noted.

Thomas Y. Crowell Company: *The Theory of Drama*, by Allardyce Nicoll, 1931.

Crown Publishers, Inc.: *Best American Plays*, Third Series—1945-1951, edited by John Gassner, 1952.

George G. Harrap and Company Limited and Harcourt, Brace & World, Inc.: *World Drama*, by Allardyce Nicoll, 1949.

Harvard University Press: *Music and Imagination*, by Aaron Copland, 1952; *Philosophy in a New Key*, by Susanne K. Langer, 1942, 1951.

David Higham, Associates, Ltd.: *The Producer and the Play*, by Norman Marshall, published by McDonald & Co. Ltd., 1957.

McGraw-Hill Book Company, Inc.: *A Life in the Theatre*, by Tyrone Guthrie, 1959.

Meridian Books, Inc.: *Creative Intuition in Art and Poetry*, by Jacques Maritain, 1955. Copyright 1953 by the Trustees of the National Gallery of Art.

Methuen & Co., Ltd.: *The Wheel of Fire*, by G. Wilson Knight, 1949.

Arthur Miller: *All My Sons*, by Arthur Miller. Copyright 1947 by Arthur Miller.

New Directions: *A Streetcar Named Desire*, by Tennessee Williams. Copyright 1947 by Tennessee Williams.

The New York Times: "That Beast, the Audience," by Rebecca Franklin, *The New York Times Magazine*, April 29, 1951; "Second

Chance," by Brooks Atkinson, *The New York Times,* July 8, 1956; "Tragedy to Scale," by Brooks Atkinson, *The New York Times,* August 1, 1957.

W. W. Norton & Company, Inc.: *Arts and the Man,* by Irwin Edman, 1928, 1939.

Princeton University Press: *Billy Budd,* by Louis O. Coxe and Robert Chapman, 1951; *Prefaces to Shakespeare,* by Harley Granville-Barker, 1946; *The Idea of a Theatre,* by Francis Fergusson, 1949.

Random House, Inc.: *Detective Story,* by Sidney Kingsley, 1949; *Plays of Anton Tchekov,* translated by Constance Garnett, 1930; *Masters of the Drama,* by John Gassner, 1940.

Charles Scribner's Sons: *The Man Who Lived Twice,* by Eric Wollencott Barnes, 1956.

Simon and Schuster, Inc.: *A Treasury of the Theatre,* edited by Burns Mantle and John Gassner. Copyright 1935, 1940, 1950, 1951 by Simon & Schuster, Inc.

The Viking Press, Inc.: *Death of a Salesman,* by Arthur Miller, 1957.

Photographs of productions at the Yale University Theatre are used with the permission of the Commercial Photo Service Company, New Haven, Connecticut; the photograph of *Measure for Measure* at Stratford-on-Avon with the permission of Angus McBean, the photographer; that of *Look Homeward, Angel* with the permission of the Teatro de Ensayo, Santiago, Chile; that of *Ah, Wilderness* with the permission of the Wellesley College Summer Theatre; that of *Othello* with the permission of the Old Globe Theatre, San Diego, California.

My thanks are due also to Mr. and Mrs. John Ottemiller, publishers of The Shoe String Press, a firm whose very name has always been associated with the theatre.

Finally, I acknowledge my deep debt of gratitude to my wife, without whose editorial and stylistic advice and assistance, patience, understanding, and devotion this book would never have reached publication.

F.M.

Woodbridge, Connecticut
December 4, 1961

INTRODUCTION

Play *interpretation* is a subject much understressed and often neglected in extant literature on play production. The space devoted to it is disproportionately small in relation to its importance. The emphasis in most publications has been on the procedures and techniques of the physical production, which are, of course, more easily explainable, less controversial, and perhaps more factual than interpretation. The "how" too often takes precedence over the "what" and the "why" in the teaching and practice of play production.

The primacy of the play establishes the principle that play interpretation, the "what" and "why" of play production, is the creative basis for the "how." The moment a director decides to use a particular setting with a particular shape, mass, line, and color he reveals his understanding of the play for which the scenery is proposed. The casting of an actor and every movement, gesture, posture, vocal inflection, and emotional expression he uses in performance stem from the director's interpretation—assuming that the director's conception of the play is the controlling and integrating factor of the production. As the coordinator of the production, the director unifies its different aspects through his interpretation. The directing, acting, ground plan, setting, costumes, make-up, lighting, and music of a production represent the purpose and meaning of a play. Play interpretation must then be conceived to make the director's interpretive and technical processes creative.

The art of play directing, like any other art, emanates from individual desire and need to be creative. These motivating forces are stimulated by the need of communicating with an audience. Quite simply, creativity expresses the common hunger of man to speak to his fellow man about mankind. The theatre director, through his directorial creativity, speaks to the audience. In the process of play interpretation the director imagines a dramatic experience for the audience. The director stands between the play and the audience. He receives impressions, stimuli, and ideas from the play and transmits them in kind, amount, and extent to the audience. Moreover, like any other artist, he responds to the original stimulus and seeks to arouse in others a pattern of responses like his own.

Creative interpretation arises out of the director's understanding of the audience and of the special nature, structure, and meaning of a play as a medium for evoking the emotional and intellectual response of the audience. The study of creative interpretation must then be, in part, a study of the audience and the play in terms of the special nature of the dramatic and theatrical.

There is no absolute interpretive formula, system, or procedure which the director can follow to assure complete success in the theatre. His individual capacity for imagination, perception, choice, and decision will always make or mar play interpretation and direction. A play possesses its own individuality and no mechanical divining rod will plumb its mystery. The director can learn to be aware of the life-giving dramatic forces lying hidden in a play. He must know whether or not they exist and in what manner to bring them to life on the stage for an audience.

The process of play interpretation is more than a matter of cold analysis of the structure and values of a play; it is an emotional activity as well. In fact, for the director, the emotional aspect of the activity is of prime importance because of its potentialities for creative stimulation. Too, the director must understand a play through its emotionalizing dynamics if he is to succeed in communicating to and arousing in the audience the dramatic nature of a play. The director interprets a play by adopting a collective personality like that of the audience. To read the play and visualize it as it will be in performance, aided by the physical elements of production, he must allow himself to respond with his full emotional capabilities. He must submerge himself in the complete imagined theatrical experience which the play intends for the audience. Imagining this experience is a creative process.

Interpretation as a creative process involves numerous readings of the play. The director's first reading and spontaneous response should be similar to the audience's reaction to the play in performance. All subsequent readings should enrich, deepen, and define this response, which should remain highly emotional and/or intuitive in nature. The ultimate intellectualization of the director's response should never drive out the emotional concomitants. His imagination must feed upon them. However, they are often elusive, transistory, and vague. They must be caught, fixed, and organized in the mind of the director if they are to be used for creative purposes. There are various ways of doing this. The one used often by directors is that of the image. Max Reinhardt used to say that he was always surrounded by images.

The directorial image, its purpose and function, is the basis of the approach to play interpretation and direction to be presented in this book. The approach and the various phases necessary for interpretation constitute the search for and discovery of images which will serve as creative food for the director.

The first phase consists of the director's immediate, spontaneous, intuitive response to stimuli provided by the play on the initial reading.

From the dialogue will emerge images of the characters and their behavior—who they are, what they are doing, and why they are doing it. These images form the basis of the director's creative interpretation of the play. His uninhibited response to the play and his subsequent search for creative images constitute this first phase of play interpretation. (The general subject of creativity is examined further in the chapter "Creativity and the Director.")

The second phase consists of a more definitely intellectual and critical response to the play. (Of course, such a response cannot be eliminated entirely from the very first reading of the play. It forms a sort of running commentary to the emotional response.) This phase is analytical. The director must approach the play with the avowed purpose of finding those inherent elements which make it dramatic and stageworthy. He asks himself how the playwright has treated his materials in order to create a potential theatrical experience for the audience. He must then determine *whether* and *how* the playwright can capture the audience's attention and involve it in the dramatic problem of the play. This is a consideration of the play's over-all compulsion. Afterward the director analyzes the play for its individual architecture: its design and structure. And finally, in this phase of the creative interpretation, he determines its unity. The emphasis in the process, it is to be noted, is on the totality of the play. (The chapters on "Dramatic Communication and Response" and "Nature and Pattern of Drama" relate to this phase.)

The director enters into the third phase of creative interpretation when he studies to determine how the playwright has, by his treatment of dramatic values, given the play individuality and set it apart from all others. In this study the director examines the parts which make up the whole. He analyzes each element of mood, theme, dialogue, character, and plot to discover the individual dramatic dynamics of each. The discovery and understanding of these dynamics is of major importance in the director's detailed work with the actors. (See "Potentials of Dramatic Values.")

The fourth phase of creative interpretation involves the focus of the play in terms of emphasis and dominance of dramatic values. The selection of a particular dramatic problem causes the playwright to arrange and organize his materials in such a way as to focus the attention of the audience upon the purpose and meaning

of the play. Whereas the director explores the dynamics of individual dramatic values in order to exploit each in production,
he must determine which one or more are primary and which
are contributory. His directorial and productional approach, procedure, and use of kind and amount of technique are dependent
upon the determination of the dominant dramatic value or values.
This phase of interpretation is the search for the playwright's
main purpose in writing the play and is the audience's key
to what the play is about. The failure of the director to
find and emphasize the dominant dramatic value can change
the author's intention and distort the specific meaning of
the play, which gives the play and production unity: The parts
find their purposed relationship to one another and to the configuration effected by the type and style of play. (See "Points
of Focus.")

The fifth and last phase consists of the integration of the
preceding four phases into an interpretive pattern based upon an
over-all image. This image, emanating from disciplined emotion
and analysis, is used as a stimulant to creativity. (See "Directorial
Image.")

In conclusion, creative interpretation consists of five phases,
which are explained in the following chapters of this book:

1. Creativity and the Director
2. Dramatic Communication and Response
   Nature and Pattern of Drama
3. Potentials of Dramatic Values
4. Points of Focus
5. Directorial Image

THE   DIRECTORIAL   IMAGE

1

Creativity and the Director

INDIVIDUAL EXPRESSION

THE HIERARCHY of artistic relationships in the modern theatre is well established and recognized. At the top is the playwright, who is responsible for originating the play, the starting point of theatrical production. His position entitles him to definite rights vested in origination and creative purpose. All the other artists of the theatre are auxiliary to the playwright and cannot work without him except in those rare instances in which they create in collaboration something to take the place of the formal play. As auxiliary artists they have certain obligations to the playwright. Chief of the auxiliary artists is the director. He stands between the playwright, his play, and the audience. As middleman he is the controlling medium for communicating the play to the audience. His function consists of interpreting the play and creating the performances and production.

In the professional theatre and in the university theatre the director may also work very closely with the playwright in the writing and shaping of the play for production. In this relationship the director can become more than an interpreter: He can become a creator. The more creative he is the more he tends to become part playwright. This tendency sometimes results in the director's usurpation of the position of the playwright and the consequent controversies, artistic and financial. The letters exchanged between Elia Kazan and Archibald MacLeish and published in *Esquire* in 1959[1] on the writing and production of *J.B.* illustrate the working relationship of director and playwright in the professional theatre. An article about the New York production of *J.B.* by Brooks Atkinson in *The New York Times*[2] discusses this relationship and the question of the director's interpretive and creative function. Kazan's work with Tennessee Williams has also been controversial, as evidenced by the comparison of the scripts of the Broadway productions of Williams' plays with the published versions. Joshua Logan's production of William Inge's *Picnic* also raised the question of the director's relationship to the playwright.[3]

However, it is not only the director's work with the original play which is controversial. His production of the established play and the classic also poses the question of his relationship to the playwright. Among others, the great English director Tyrone Guthrie has been accused of deviating from the author's intended meaning and even distorting it. In his *A Life in the Theatre* he says, "Throughout my own career I have been criticized for impertinently attempting to express my own subjective, and admittedly limited, comment upon the masterpieces which I have been privileged to direct."[4] He and other directors, it has been alleged, have given themselves too much latitude in interpreting plays. The noted critic T. C. Worsley takes him to task specifically in his review of Guthrie's production of *Henry VIII* and implies that he is an exemplar of the " 'Wouldn't-it-be-fun (just for a change)' school" of directors.[5]

Actually, the indictment is against stepping over the bounds of pure interpretation into the realm of personal expression. The problem then involves the role of the director as interpreter and creator, and the problem has been complicated by the fact that interpretation is usually thought of as an objective process and creation as a subjective one. The truth of the matter is that interpretation involves creative work and is largely subjective.

As a work of art a play must appeal to the imagination not only of the audience but of the director and all those intermediary artists that communicate it to the audience. When a director's imagination is stimulated by a play he responds by visualizing and hearing it as a series of images.

The first image evoked by the play is a stimulus for expression. The moment the director reads the title of the play he responds imagistically and consciously or unconsciously formulates an attitude toward it. This attitude is the result of mental associations and feelings. His past experiences and knowledge—the sum total of his intellectual and emotional make-up—formulate his response. As he reads the names of the characters and their brief descriptions and relationships in the list of *dramatis personae* he takes another step in the process of expression. The description of the setting of the play, the time of day, the season of the year, the weather, and the historical period stimulates his mind and emotions further. The reading of the play, word by word, speech by speech, scene by scene, and act by act, works upon his thoughts and feelings to evoke a sequence of images which forms a pattern resulting in a larger image of the play as a whole. Needless to say, each image and the whole pattern of images are individual to the particular director. They cannot be evoked or conceived in the same way by

anyone else. This means that each director will imagine and perceive and produce a play in a way different from that of anyone
else. Then can each one express the playwright's image of the
play or his over-all intention in writing it?

Tyrone Guthrie answers this by saying that "The meaning of
any work of art is subjective. It is not what the author thinks it
means. If the objective meaning of a work of art were known,
there would be no point in its existence. It exists merely to suggest
many ways in which an undefined truth may be approached. Every
interpretation is subjective. Some will be nearer to objective truth
than others, but not on that account necessarily more interesting
than others."[6] The difficulties inherent in discovering the objective
and exact intention of the playwright support this view.

How can the director find this intention? If the playwright is
alive he can say what it is. But when he says what the intention
is he may be relying primarily on his imagination, and he may not
be fully aware that what he imagines will undergo a transformation
when it is placed on the stage. The corporeal existence of the characters as projected by the personalities, voices, and behavior of the
actors can be quite different from what has been imagined from
reading the printed page. Qualities, values, and meanings can
undergo changes. Even experienced playwrights often fail to take
this into consideration. Eric Wollencott Barnes, writing about
Edward Sheldon's reaction to the production of his play *Salvation
Nell*, starring Minnie Maddern Fiske, gives us an example of this
when he says "It was one thing to have written the play, and quite
another to see it take on life under the combined efforts of director,
actors, and scene designer.

"What struck him as truly wonderful was how much the play
contained that he had never been aware of himself, especially when
Mrs. Fiske began to work on the character of Nell. It was like
some miraculous growth, as day by day the personality born in
Ned's mind became merged with that of the actress, flowering in
unexpected ways as it did so."[7]

Another aspect of the matter is that the playwright can say
that the intention of the play is thus and so but the play as written
may not project that intention. The playwright may *intend* one
thing and actually *write* another. Directors who have worked with
original plays, professional or student, know this to be true. The
matter is further complicated by the fact that sometimes a playwright writes out of purely spontaneous feelings and thoughts
and afterward reads into his work a so-called intention.

Others reading the script or seeing it performed may or may
not have this intention communicated to them. Sometimes a play-

wright can formulate an intention and consciously write to dramatize it. Even so, he may fail to project it in the writing. But what
of the classics which, by virtue of the excellence and artistry of
their writing, do project their meaning and intention? The plays
of Shakespeare, the greatest classics written in the English language,
which are produced more often than any others, can be considered
in this connection.

The history of Shakespearean criticism and production gives
ample proof that each play has been interpreted and produced in
a variety of ways. The definitive "objective meaning"[8] has not yet
been discovered and universally agreed upon for a single one.
There have been many successful and effective interpretations and
productions of *Hamlet,* for instance. In the modern theatre the
productions of the play with John Barrymore, Maurice Evans, and
John Gielgud playing Hamlet are memorable. Not only Hamlet
but the other characters, as well as the various scenes of the play,
were differently interpreted and presented. As a consequence, the
directing and the elements of the physical production were different.
However, it can also be said that each of these productions was
similar to the others in certain definite aspects. Each interpretation
and production did project the tragedy and the quintessential
meaning of the play. The subjectivity of the director and the actors
of each did permit a degree of latitude of individual expression
but a limit was set by the frame of reference established by the
play. What has been said about *Hamlet* can be said in general
about the other great tragedies. *Macbeth,* though, is sometimes presented as a violent Elizabethan melodrama with the approval of
many scholars and critics. The Shakespearean comedies and the
"dark comedies" particularly have had a wider and more divergent
variety of interpretations and productions than have the tragedies.
Directors have allowed themselves almost unrestrained freedom
in producing these plays, evincing little regard for traditional interpretations and what can be considered their general meaning and
tone. The generally recognized great tragedies, about which the
differences of critical opinion are narrowest, have been subject to
more limited directorial expression than the other plays. Yet the
fact is that all the plays of Shakespeare have lent themselves to
the highly subjective interpretations of directors. There has been
merely a question of amount of personal latitude.

Some directorial latitude must be permitted because of the
practical problems inherent in the interpretation and production
of plays originally written for stages and audiences quite different
from ours today. The classics demand a certain amount of restate-
ment for modern audiences, and their original intention cannot

be communicated in all aspects. Not only have the physical conditions of staging changed but so have audience attitudes. To give only one example, *The Merchant of Venice*, originally conceived according to most scholars as a play about a comic Jew, is seldom so interpreted and produced today. Dramatic values shift with the passage of time. Even the plays of the last few decades are subject to reappraisal because of changes in world thought and feeling. Therefore the director now finds it necessary to stress certain values which were not most important when the plays were conceived and written. For instance, *Ghosts* cannot today have the same meaning that it had for the original audiences. Its interest for us today lies mostly in the character of Mrs. Alving. The long thematic scenes between her and Pastor Manders have difficulty in holding the interest of a modern audience. Even many plays written since World War I have lost their original meaning and necessitate a different emphasis if they are to be made acceptable at all to audiences today. Dramatic literature is strongly subject to temporal factors, and if the director is concerned with audience psychology and reactions he must consider this. The author's original meaning and intention must possess interpretive elasticity in order to endure. Surely the intelligent and practical director must possess the imagination and flexibility of thinking necessary for production. Creativity is necessary in interpretation. But, for example, does his creativity extend to willful and arbitrary changing of a play's values in order to take advantage of temporary world political conditions?

This question can be asked about some of the Shakespearean productions presented just before and during World War II. It can be asked particularly about productions of *Coriolanus* and *Julius Caesar*, which were so interpreted as to emphasize the theme of fascism in conflict with democracy, a theme evidently not originally intended by Shakespeare. The Orson Welles production of the latter on Broadway in 1937 was brilliantly timely and exciting to audiences painfully aware of the evil and predatory dictators Mussolini and Hitler. The entire production of the play was predicated upon an interpretation capitalizing upon its timely meaning. The bare stage, the modern military uniforms worn by the actors, the harsh, stabbing rays of light, the heavily rhythmic atonal music, and the quietly realistic style of acting took the play out of its era and, except for its verse, made it contemporary. But was it Shakespeare, the scholar may ask. It was certainly not the Shakespeare that audiences had come to expect. It was not the Shakespeare they had studied reluctantly in high school and it was not the Shakespeare the college English professor passed on from

Granville-Barker and Caroline Spurgeon. But it was theatre and it was successful Shakespeare seen in a new and meaningful light for modern audiences. A traditional production of the play, even with star actors dressed in Roman togas and giving the well-known speeches on steps that are often reminiscent of those at the county courthouse probably would have had little interest and meaning, much less excitement, for people on the brink of another world war. Is a director doing a disservice to a play even if it is a classic by placing it in the context of contemporary thought? Is Shakespeare of an age but not for all time?

Another illustration of directorial interpretive latitude is the tendency of some directors to "kid" plays. The melodramas of the nineteenth century and the first two decades of the twentieth century, particularly, have been subjected to kidding. Period plays, including the classics, have also been victims. In productions so approached the plays become chronological jokes. The directors make little attempt to interpret the plays except to comment upon them in such a way as to make fun of the original dramatic values. Recent productions of *Ten Nights in a Barroom, East Lynne,* and similar romantic melodramas have been treated this way, to the delight of the twentieth-century audience. Plays and musicals of the twenties have also been held up to ridicule and laughter. Some of the minor Elizabethan and Restoration plays have been similarly treated by directors. Even the lesser known works of Shakespeare have not escaped such maltreatment. Is there then no limit to the director's freedom of individual expression?

The answer probably lies in the individual director's philosophy regarding his position in the hierarchy of artistic relationships and obligations in the theatre. Specifically, he must decide whether he serves the drama or the drama serves him. If he decides the latter, he can use the play as a skeleton of a dead play upon which to embroider an evening's entertainment for his own personal exhibitionism and the audience's momentary pleasure. In serving the drama he can strive to find the playwright's general intention, difficult as that is. This can be done even though the exigencies of the times and staging conditions may force him to emphasize certain aspects of the play not originally intended. By adhering to the frame of reference established by the play, by preserving the spiritual and intellectual qualities of the play, by refusing to distort the original so as to create something new and in violation of the original, the director can achieve a high degree of art in his own work through "the power of acting creatively under the laws of its own origination."[9] With "the play as a work of art in an individual creation requiring individual assessment even when the playwright has made a commitment to specific principles"[10] he can "learn to create theatre with the text . . ."[11] He must see himself as an auxiliary creator one step removed from the main creator, the playwright, and thus lacking absolute freedom of expression. He is interpretive and creative, basing his creativity upon interpretation and the media of play production. As such, he works as all creative artists do, using his imagination, perception, and judgment to originate something: his particular and individual interpretation and production. His creativity begins with the impulse to create.

THE CREATIVE IMPULSE

The creative impulse is possessed by everyone and finds expression in everyone. This expression is not always artistic and it varies in imaginativeness and intensity from individual to individual. At its most imaginative, intense, and powerful it can achieve the heights of art. At lower levels the creative impulse and self-expression take the form of pastime and diversion. In the artist-director expression is based on a desire to say something about life. To be creative is to be godlike and, at the same time, to express the relationship between God and man. It is a source of deep spiritual satisfaction. Moreover, the urge to creativity is forever resurgent and never satisfied. Aaron Copland writes of this in the composer of music and also points out that "The reason for the compulsion to renewed creativity, it seems to me, is that each added work brings with it an element of self-discovery." He goes on to say that creativity is continuous throughout life because man's "self-knowledge is a never-ending search . . ." Thus creativity is important to the artist; but why is it important to others? Copland's answer is: ". . . just as the individual creator discovers himself through his creation, so the world at large knows itself through its artists, discovers the very nature of its Being through the creation of its artists."[12] This is as true of creativity in the theatre as in music.

The theatrical director-artist, when reading a play, hearing about one, or seeing one, may say to himself, "I must do that play." This expresses a desire to create. His directing one play after another is an attempt to assuage this desire. With each succeeding play he discovers something about himself and life through its characters, language, and action. He in turn reveals to the members of the audience something about themselves and himself.

THE CREATIVE PROCESS

Creativity may occur as a matter of inspiration or it may be induced, consciously or subconsciously, by stimuli emanating from life, the play, and the media for its production. The presence of stimuli for creativity is felt in a moment in which the creator is possessed by what Coleridge called "a more than usual state of emotion."[13] This is the creative state. (De Quincy is said to have taken opium and Edgar Allan Poe drink to induce the creative emotion.) This state is one of heightened emotion in which the creator is hypersensitive to aural, visual, mental, and sensory stimuli. In response to these stimuli an image is formulated, which may be a conceptual idea, a mental picture, a symbol, a metaphor, a simile, or some other vivid embodiment or representation of the director's emotional reaction to the play as a whole and to the parts of the play making up the whole.

To illustrate the use of a conceptual idea by the director we may cite a particular scene from a play. If, for example, we are directing Thornton Wilder's *The Skin of Our Teeth* and come to the scene near the end of Act I in which Mr. Antrobus is teaching Henry the multiplication table and Mrs. Antrobus is teaching Gladys the beginning of the Bible, the question naturally arises regarding the meaning to be communicated to the audience. If the director can arrive at a conceptual idea which sums up the meaning of the scene, he can take the first step in directorial creativity. The second step consists of determining the technique needed to convey this conceptual idea. The conceptual idea for the scene might be expressed by the words "Together, the human race can be saved by knowledge." To communicate this to the audience in visual terms Mr. and Mrs. Antrobus must be near their children to teach them. The director might place Mr. Antrobus and Henry on one side of the stage, with Mrs. Antrobus and Gladys on the other—the two visual units separated. This staging, however, fails to convey the "togetherness of the family." If the human race is to be saved, the family must stay together. And it must help one another, just as all members of the human race must stay together and help one another. Therefore, if the director places the family together around a table, center, or together with father and mother seated on a sofa and children on the floor in front of them, this togetherness will be graphically conveyed to the audience. The meaning of the entire scene—involving the Muses, Judge, Homer, Doctor, and Professor, as well as the Antrobus family—can be made clear visually by placing the family in the center of the stage surrounded in a semicircle by the other representatives of the human race. Thus a conceptual idea is dramatized creatively.

This creative activity involves what Susanne K. Langer calls "the comprehension of an unspoken idea." She goes on to say that it "must be sustained, complete, and intense; his [the artist's] intellectual excitement . . . at fever pitch. The idea is his own, and if he loses his command of it, confused by the material or distracted by pressing irrelevancies, there is no symbol to hold it for him." (This thought is the outgrowth of her philosophy of "symbolic transformation.") "His mind is apt to be furiously active while an artistic conception takes shape."[14]

Regarding symbols Miss Langer says, "The material furnished by the senses is constantly wrought into *symbols,* which are our elementary ideas. Some of these ideas can be combined and manipulated in the manner we call 'reasoning.' Others do not lend themselves to this use, but are naturally telescoped into dreams, or *vapor off in conscious fantasy . . .*"[15] Let us look at an example of the director's practical use of the symbol.

When Jed Harris directed *The Green Bay Tree* in New York, James Dale who played Mr. Dulcimer had a piece of business at the end of the act which symbolized his whole attitude as a character. The boy Julian, whom Dulcimer had adopted and reared, had brought home his fiancée to meet his foster father. At the end of the evening they left to go to the girl's home. Immediately after they made their exit, Dale turned his back to the audience and slowly clenched his fist. This symbolized his thought and attitude far more eloquently than words could express. Not only was the clenched fist connotative to the audience but the fingers, looking like so many tentacles of an octopus, slowly closed on the invisible Julian and his fiancée in the hollow of Dulcimer's hand. Now, this symbolization must have been consciously or subconsciously in the mind of the director or the actor or both. The director and the actor often create without being conscious of their stimulus. Perhaps this bit of business came not from the use of symbols but from a knowledge of the psychology of the behavior of the character. Yet certainly the symbolism made the psychology clear.

In a production of Ibsen's *Ghosts,* Madame Nazimova or her director consciously used the symbol of the cross at the final curtain when she stood at the window with outstretched arms as Oswald cried out, "The sun. The sun."

The importance of the image to the director is its value as a stimulant to creativity. It stirs the emotions as well as the mind, exhilarates, and encourages inspiration. It can represent a vague and fugitive or a definite and everlasting feeling, an abstract or concrete idea. Harold Clurman, in writing about "The Principles of Interpretation," speaks of the director's crystallizing

> in himself a general sense of the play . . . The sense of the play [which I call mood; see pp. 71-76] is not an intellectual perception of the play's theme—this is a critical function . . . It is a personal image or feeling peculiar to the director. My first reaction to Clifford Odets' *Awake and Sing!* was a sense of chaos. This chaos could be described in terms of conflicting colors laid on "cubistically" in uneven patches one over the other, or of incongruous combinations of objects, of voices in counterpoint. While this chaos, like all disorder, had its comic side, it was, in this instance, essentially melancholy.[16]

Robert Lewis, another highly esteemed director, illustrates the use of the image in the practical realm of directing when he writes about his production of Saroyan's *My Heart's in the Highlands:*

> . . . the nature of the script, which was an episodic and poetic treatment of an idea, demanded a production which would crystallize it in theatre terms; for without this treatment, it would have seemed disjointed and choppy. In addition to the usual work on the psychological meaning and development of the performance, it was necessary therefore to find the *poetic* expression of that content, the clearest way to say it, the simplest, or if you will, the most "refined" way; to look for the highest expression of a given impulse . . . to arrive at an *image* to convey the feeling.
>
> For example, at one point the old man with the trumpet plays a song for the villagers and they give him food. The feeling I had about this moment was: the people are nourished by art. The image that came to my mind was: *a plant flowering as it is watered.* I translated this into staging by having the old man above on the porch, playing his trumpet, with the villagers below grouped tightly together built up like a tree. This picture was built up from people kneeling, to a child held high on somebody's shoulders; by having each person conceal his colorful article of food, and slowly, as the music played, having all of them hold aloft their offerings, as if these were growing out of the branches of a large tree . . .[17]

These are two illustrations of the use of the directorial image. The first shows how, in terms of interpretation, it can represent the play as a whole, and the second shows how interpretation can formulate the actual pictorial dramatization of a scene. When directing the last act of Shaw's *Heartbreak House*, the director conceivably might have the image of a graveyard, suggested by the decadent, dying Europe symbolized by this house—a ship of state. The characters sitting immobile on the terrace are so many tombstones, cold, moss covered, straight, and unbending.

Another practical example of a director's evocation of imagery might be illustrated by the scene involving the wedding in *The Taming of the Shrew*. When studying the scene in which Gremio describes the wedding ceremony which took place off stage, the director might visualize it and be so stimulated by the various images called up that he decides to show it on stage. This, as conceived, would involve a wedding procession. Since the spirit of the play is slapstick comic, the procession could not be executed seriously or realistically. Consciously or unconsciously, it could be seen as though it were a locomotive (the priest at the head of the procession), followed by the various cars (the other characters). But this train would not slide along the tracks smoothly and continuously. It would go forward, then backward, to a syncopated beat. Accordingly, music would be composed to accomplish this. This is an example of a piece of business evolving from an image. Another is exemplified by so staging Hamlet's death scene that he dies on the throne. The image could stem from the ironic thought that Hamlet occupied in death the throne that he never held while living. Claudius was out of the way and no longer usurped his rights. Another director's image is obvious in Forbes-Robertson's having Hamlet borne aloft on a shield to the singing of an angel choir.

The use of imagery in the director's work with actors is very stimulating to both director and actor. For example, the director may conceive of a character shaped like a barrel. His barrel-like qualities may be expressed not only in his enormous stomach but in his deep vocal tones and in his barrel roll of a walk. Michael Chekhov, in *To the Actor*, has a chapter on images and says that once you have an image you must ask it questions, "see" the image of a character making certain movements and participating in different character relationships. He says, "The images which I see with the mind's eye have their own psychology, like the people surrounding me in my everyday life."[18]

It is reported that, when Elia Kazan told the designer for the setting of George Tabori's *Flight into Egypt* that it should be a hole-like trap with a long escape corridor, he had an image of the characters in this environment, which in physical and psychological terms expressed the meaning of the play.

Obviously, the directorial image can be translated into all the various aspects of play production.

In seeking stimulation for imagery, the director will find the words and word patterns helpful sources. A. C. Bradley, in his *Shakespearean Tragedy*, clearly shows the importance of atmosphere and imagery emanating from the poetry of the plays. His discussion of the blackness of night and the redness of the bloody deeds in *Macbeth*[19] may be considered a key to the mood, theme, and total interpretation of the play. Caroline Spurgeon's studies in word imagery which followed the pioneer work of Bradley pointed the way for a general interpretive procedure for the plays of Shakespeare. G. Wilson Knight, in his *The Wheel of Fire*, brilliantly illustrates his use of image, symbol, and metaphor in interpreting Shakespeare. His suggestions regarding the creative process of interpretation for Shakespeare are equally valid for all drama.

In order to interpret creatively the director must submerge himself in the play and merge himself with it. In writing "On the Principles of Shakespeare Interpretation" in *The Wheel of Fire,* Knight points out that the "Interpretation . . . tends to merge into the work it analyses . . ." In merging with the play the director becomes a part of the world of the playwright. It is only then that he can make, in the words of Knight, "interpretation a reconstruction of a vision."[20] This is the creative vision of the playwright. The feeling and understanding of the vision are the beginning and goal of interpretation.

The play itself is the basis for this reconstruction, but the knowledge of the author's world, his life, his dramatic work, and his creative intentions and technique contributes strongly to this understanding. For example, O'Neill wrote *The Long Voyage Home* and his other plays about the sea from his actual experiences and observations of life at sea. They represent things seen, remembered, and felt. They were created out of emotions and attitudes. In order to understand *The Long Voyage Home*, the director should study and absorb the feeling and meaning of O'Neill's other sea plays, his own writings about them, and the various accounts of his way of working as a playwright. A study of the general conditions of seafaring, a study of national and world social, economic, political, and cultural conditions at the time of the writing of the play, and a study of O'Neill as a person at this particular time of his life will help the director to understand the play and particularly the writer's view of life as exemplified by it. A study of the physical theatre, the actors, and the audience for which O'Neill wrote is also helpful. A knowledge of the dramatic literature, its subject matter, techniques, and conventions, and the dramatic criticism of the era is essential.

The discovery of the world of the playwright and his creative vision will serve as a definite source of imagery for interpretation and production. However, the director's response to and evocation of imagery require a certain state of mind.

Willing and positive receptivity without the disturbing forces of questioning and criticism is necessary for achieving complete creative feeling and understanding. As Knight points out, "We should not, in fact, think critically at all: we should interpret our original imaginative experience into the slower consciousness of logic and intellect, preserving something of that child-like faith which we possess, in the theatre."[21]

In responding to the play for creative reasons, the director must give his feelings and thoughts free rein in order to open himself up for creative preparation. The first readings of a play should be used specifically to evoke completely free spontaneous images. These images may be the literal picturization of the behavior of the characters in their particular scenic environments—like a sequence of motion picture "frames" of detailed action—or they may be metaphoric or symbolic. Both kinds of images are stimulating and creative. The metaphoric and symbolic, however, being suggestive rather than specific, tend to stir the director to continuous creativity rather than terminal creativity resulting from the literal picturing of something. If on reading *The Long Voyage Home* the director pictures in detail a water-front bar with the characters moving in a series of literal images, he tends to stop creativity. He merely waits until he can duplicate in actual production everything exactly as he imagined it, whereas if he uses metaphors or symbols to represent the play in its various aspects his images become emotionally and intellectually evocative and generative of something that feeds the imagination to increased and ever-flowing creativity. These kinds of images may not come so freely or so easily as the literal ones. They must be encouraged and even sought after.

The selection and ordering of images will begin to take place through the director's subconscious and intuitive perception of relationships and patterns inherent in the playwright's concept and intention, and his dramaturgical design of the play. When the director arrives at the last step in his interpretive procedure he should consciously seek images which will conform to the order and concept emerging from his interpretive vision of the play. Individual images of the components of the play will order themselves into a perceived pattern which is telescoped into one large over-all image of the play as a whole.

In seeking an over-all image for *The Long Voyage Home* the director might conceive of the play as a trap. Specifically, this large image could evoke for the director feelings and thoughts which emerge from the smaller images of the trapping of animals by hunters. This result could be gained from the characters, plot, and theme of the play imagistically perceived. Then, applying his imagery to the play, the director might divide the characters into hunters and the hunted, thus activating his image by changing the noun form of the word into the verb form: to entrap. The image "to entrap" could be the basis of all creativity for the production of this play—directing, acting, scenery, costumes, lighting, and sound. A concrete expression of the image can be illustrated by the following.

A low ceiling and raked walls of a set shaped like a triangle could enclose the action of the play in such a way as to *entrap* the sailors, especially Ollie. The dim lighting, the drinking, the knock-out drops, the seductive sounds of the phonograph music, the presence and behavior of the girls, the behavior of Joe, Nick, and their henchmen could all assist in the baiting and the springing of the trap. (The director's use of the image of a trap and the verb form of the word would also stimulate the imaginations of the designers of the setting and lighting and the actors as well.)

The director might then divide the play into scenes and find an image for each. For example, the first scene in which Nick and Joe plot to attract the sailors to the bar for the purpose of kidnapping one of them might be conceived in terms of the image "the decoy," another hunting image. Nick is set up as the decoy, of course, and the word could serve as an image for creating his character. Translating the image into a verb, the actor playing Nick can find his over-all objective to be "to lure." His movement and speech can be accordingly based on the words "to lure." Furthermore, extending the use of the image, the director and designer might dress Nick to *suggest* a sailor to attract other sailors to him to lure them into the trap. Images then could be used for the rest of the scenes and the characters.

Certainly the directorial techniques could be based on images for the pictorial dramatization, movement, and sound of the play. The over-all interpretive image will integrate and unify these aspects and will place upon the production of the play the director's individual creative hallmark.

The over-all interpretive image, however, should not harden the director's emotions and freeze his inspiration but rather should be a continuous source for creation. In order to arrive at his image he has to progress from free and spontaneous imagistic responses through phases of objectification. Emotion and thought become disciplined. But it must be remembered that discipline should be invoked to control and not to destroy emotion. Creative emotion should flow freely, though channeled according to the needs and purpose of the play.

CREATIVITY AND SUDDEN WONDER

Possessed of the aesthetic emotion, the director conceives of a moment imagistically or metaphorically in such an original and unexpected way that the audience will be taken by surprise and moved to sudden delighted laughter or thrilling excitement. The creative process consists of bringing into being something that never existed before or of varying something already in existence in a new way. This element of the unexpected evokes the suprise and astonishment which accompany all that we associate with imagination, originality, and creativity. Tyrone Guthrie is one of the few masters of such directorial creativity, as shown by his New York production of Pirandello's *Six Characters in Search of an Author* in 1956. One example was the breath-taking appearance of the six characters in the midst of a scene of the play-within-the-play being rehearsed on stage by the comic actors. The scene in progress consisted of wildly amusing antics and quick swirling movement in one direction and the surprising entrance of the black-swathed members of the family from the opposite direction. Here was theatrical magic in a play whose meaning revolved about the difference between illusion and reality. The directorial principle of contrast was beautifully illustrated here: contrast in mood emanating from contrast in movement, tempo, and audience focus of attention. Peter Brook also illustrated this in his 1946 production of *Love's Labor's Lost* at Stratford-on-Avon, when the tall, black-caped messenger arrived during the nonsensical caperings of the characters near the end of the play and announced that the king was dead. Alfred Hitchcock employs this principle often in his melodramatic films. *Rebecca* abounded in scenes illustrative of it. His technique involves rapid and unexpected changes in rhythm which result in contrasts in mood, usually breaking suspense with laughter and heightening suspense by a sudden switch from laughter or a moment of calm and peace.

Such creativity is part and parcel of the art of the theatre, which is the art of sudden wonder and astonishment. It stems from interpretive originality and individuality marked by a synthesis of inspiration and discrimination.

CREATIVE DISCIPLINE

In all this we see the workings of the director's creative and interpretive mind. The process, in addition, must include the exercise of mind over unrestrained emotion. Ratiocination must accompany the aesthetic emotion. The director, in all his creativity, is presented with many choices and must make aesthetic and theatrical judgments and decisions. Wordsworth's saying that poetry "takes its origin from emotion recollected in tranquility"[22] implies the need of thought to shape emotion in artistic creativity. And thought is at the peak of its possibilities when it is free from emotional disturbance. Quoting Copland again, "The creative mind, in its day-to-day functioning, must be a critical mind. . . . Beethoven's genius was once attributed by Schubert to what he termed his 'superb coolness under the fire of creative fantasy.' "[23]

Emotion controlled, guided, and shaped by reason involves for the theatrical director the application of the fundamental principles and laws underlying the various aspects of theatrical art. Precisely what these principles or laws are is sometimes baffling. They are in any case a part of what Jacques Maritain calls "working reason." However, he says that "the intellect or reason which plays the principal and royal part in them [the fine arts, and I include the theatre among them] is not conceptual, discursive, logical reason, nor even working reason. It is intuitive reason, in the obscure and high regions which are near the center of the soul, and in which the intellect exercises its activity at the single root of the soul's powers and conjointly with them." Thus, like all artists, the director is subject to intuitive reason and working reason, both necessary in all creative work. Maritain points out that the working reason plays a

> necessary—though secondary—part in the fine arts . . . As soon as it gets the upper hand, the work is but a corpse of a work of art—a product of academicism. But when the resourcefulness of discursive reason, and the rules involved . . . secondary rules—are used as instruments of a master *habitus,* and as the fingers, so to speak, of creative intuition, they compose the indispensable arsenal of prudence, shrewdness, and cleverness of the life of art. . . . To make fun of the rules, in proclaiming the liberty of art, is just an excuse provided by foolishness to mediocrity.[24]

This is the answer, I think, to the young director-artist who is impatient with and rebels against artistic discipline. Even in art one must exercise freedom with reason. This rule holds for the genius as well as the merely talented. Maritain quotes from Coleridge: "'As it must not, so genius cannot, be lawless; for it is even this that constitutes it genius—the power of acting creatively under laws of its own origination.'"[25]

CREATIVE BOLDNESS

Though the director, like other artists, may feel restrained by the discipline of his art, he nevertheless can be and must be *bold* in whatever he does. He must "give the impression that chances are being taken."[26] This is a true expression of the artist's spiritual freedom. This boldness or sense of danger is unconsciously felt by the audience and engenders the kind of excitement that circumscribes all great art. This can be expressed in directing by the interpretation and creation of character, emotional and atmospheric effects, theme, and, above all, theatrical style. The modern theatre has settled into the rut of a conventional style: realism. It should be violently and boldly pushed out by the creative and interpretive mind of the director. The director's own individual style, apart from the style of the play, can in itself give impetus to the excitement essential to the highest form of theatrical art. Every play he approaches demands a scheme of production which may present the opportunity for freedom of expression. However, if this freedom involves a departure from the traditional and conventional, it must be expressed explicitly and without timidity. The audience wishes to be commanded and guided positively. The director must be bold in his imaginative and emotional flight. The machine-like, smooth, polished, and conventional theatrical production is arid and ungenerative of emotional or intellectual excitement. It emanates from the craftsman of the theatre, not the artist. The artist is uninhibited and adventuresome, and courts danger no less than the wild-game hunter who stalks the lion. He is aiming for high stakes—the pinnacle of artistic achievement.

COMMUNICATION

If the director has the creative impulse to say something about life, he must say it to someone. An artist cannot create in a vacuum. And certainly the production of a play should not be conceived in a void without reference to the audience.

The director finds it difficult to know to what extent he is communicating his thoughts and feelings. He is often amazed that individual members of the audience fail to perceive certain points and values in his production. A great deal is perceived emotionally and subsconsciously which is not translated into conscious, coherent thought. A member of the audience may say he does not understand the theme of a play, whereas upon questioning he may reveal an emotional understanding which needed thought and discussion to give it coherence. The director, of course, cannot speak privately to each member of the audience to get his reaction; he must depend upon those audible and visible reactions emanating from the audience during the performance and the intermissions, and as they leave the theatre.

One of the great difficulties of theatrical communication stems from the fact that the rapid and continuous flow of the performance permits the possibility of visual and aural failures. If the audience could stop the play and say "What's that?" or "Would you please do that again; I didn't quite get it," many communication problems could be solved. The novelist and the poet have an advantage in that their audience or readers can stop to ponder a passage or turn back the pages and study a line or paragraph. The playwright, with the director's help, must present a thought, phrase, or moment so clearly and emphatically that the audience can perceive it in the flow of the dramatic action. Sometimes he must communicate at once through clarity of dialogue and action or he can communicate cumulatively by repeated implication or control of information.

In order to communicate clearly and emphatically each moment, the director must focus the audience's attention not only on the stage in general but upon the important character, line, word, and situation as these shift and change. The various techniques employed by the director in pictorial dramatization and movement include ways and means for establishing and guiding the audience's attention. Once attention is controlled, techniques for achieving emphasis may be utilized. The director's proficiency in these techniques can guarantee a high degree of communication.

Audience communication is, perforce, an integral part of the director's interpretive and creative thinking. Communication with the audience through the play via the actors and the other elements of production involves certain steps in sequence for the director. First of all, he must interpret and understand the audience before he can communicate with them. Then he must interpret the play and utilize the actors and the production as channels of communication. This sequence is a chain of action which might be summed up as creative interpretation. A special kind of imagination, vision, intelligence, and perception are needed by the director in order to be both creative and interpretive. This is essential in considering the two components of dramatic interpretation: the audience and the play. Neither can be approached factually with the expectation that formulas exist or can be evolved to solve their mysteries. Hard and fast rules cannot apply. Principles cannot be followed, though they may be deduced. The audience and the play are undefinable elements whose ambivalence and everlasting elusiveness confound both theatrical theorists and practitioners. Yet the director must try to understand both the psychology of the audience and the art of the play. If he succeeds even partially in understanding one, he has made genuine progress in understanding the other. His first step in understanding the audience is to see clearly his relationship to it.

2

Dramatic Communication
and Response

THE DIRECTOR AS A COLLECTIVE PERSONALITY

THE DIRECTOR can perceive the nature of drama in general and the dramatic potentials of a particular play only through a knowledge of the psychology of audiences. The subject matter and materials of a play are selected, organized, written, and produced to evoke specific emotional and mental reactions from the audience. These reactions constitute the play's dramatic effect. The dramatic effect of each play, stemming from its own subject, structure, and production, is unique. The knowledge of this fact is basic to the understanding of play interpretation and direction.

In analyzing a play for production the director must seek its potential emotional and intellectual individuality, the reality of which he can learn only later when the play is produced before an audience. Nevertheless, it is his problem to predict what it is and the reaction of the audience to it. Speaking strictly, a play does not exist until it is produced and brought to life by audience response. During and after the performance the intelligent director sees, hears, and feels the audience response, which tells him what the play is. (A different production and a different audience create a different play. However, the main dramatic qualities of a play remain the same regardless of the production or audience.) If the director is able to watch the performance of a play before many different audiences over an extended period he should learn the basic intellectual and emotional values of the play. When the director is unable to obtain this experience, he must rely upon his knowledge of audience behavior, learned while watching other plays, and upon other people's knowledge. In addition to these external and objective sources of information, he will find in himself subjective sources which will aid him in discovering possible and probable audience response to a play. In fact, the director deprived of the foreknowledge which comes from having witnessed an audience's response to a play must rely upon his own personal reactions. These reactions, however, are trustworthy only to the extent that they reflect, suggest, and resemble those of the play's future audience. This means, then, that he must be able to determine when and how his own individual reactions differ from or resemble those of the individuals making up the audience.

In order to do this he must imagine himself to be each member of the group of people who compose the audience; he must identify himself with them and empathize with them. This presents a problem which even the most sensitive, imaginative, and experienced director cannot always solve. The crux of the problem lies in the fact that he as one individual must anticipate the responses of many individuals. Perhaps he can imagine himself in the place of one person whose appearance and attitude are typical enough to warrant the director's anticipating certain reactions and behavior from him, but it is less possible to imagine himself in the place of a large group of disparate persons. Yet that is the director's job. He must learn to be a kind of barometer anticipating audience response before a performance and, moreover, recording their response during a performance. The anticipated response will dictate what he will think and do in terms of play analysis and direction before the audience sees the play. The audience's recorded response will tell him how he has failed or succeeded in his analysis and direction of the play. In the process of acting as a barometer of audience response the director changes himself from a single personality into a collective personality.

Becoming a collective personality, the director, in one respect at least, undergoes the same change experienced by the individual member of the audience when he becomes amalgamated with the group; that is, he tends to lose his identity and take on the characteristics of the group, with the specific result that he tends to become more emotional and less intellectual.

In comparison with the isolated individual, an audience is more easily and quickly stimulated into response because of its highly subjective and spontaneous receptivity to stimuli. Being thus receptive, it is less critical and more readily willing than the individual to believe and become involved in the fictional facts of plot and character and the playwright's thematic propositions. This must be borne in mind in play analysis and rehearsal. During rehearsal the director attempts to combine analysis with technique. He must realize that in the process the play's emotional qualities of surprise, suspense, humor, beauty, and sadness have been weakened in their impact on him by his analytical study and rehearsals. The audience reacts with more intensified emotions because it is unrestrained by such conditioning and also responds as a collective personality.

The intensification of emotions resulting from group response, for example, can most easily be perceived from two performances of the same comedy by the same actors, one before a small audience and the other before a full house. Laughter will be spotty and halfhearted with the small audience. With the full house the laughter will be louder and more general. An audience creates emotional contagion. Radio and television producers know that the laughter of a studio audience makes a show funnier to the individual sitting at home alone before his set. Hearing others laugh gives the individual a sense of contact with them, and through the power of suggestion he will laugh too. The belief in this theory has prompted television producers to incorporate audience laughter in the sound track of filmed TV shows which originate from stations without studio audiences. The techniques used are described in a *Time* magazine article called "Can the Laughter."

> Some shows, e.g., *Lucy, December Bride, Phil Silvers,* are filmed before a live audience whose real laughter is recorded with the show itself. Then the film's sound track is judiciously "sweetened": coughs are erased, idiot giggles toned down, chuckles reinforced and silences sprinkled with gaiety. Another common technique, used by *Jack Benny, Burns & Allen,* the *Bob Cummings Show* and *Private Secretary,* is to film the show without spectators, then show the film to a movie-house audience monitored by microphones. The sounds of the audience reactions are dubbed in—and again doctored on the theory that he who laughs most laughs best.

The article also points out that a TV show, "Dear Phoebe," on its sponsor's orders eliminated the canned laughter and its ratings fell. "Just to make sure, the advertising agency tried an experiment with the show in two cities: one station showed it with laughter and another without. The laugh-packed version ran 25% higher in its ratings."[1]

An intensification of the serious emotions can also be brought about by the power of suggestion and contagion. Understanding this, the French theatre has long employed *pleureurs* as well as *rieurs* in its claque. Professional mourners and "sob sisters" can be as effective in the theatre as at rigged funerals or rigged mob demonstrations. Nero capitalized on this knowledge when he employed 5,000 soldiers to show their appreciation of his acting ability in a play, and so did Shakespeare's Richard III when he hired people to shout for his election as king in order to influence emotionally the innocent citizenry.

Thus the Hydra-headed and many-hearted mass group possesses a psychology of its own. The director in assuming its collective personality must study it and understand it as though it were a character in the play. It has physical, psychological, and sociological traits. The director's relationship to the character of this collective personality is similar to that of the actor to the character he wishes to impersonate. The actor impersonates the character in the play, the director the character outside the play—the audience. In both cases the individuality of the interpreter must be absorbed in the assumed character. An important aspect of the character of the audience to be assumed by the director concerns motivations.

AUDIENCE MOTIVATIONS

Why do people go to the theatre? Like all human conduct, playgoing meets some desire and need. It is comprised of a number of psychological drives, conscious or unconscious. The strongest drive is to satisfy the desire for emotional relaxation, stimulation, and enrichment. A playgoer wants to be relieved of the daily obligations and responsibilities which cause emotional tension. Call this escape, if you will. Hebbel, the great German critic, said that playgoing was the only pause possible in man's life. It is a pause in the sense of cessation of one's own activities and in the sense of emotional and mental refreshment. The desire for emotional relaxation is great in this twentieth-century world of anxieties and tensions. The theatre does not de-emotionalize; it redirects and controls the emotions on the level of theatrical illusion. It causes a removal from life. Participation in the fictional life of the stage implies objectivity and superiority to what is seen and heard. The audience is in a godlike position of omniscience regarding character background, motives, and attitudes. It possesses knowledge of persons, events, and ideas not possible to the people of the play. Moreover, it has the ability to vary its degree of objectivity and subjectivity of response. It can identify itself with the characters and involve itself in the action to the extent it desires. It can also withdraw identification and participation at will. The audience has the cheerful knowledge that the characters are to entertain it but that it will never be asked to entertain the characters.[2] Here are superiority, security, and diversion.

The instinctive will to make believe which is a part of the "play" drive is common to mankind. This willingness to pretend, to substitute fiction for fact, to play the game according to the rules is manifested in all kinds of diversionary activities. If the playgoer is to have a rewarding theatrical experience, he must have this willingness in strong measure. It induces belief and vicarious participation in the emotions and thoughts of the characters. This is a stimulating experience. Emotional exercise on the plane of play-going is titillating and exhilarating, and lacks the danger of traumatic effects resulting from emotional disturbances in life. Many people go to the theatre for a good cry or a good laugh. They seek emotional outlets not provided them otherwise. Moreover, they seek emotional experiences denied them by the conventions, mores, laws, and circumstances of the society in which they live.

The theatre allows the playgoer to travel all over the world and be anyone he pleases. The human imagination is able to transform the meek and mild into the aggressive and passionate. The possibilities for adventure are limitless in the land of make-believe. Traveling on the magic carpet woven by theatrical illusion, we go to far-off places and become kings, queens, princes, princesses, beggars, or thieves or whatever our fancy dictates. We perform deeds of derring-do and think sublime thoughts. We can seek and find world renown, become prophets honored at home as well as abroad. We can be as funny as any clown and as witty as Congreve, Wycherley, Sheridan, Wilde, Shaw, Coward, or Kaufman and Hart. Visiting strange lands and people, and becoming acquainted with strange customs, we can indulge passions, experiences, and thoughts foreign to us. Anna and the King of Siam, Hamlet, Macbeth, Stanley Kowalski, Willy Loman, Medea, and Henry VIII, out of the present and the past, extend our emotional experiences. They enlarge our social sphere, stimulate and intensify our love and compassion for mankind.

Attendant upon emotional relaxation and stimulation is emotional enrichment. The theatre provides vicarious experiences which are purgative. Our own emotions are cleansed, broadened, and deepened. The human spirit is uplifted.

People go to the theatre out of a desire to be with other people. Gregariousness is akin to social conformity. Keeping up with the Joneses who go to the theatre is sufficient motive for many. Besides, the theatre provides a subject for conversation and enhances social life. The theatre is a social outing. After cocktails and dinner the theatre makes an evening of it. It is somewhere to go, something to do. It satisfies the desire for close contact with others, companionship, and a sense of security. The common experience of like and simultaneous response provided by a theatrical performance is a source of good will and feeling. It makes for identification with the crowd. Like Yank in O'Neill's *The Hairy Ape*, the individual wants to belong. Identification with the characters in the play meets the need for belonging. The theatregoer sees himself as the character. He usually identifies himself only with the strong, wise, powerful, witty, and heroic. This is aggrandisement of the ego. Even identification with the weak, stupid, and cowardly enhances one's own estimation of himself. This feeling of superiority continually brings to members of the audience the strength, wisdom, and stature denied the play's characters.

The love of the beautiful is demonstrated in many ways. The planting and nurturing of a single petunia at the doorstep of the meanest hovel is to satisfy a hungering spirit. Surely the beauty of sight and sound created by a theatrical production satisfies the drive for an aesthetic experience. Theatre appreciation differs among individuals, depending upon experience and knowledge. The person who sees a play for the first time, the one who has seen many plays, and the jaded playgoer respond with highly contrasting degrees of appreciation. The aesthetic experience provided by the theatre includes a certain amount of artistic creativity for the audience. Inasmuch as the performance and the various aspects of play production do not come to life without audience response, the individual members help to create a work of art. The conscious or unconscious knowledge of this fact is pleasurable to the audience. Creativity which is concomitant, peripheral, or even involuntary satisfies a need in man.

The need for intellectual stimulation and provocation can be one of the reasons for theatregoing. From the beginning the theatre has provided insight into man's relationship to God, to his fellow man, and to himself. It has been the medium for public discussion of ideas new and old. The exhilaration from the exercise of thought is satisfying.

An understanding of the composition and character of the audience in terms of interests and motivations leads to a consideration of some of its basic traits and ingredients.

NATURE AND CONTROL OF AUDIENCE RESPONSE

Other works of art like the novel, poetry, sculpture, painting, and even music depend upon individual response. Not so the theatre. The theatre is a social art, depending upon group response. The reading of a novel is an experience in some ways similar to playgoing. Both the novel and the play are fictional; both have character, plot, dialogue, and theme; both demand varying degrees of character identification and empathy; both require "suspension of disbelief." Yet the fact that a novel must be read and responded to by one individual at a time whereas a play receives the group response of an audience constitutes the fundamental difference between the two art forms. While a person is reading a novel he is not influenced by the reaction of others; nor is his response shared with others. The quality and quantity of his responses are tailored to his individual mental and emotional reflexes. A member of a theatre audience, on the other hand, shares his experience concurrently with others and is affected by the response of others. The novelist appeals to individual psychology, the playwright to crowd psychology.

Clayton Hamilton, in citing the theories of Gustave Le Bon in his *Psychologie des foules,* observes an important difference between the individual and the mass when he says that "The mental qualities in which men differ from one another are the acquired qualities of intellect and character, but the qualities in which they are one are the innate passions of the race."[3] This means that the individual when a part of a crowd partially loses his acquired identity, his characterizing traits, and tends to revert to his original state when he was a creature of emotions. Thus his response to a theatrical performance is primarily emotional. If he thinks, he tends to think as a result of his emotions. A corollary to this fact is that to be effective a play must appeal to certain basic human emotions and instincts. When the ability to reason is subverted by the emotions the response to stimuli is not easily controlled. In an article called "That Beast, the Audience," Rebecca Franklin quotes Joshua Logan, an audience-wise Broadway director, as saying,

> I think of an audience as a tremendous, frightening beast, a behemoth which has to be licked. It is many people suddenly fused into one, and it can be loving or vicious. The challenge is: "Do we lick you or do you lick us?" There has to be the calm, attractive arrogance of a champion in the work of an actor, director or an author, or else he is lost. An audience will accept on the stage only complete authority and the relaxation that comes with it. When it gets that, it settles back, becomes tame and listens. It smells insecurity, as a horse knows fear in its rider.[4]

In order to "lick" the audience the director, like any fighter, must be able to anticipate and control his opponent.

The first step toward audience control is unification. The director, unlike the military commander, cannot divide and conquer. The modern audience, individualistic and pulsating with variant hearts, comes to the theatre with highly contrasting thoughts, feelings, and attitudes—social, political, religious, and philosophical. A play can come completely to life only when the many-headed audience singlemindedly concentrates on and becomes absorbed in the fictional life revealed on the stage. Whenever a performance went badly and the audience got out of control at the famous Vieux-Colombier, Jacques Copeau would say it wasn't an audience but people. By this he meant that the audience was responding not as a unified group but as individuals.[5]

To create a unified response to the play and control it is today difficult because of the lack of unity of audience attitude. As Francis Fergusson has pointed out in his *The Idea of a Theatre*, the audiences which came to the first theatre in Western civilization were molded into cohesion as a result of "the perspective of the myth, of the rituals, and of the traditional *hodos*, the way of life of the city."[6] Theatregoing was ritualistic and religious. The resultant unity of attitude tended to unify audience response.

The Elizabethan audience went to the theatre not for religious reasons but for social and educational reasons. The Globe was the convivial center for those who came to relax and pursue amorous adventures, to yield to the magic of words, to be stirred not by myths or legends but by history—the fictionalized accounts of the true exploits of kings and queens who symbolized England. Here was audience cohesion too. Perhaps basically it was unity through deep nationalistic fervor. Elizabeth succeeded more than any other monarch in molding the nation into unity of strength, pride, and devotion to motherland. The underlying integrating forces manifested themselves in every gathering, and theatre audiences were no exception. Shakespeare and any other playwright of the day could depend upon a kind of unanimity of audience response. The popular audience of today, though in general the product of the concomitant forces of the twentieth century, is segmented and diversified by educational, social, racial, political, and environmental backgrounds. It is a disorganized monster, unpredictable, fickle, and chameleon—a heterogeneous and undirected audience.

Yet it is possible for the director to find a homogeneous audience, assembled out of a common desire and the product of the same special background and interests. The so-called "experimental" and "off-Broadway" theatres have been established for such audiences. They are usually interested in the seldom-produced classics or in the *avant-garde* or esoteric works. Plays have even been specially written and performed for particular groups: unions, clubs, industry, the armed forces, schools, and other associations. Before World War II during the depression years the Group Theatre and the Theatre Union produced plays of social reform consistent with their social and political ideology. The so-called "agit-prop" plays have sprung up from time to time demanding social and political action. The Fascists under Hitler and Mussolini no less

than the Communists throughout the world have not only created
their brand of theatre but have instituted principles of art to conform with their political philosophies.

Audiences in general are intellectually conditioned by the
period in which they live. The history of the theatre shows that
Aeschylus, Sophocles, and Euripides wrote for a mythologically
minded audience, the medieval playwrights for a nonreading,
Bible-minded audience, Shakespeare for a nationalistically conscious
one, Congreve and Wycherley for an amoral one, and Tennessee
Williams for a Freudian one. Whatever may be the popular and
general emotional and intellectual posture of a period, there are
also special attitudes resulting from particular intellectual and
artistic interests and motivations.

Such attitudes and interests form special audiences which
are necessary for the appreciation of some plays of foreign origin,
for example. Even modern foreign playwrights such as Pirandello,
Strindberg, Lorca, Brecht, Chekhov, Genêt, and Beckett have a
limited chance of commercial, popular success because of their
special appeal. However, university theatres have proved that
there is an audience away from Broadway for these writers.

Similarly the classics must find their particular audiences.
Stars can attract the general Broadway public to the classics for
a limited time. Olivier can pack them in when he plays Shakespeare
or Sophocles; the Lunts when they perform Chekhov; Evans, Shaw;
or Jean-Louis Barrault, Molière. The educational theatre and the
off-Broadway theatre must content themselves with the special
audiences who are specially interested and directed. It is they
and not the commercial theatre who are the custodians of our
dramatic heritage.

In addition to these special audiences brought together because of similar intellectual backgrounds and outlooks are those
particularly interested in folk and regional drama. Folkways, dialects, and local problems have a fascination for some and repel
others. American plays about New England and the southern
mountainous areas in North Carolina, Kentucky, and Tennessee,
as well as Irish plays, have limited appeal. This is so especially if
the dramatic values lie principally in the environmental and folk
aspects. After the first world war considerable interest was manifested in American regional drama. And some of it has managed
to reach the New York stage. Paul Green, Hatcher Hughes, E. P.
Conkle, and a few others have made notable contributions, but
their audiences have been generally small. Today very little regional
drama is being written. The Irish dramatists have, by and large,
commanded larger audiences in this country than have our own

native regionalists. The reason for this is that they have managed to create more universal appeal in character and language. Synge, O'Casey, and Paul Vincent Carroll have had some success on Broadway and in the educational theatre. Yet neither the American nor the Irish folk dramatists have had wide popular appeal.

These are examples of special audiences who assemble for reasons of similar cultural interests, and their directed response is accordingly more easily anticipated.

The director can also anticipate audience response if the audience is conditioned by the exigencies of the times. Special circumstances can tend to unify an audience today and predispose it to certain ideas and emotions. The nature of these circumstances can be national, regional, group, ideational, social, or political. For example, an audience can be integrated by war.

Such an audience comes to the theatre in an emotional and mental state conditioned by the war; it is a pushover for the play because of its heightened emotions and uncritical attitude; it is ready to believe anything and everything. A play related to the war merely ignites emotions already smoldering and gives concrete meaning to abstract ideas. A national catastrophe not only brings such cohesion but, on the other hand, often causes mediocre playwriting and production to appear superior because of their ready and excessive emotional impact. Too, timeliness of subject matter can create its own statute of limitations. Even such war plays as *What Price Glory?*, *Journey's End*, *Watch on the Rhine*, and *There Shall Be No Night*, all of them great successes at the particular time of their initial performances, now, in the proper perspective of comparative objectivity, both fail to elicit uniformity of audience appeal and have lost considerable dramatic musculature. The economic crisis of the early 1930's in this country created a special audience for plays of social protest. Such plays, produced in New York by the organization known as the Theatre Union, were wildly cheered when presented to members of the audience unified by their strong feelings and political ideology. Playwrights writing and directors staging plays in such special climates will always find it comparatively easy to predict, influence, and control audience behavior. That beast, the audience, becomes tamed, domesticated, and docile.

Although varying factors underlying audience behavior tend to produce disparate responses, there is nevertheless a universal element which aids audience integration. This is the play or make-believe tendency in people. "Let's pretend" appeals to every human being, young and old. To a large extent it depends upon illusion and belief. Children yield most readily to the imagination as the basis of belief. This may be true because children often cannot distinguish between illusion and actuality. They do not possess the experience of maturity which teaches the distinction. Generally speaking, the older we grow, the more we distrust outward appearance, the more we question, the more we evaluate and select, and the more we disbelieve. Nevertheless, when we decide to go to the theatre we voluntarily agree to self-deception. The barriers of disbelief are down and we are willing victims of pretense. Our degree of willingness will vary according to our individual backgrounds of psychology, education, playgoing experience, physical state, and circumstances surrounding our going to the theatre.

It has been said that national and international crises, inclement weather, income-tax deadlines, Christmas, Easter, and New Year's make the general public less receptive to the state of mind for playgoing. Every play and its production must combat these factors and, if they are to succeed, must overcome all resistance to belief. The audience must be induced to believe at the level of reality projected by the production. A state of reciprocal communication and response must exist between audience and play.

STIMULATION, ATTENTION, AND ABSORPTION

An audience comes to the theatre disposed to believe, and its induction to a state of belief depends upon the aural and visual stimuli emanating from the theatrical production. First of all, the audience's attention in the darkened theatre is directed to the only area lighted—the stage. An empty lighted stage can serve to focus attention and create an atmosphere of expectancy which can be absorbingly stimulating. The depth and duration of such expectancy will depend upon the time lapse before something is seen or heard on the stage. The awareness of the arrival of actors or the awareness of sound will deepen or relax the intensity established. From then on throughout the performance, the variety and power of stimuli will vary the kind and amount of attention and depth of absorption. Frequent change of stimuli is necessary for continued attention and interest. Repellent stimuli, shocking sights or sounds, unconvincing character behavior, or theatrical ineptitude, for example, can destroy attention and break the illusion.

Audience unity of attitude depends upon certain psychological pressures. The creation of what has been called "polarization" or audience "line-up" or orientation physically and psychologically to stage stimuli depends on: "social facilitation" (the intensity of the stimuli, the power of suggestion), "social anonymity" (submersion of the individual in the crowd), and "regimentation" (audience seated in rows and close together to effect loss of individuality and psychological conformity).[7] Unification of response to stimuli increases the intensity of separate responses. If the audience is unified in its depth of attention to a comic situation, for example, the laughter at the comedy will be louder and greater. The same is true of serious emotion experienced by the audience.

Unity of audience response also depends upon unity of attitude and mood evoked by the stimuli provided by the playwright and director. They must provide signposts indicating what the audience's attitude should be. Inexperienced playwrights and directors often bewilder and confuse the audience. "Is that supposed to be funny or serious?" the audience asks. The reading of a line of dialogue, a piece of business, a reaction can signal the audience. The practice of the modern playwright of mixing farce, comedy, melodrama, and tragedy all in one play destroys unity of response and generally frustrates the audience. It says, "I want to play the game but I don't understand the rules." (See Chapter 3, "Nature and Pattern of Drama," for a further discussion of unity.)

ATTENTION, INVOLVEMENT, AND BELIEF

Modern playwrights no less than the Greeks realize the advantages of placing a character in a crisis at the outset of a play in order to capture audience interest immediately. *Death of a Salesman* and *Oedipus Rex* illustrate this practice. Once attention is engaged, emotional involvement will follow and hold if the span of attention or absorption can be prolonged sufficiently. Variety of mood will guarantee audience attention and sympathy and concern over the characters' problems and will assure depth of absorption. Audience absorption in a play can be mental as well as emotional. Most of the plays of Shaw appeal primarily to the mind. *Man and Superman* is an example. We are never involved emotionally in Tanner's or anyone else's problems. Our sympathies are not aroused enough to touch our deep emotions. The members of the audience are absorbed by Shaw's dialectics and humor in proportion to their ability to respond intellectually. Being so detached emotionally, they participate at will and withdraw at will. An audience following the involuted thought of Shakespeare, Eliot, or Fry is first mentally titillated, then imbued with aesthetic feeling. A play like Williams' *A Streetcar Named Desire* and Miller's *Death of a Salesman* can absorb an audience profoundly and shatter it emotionally. The frivolous humor of *Three Men on a Horse* and *No Time for Sergeants* elicits attention and carries compulsion commensurate with the fascination and diversion of complex situations and obvious comedy. Melodramas like *Angel Street* and *Dial "M"* *for Murder* allow audiences to watch with a degree of fascinated detachment. They realize how unlikely the events are but find them pleasurable despite the constant admonishment that they would be horrible if they were true.

Audience desires and emotions make truth out of fiction. An audience believes not what is true but what it wishes to think is true. Never was war like *Journey's End, What Price Glory?, At War with the Army,* or even *Mister Roberts,* but with the perspective of time and sufficient veneer of truth highly polished with wishful thinking, audiences have accepted them as actuality. Never was a newspaper office like that in *The Front Page,* but it is fascinating to an audience to think so. A so-called slice of life like *Dead End* is some distance from actuality, but it is so emotionally compelling that it is acceptable as truth. The mental elasticity of the audience is such that the implausibility of melodrama, farce, and fantasy achieves the appearance of truth through the appeal to the imagination and the willingness to play the game of make-believe. In these types of plays and in the nonrealistic styles of writing and production the audience becomes a true collaborator. It meets the play halfway and sometimes more than halfway. (Actors, by their own belief and the conviction of their behavior, play a not inconsiderable part in stretching audience belief.)

AUDIENCE PARTISANSHIP

Crowd psychology includes the desire to take sides in a conflict or struggle within a play. An audience must root for somebody or some idea. If a play does not possess the ingredients to bring about audience partisanship, its emotional impact is the less. The most obvious opportunity for this occurs in melodrama, where the issues involving a distinct hero and villain are clearly drawn. Here audience sympathy revolves around a certain character and is alienated from another. Tragedy and drama permit the audience to take sides too, but inasmuch as the characters are more rounded and truer to life, the right and wrong of a struggle are not so categorically marked, and neither is audience partisanship. In this kind of play, sympathy and understanding for all sides are possible. Thus the kind of play will determine the degree of partisanship. Nevertheless, this aspect of audience response makes it quite clear that an audience must *care* sufficiently about the characters and their problems to be interested in their resolution. An audience's sympathies must be aroused to some extent, in serious drama more than in comic. In the latter, sympathy may be diluted to plain liking for the characters and objective concern about their problems; yet, however slight, audience emotion must be appealed to.

AUDIENCE RESPONSIBILITIES AND SIGNS

Audiences come into the theatre with certain backgrounds—sometimes disparate, sometimes similar—motivated by definite psychological drives, tendencies, susceptibilities, and attitudes. The director must study them as guideposts to govern the interpretation and direction of plays.

A pebble is dropped into a pool and forms a tiny circle of waves which multiplies into larger and larger concentric waves breaking against the perimeter. The larger the pebble, the larger and deeper the waves churning up the pool. This pool is like a theatre audience activated by the words, looks, gestures, and movement of the actors in their scenic environment. Waves of auditory and visual vibrations emanate from the play and work upon hearts and minds to evoke emotions and thoughts. The design of the play creates a mosaic of feelings and ideas which constitutes a theatrical experience for the audience.

As John Mason Brown points out, this experience is not the "shortest distance between 2 hours"—a mere waste of time during which the audience "check their judgments and their perceptions with their hats."[8] It is not the privilege of the audience to come to take their ease and sleep an hour or two. They must come to make the theatre justify the "theft of time," to make it live, memorable and crowded with "all the insistent joys of complete awareness of the heightened chronology of a heightened world."[9]

Though the audience must suspend its disbelief, it nevertheless must, as Brown tells us, retain what Colly Cibber called "resistant flexibility."[10] It must not throw away its judgment and taste.[11] It must be actively receptive, alert, and perceptive, with the ability to discern the meretricious from the genuine.

Audience decorum has changed considerably since Elizabeth's hearty, swaggering, nut-cracking subjects stood in the pit and galleries or sat on the stage hurling insults or raucously expressing approval. Today's American audience in general is polite, quiet, and attentive. It is also unvocal. Not so the Italians, French, or even the Irish (though they, since the golden and turbulent days of the Abbey Theatre, have relaxed into respectability). It is difficult sometimes to find out what the audience thinks and feels; that is, during a performance. Creaking seats can be an indication of restlessness and inattentiveness. The more comfortable the seats, the deeper the sleep and the louder the snoring. That situation is, of course, indicative. The cosmopolitan evening audience, loaded with good food and slightly befuddled by drink, is either lethargic and dull or silly and conspicuous, depending upon its intake. Audiences need not shout or pitch decomposed edibles or other missiles like paper airplanes constructed from the pages of the program, but they can express their approval by laughter and tears and applause. Moreover, it is their obligation to do so. The play and players depend upon demonstrative audience reaction in creating a genuine theatrical experience.

Laughter, if the result of genuine comedy and not theatrical ineptitude, and audible sobbing are unmistakable signs. Applause, on the other hand, can be misleading. This is particularly true if the applause at the end of the play is to be taken as the barometer of approval. Often there is hearty and enthusiastic applause at the last curtain. Of course, the theatre-wise stage manager who continues to raise and lower the curtain for curtain calls and keeps the auditorium dark to hold the audience captive can "milk" heavy and sustained applause. Friends of the author and actors can spark the audience into applause any time during the play and especially at the end of the performance when they can stand behind the orchestra rail to clap their hands, shout "bravo," whistle, and otherwise demonstrate their approval.

Genuinely enthusiastic applause is often for the performers and the production rather than for the play.

Audience response at the final curtain can be most deceiving. The actors, director, and all others connected with the production and hoping for its success are the most easily deceived. The amount and duration of applause are usually overestimated by wishful thinking. Seldom do those involved in the show consider the motives and reasons for applause indicated above.

Applause during a performance to indicate approval of a good scene or a witty line can be spontaneous or induced by one or more individuals in the audience or by the actors' friends standing at the back. Audible signs of approval during the play and at the ends of scenes and acts are usually reliable indications of the success of the play itself. Tepid applause at the end of an act is without doubt an indication of the audience's lack of interest and approval. (Sometimes an audience is so moved at the end of an act or even of the play that the applause will be scattered or absent.)

A quiet, watchful audience may indicate real interest and involvement or it may indicate surface interest or, more exactly, merely focus of attention. When the theatre is darkened and the stage lighted, the audience is naturally attentive to what is happening on the stage. The question is "Is this kind of attentiveness the result of focus or of absorption in the play and performance?" The attentive, quiet, relaxed audience may be interested and enjoying the play or it may be simply polite. (The school and university theatre audience is usually the most polite and it is also the least demonstrative, particularly if it is made up of middleaged professors and their wives together with the conservative town and gown playgoers. A sprinkling of students among their elders helps to ferment audible response.) The experienced and trained actor, director, or critic is easily made aware of the hushed, absorbed, breathless audience during a scene or act which has definitely taken hold of the audience. The last scene of Joseph Hayes' *The Desperate Hours* evokes such audience response.

The silent, immobile audience, deeply moved, is absorbed and tense, and an atmosphere is created which is unmistakable. Even after the scene is over and the curtain is down, a count of several seconds will elapse before this audience moves and applauds; or it may even refrain from applauding. The "requiem" scene from *Death of a Salesman* affects the audience in this way, or the audience breaks down into audible sobbing. The end of *A Streetcar Named Desire* usually leaves the audience stilled, shocked, and emotionally overcome. It takes a few moments for it to recover.

Audience response is often difficult to diagnose during and after the performance. Perhaps the surest sign of approval or disapproval is the response indicated by the box-office returns. However, the continuance of a Broadway play sometimes does not mean favorable audience response. The backers may run the play at a loss, hoping to stimulate interest by word of mouth and other kinds of advertising. The brief run of a play is, conversely, not always an absolute indication of artistic failure. The play may have been killed by unfavorable reviews, lack of time for it to catch on, high operating costs, or loss of the star. Vocal, unmistakable audience response during and after the performance shows a cooperating and responsible audience aware of its appreciation and perception of the values of the play and performance. The audience must show signs which the director and critic can read. Lethargy, silence, and politeness on the part of the audience can destroy its own chances for a true theatrical experience and thus frustrate the desires which motivated its coming to the theatre.

No discussion of the audience can be complete. In the first place, we do not know enough about general audience psychology and, in the second place, every audience is different from any other. Although all audiences have certain common traits, no two audiences will express them in the same way. For example, a play through repeated performance can prove itself to be a comedy—laughter is the predominant mood. Nevertheless, the amount, kind, and duration of the laughter will vary with each individual audience. Actors and directors have found that, whereas certain patently comic lines, situations, and business provoke laughter some nights, they do not on other nights. This can be explained only by the fact that audiences come to the theatre in different moods and vary in their willingness to surrender themselves to the play. They will vary too as to what they consider comic. You hear actors say, "The audience is cold tonight," or "The audience is slow," etc. Variation in audience reaction can, of course, be caused by the actors, who may not be so effective as usual. There is a circular and reciprocal action between audience and actors. They affect and guide one another.

Because of the infinite variety of audiences, the study of them never ends. It is a lifetime study for the director. Yet the director can formulate certain generalizations about audience behavior and then wait to see them confirmed or disproved. His knowledge cannot be reduced to rules but it can be used to denote signs, tendencies, or possibilities. At least it can encourage alertness and awareness. The young, inexperienced, or idealistic director often blames the audience for not reacting in the desired way. An audience may be relatively inexperienced and untrained or slow to react to strange theatrical ideas and styles, but it is never to blame. The director's job is to analyze each particular audience and base his ideal interpretation and production of the play upon this analysis. In general, then, the audience is the director's guide. Does this mean that the director must "play down" to the audience? No, because audiences usually know when they are underestimated and they react in protest. Furthermore, it is possible for the director to create for the mass through the universalities of a play and appeal to individuals at the same time. As Henri Gouhier points out in *L'Essence du théâtre,* "The drama talks to each of us in particular in order to obtain the applause of all."[12] It does not matter what the general meaning of a play may be; each individual will understand and interpret it in his own way, according to his capacities and needs.

The understanding and anticipation of audience feelings and thought must be reflected in the director's analysis, interpretation, and direction of a play. We must now turn to the special nature of drama as a literary form which is based upon its function of communicating its content to an audience.

3 _Nature and Pattern of Drama_

THE PRECEDING study of audience response, its nature and control, factors of attention, involvement, credibility, and other characteristics, is the basis for understanding what constitutes drama, its traits, and its techniques. The playwright selects his subject and organizes the elements of a play specifically for an audience. Thus the play differs from other literary forms. The director must bear in mind the distinguishing characteristics of the form of drama when he judges a play for its stageworthiness. Also he must remember that such characteristics dictate his choice of the media for communicating to the audience those aspects of the drama which are implied and are not said directly by the written words. What the play says between the lines and under the lines of dialogue complements and supplements the words. The director finds here the psychological basis of the characters of the play and the source of significant material which must be conveyed to the audience with his help and without which the play would fail in its effectiveness. The greatest difference between drama and other literary forms is that a play is restricted to dialogue, whereas poetry, the short story, and the novel can use descriptive matter as well. As a general principle, the playwright must allow the characters to speak in accordance with their own thoughts and feelings and not those of their creator. This obtains particularly in realistic drama. Other styles of drama permit the playwright to inject himself in varying degrees. Shaw, of course, quite frankly presents his characters as mouthpieces for his thought and philosophy.

Another distinguishing trait of drama is the fact that the playwright cannot directly describe persons, "places, sounds, sights, smells—upon which both fiction and poetry heavily depend . . ."[1] Moreover, the drama, because of the physical limitations of the stage, is restricted in its locale, while fiction and poetry can range over the face of the earth. The playwright may not comment directly on the situations, actions, or meanings in the play; he must convey his thoughts by implication. In order to communicate these implications he must present his dialogue, characters, and plot with such clarity and emphasis that they can be understood in the rapid

action of the stage performance. The indirect presentation of the
inner action of the mental life of a character is difficult for the
dramatist. Modern playwriting eschews the soliloquy and the
aside, though certain attempts have been made to use them in
the more experimental modern drama. Poetry and fiction can
present such action directly. It is interesting, incidentally, to note
how difficult it is for fiction writers and poets to become dramatists.
Witness the efforts of Henry James and Lord Byron: They managed
to turn out only closet drama. (It is ironic that the works of James
have recently been successfully adapted for the theatre: *The
Heiress* from *Washington Square* and *The Innocents* from *The
Turn of the Screw.*)

The director, then, uses his actors and the other elements of a
production to compensate for the restrictions imposed upon the
drama as a form. The way the characters behave, their scenic
environment, and other productional elements must make clear to
the audience what a playwright cannot say with words but a
novelist or poet can describe. The actor's voice, movement, and
general comportment when alone and when in visual relations
with others must communicate the author's attitude as well as the
character's. The director can say by various means much that
may be merely suggested and implied by the playwright.

Though of late years playwrights have tried to break away from
the structure of the well-made play and have written with less
discipline, compression and general tightening are special characteristics of most drama. The novel can take hundreds of pages to
present its characters and story; the length of a play must conform
to the conventional playing time of about two and a quarter hours.
(The experiments of O'Neill and the production of the uncut
Hamlet are rarities.) The drama, in order to develop its characters,
must limit the number. Fiction and poetry may have a larger canvas
and depict a greater number of subjects. The drama is most successful when it concentrates on a single character with a small
group of characters related to him. The story in drama is most
effective when it is unified, compressed, and intensified. Subplots,
in general, went out with Shakespeare. Plays with a group of characters who receive approximately equal attention, like those of
Chekhov, seem to be less popular than those with a strong central
character like Hamlet, Lear, Oedipus, or Electra. Dialogue in the
drama must be selected rigorously to ensure clarity and understanding. The characters cannot meander; they must speak to the point.
A play is constructed for tension. The theme in drama is most
easily perceived when it is demonstrated through the actions of
the characters and through the whole plot. In fact, the play that

depends upon a particular line of dialogue alone to convey its theme usually fails in its purpose. The simpler the theme, the more easily it is conveyed in the theatre. Labyrinthine thematic threads cannot be untangled in the continuous flow of drama. The levels of meaning so dear to the writer of fiction and poetry present many dangers to the dramatist. Few members of an audience can consciously perceive on more than one level at a time, except when witnessing the simple allegories. Dual consciousness is the privilege of only the most sensitive and experienced. The general audience tends to be more literal minded than symbolic and metaphysical.

In summary, the drama demands a greater attention to *clarity, simplicity, definition, the specific, heightening* and *intensification,* and *compression* than the other forms of literature. (See "Potentials of Dramatic Values" for a more elaborate study of these characteristics in the playwright's treatment of theme, character, plot, and dialogue.)

Basic Essentials of Drama

The dramatist's first problem is to select a basic situation which is dramatic, that is, one which is the result of conflict and will develop into more conflict and overt action. The action must be not only overt but demonstrative action, which is more dramatic than descriptive or narrative action. An old adage in the theatre is "Show 'em, don't tell 'em." The messenger who comes into so many old plays to *tell* of events off stage could be used originally for plot purposes and to capitalize on contemporary audience love of rhetoric, but the modern audience usually finds his recital undramatic and boring. The audience wants to see all pertinent and important action. The director should beware of the play in which very much action takes place off stage. The inexperienced playwright will sometimes become so involved in writing dialogue for its own sake that much of the dramatic action in his play takes place off stage and between the scenes or acts. (Brooks and Heilman point out quite significantly that *A Sum in Addition,* though written for the most part in dialogue, is not a play and cannot become one because it lacks this essential—overt action.[2] Many people often mistakenly think any work expressed in dialogue is stageworthy. It may be characteristic of the dramatic but it may not be capable of being drama.)

To be dramatic, the basic situation of the plot of a play must demonstrate a state of imbalance. The status quo must have been upset. A dramatic problem must be solved by the characters. This

may be exemplified by citing *A Streetcar Named Desire*. At the
opening of the play Stanley Kowalski and Stella are living in peace
and love with one another and their neighbors. Everything is
comparatively calm. Then Stella's sister Blanche DuBois arrives.
She is the catalytic agent who changes the dramatic balance to a
state of imbalance. The resultant situation and crisis catapult the
play to its inevitable tragic climax and resolution. In addition to
being dramatic, the basic situation must be specific and limited
in scope. The dramatist may gradually reveal many contingent
factors and the events leading up to it, but the situation must
remain comparatively simple, clear, and compact. The selection
of the starting point of a plot is very important. It may occur
before the basic situation and develop into it, but the author must
not spend too much time before he arrives at it if he wishes
to hold the audience's interest. *King Lear*, for example, begins
before the basic situation or point of crisis but wastes little time
in reaching it. The same is true of *Macbeth*. Some of the great
classics begin at the point of crisis: *Hamlet, Antigone,* and *Oedipus
Rex*. Beginning at the point of crisis ensures the play's immediately
engaging the attention and interest of the audience. The plot then
may go backward to reveal the past as does that of *Oedipus Rex* or
may go forward while revealing the past. Ibsen has the great
artistry to move his plot backward and forward with simultaneity
so that the cumulative tension is greatly felt. In this double action,
however, the past is revealed more than the present is developed.
(Of course fiction and poetry may use this same retrospective technique.) Regardless of how the playwright presents the plot, the
crises must lead up to bigger and bigger crises which eventuate
in the climax and resolution. This progress must proceed without
delay or the introduction of side issues or subplots which deviate
from the main line of development. Here again is another example
of the economy, compression, and intensification characteristic of
the drama. All the highest expressions of tragedy and comedy
demonstrate this principle.

The director's knowledge of these basic essentials of the drama
will guide his thinking as he analyzes a play for interpretation,
and will tell him how to direct it. His awareness of what constitutes the dramatic will remind him of the need for the demonstrative and the graphic in action and stage pictures, for emphasis,
and for the emotional shaping of the performance, in order to
establish and maintain clear and stimulating communication with
the audience.

Bearing in mind the nature of drama, the director next proceeds to consider the pattern of drama followed by the playwright.

This pattern will also dictate interpretation and direction. It serves to alert the director to the totality of the play before he becomes absorbed in its constituent parts and defines the shape of the play's production. Mindful of how the playwright works, the director will understand better how he too must work.

ARCHITECTURE

A play, like a house, has architecture. That is, it consists of a design and a structure. Out of the situation, characterization, dialogue, and theme—the bricks, mortar, lumber, and nails of drama —the playwright will plan and build the play. First of all, he must understand the principles of design and the characteristics and functions of materials. Then he can make some rough sketches which will eventually take final form in blueprints for the builder. Since principles can be understood only in relation to materials, we will investigate them together. First let us see what design means.

1. *Design*

The design of a play usually starts with an idea, which may be in the form of a situation together with the characters, a fragment of a story, an incident, a character, a group of characters, or a central theme. The idea may come directly from observation and experience or from a secondary source like a newspaper article, a story told by someone else, a book, etc. The idea is developed by means of a scenario—the outline of the play. This is changed until it takes form in terms of character and dialogue. The characters, above all, will bring order out of a jumble of thoughts, if the playwright will allow them to come to life and will not restrain and control them excessively. They will tell the playwright whether the play is to be a comedy, a tragedy, or something else. They will also indicate the distance from life and reality to be measured by the audience. Thus the playwright arrives at the style of the play. The characters, together with the other elements, will define the limits, the points of reference, and will give shape and emphasis to the design of the play. Thus the *germinal idea, kind,* and *style* of a play create its plan or *design.* Design is the art form and structure is the technique. Design determines structure.

2. *Structure*

a. Curve of intensity

The framework determined by the design of the play is supported by a structure consisting of the organization of the interrelated parts of drama dictated by the general character of the play. The playwright imposes such an organization of materials in order to affect the audience in a specific way and create a pattern of response. This response might be considered a curve of intensity marked by what has been called rising action and falling action. Rising and falling action is the basis of what is reputed to be the noted Broadway director George Abbott's formula for a play: Get a man up a tree in Act I, throw rocks at him in Act II, and get him down in Act III. In technical terms such action is made up of *exposition, inciting action, the dramatic problem, complication, climax,* and *resolution. Exposition,* as I have pointed out earlier, consists of explanation to the audience of all facts—past and present —of character, plot, and theme. *Inciting action* is that which results from character or circumstance and serves to propel the entire action of the play forward from a state of balance of forces to succeeding crisis, climax, and resolution. A catalytic agent is necessary for such action, who, by word, deed, or other force, causes the upset of balance. This imbalance creates *the dramatic problem:* the predicament, dilemma, or state of maladjustment. (If a play does not have a dramatic problem it is not dramatic and stageworthy.) The characters must extricate themselves from the predicament, make a choice, or adjust themselves. The dramatic problem is the springboard for action and creates, controls, and unifies all subsequent action. It is the source of the play's dramatic energy, which the director will express in the rhythm of the performance. The theme of the play evolves from the dramatic problem and expresses what the play is about. The catalytic agent is of course a source of *complication,* but other characters and circumstances can cause and affect action. Complications are needed to keep the action of a play flowing. And action must flow inevitably toward the highest peak of emotional intensity, which is the climax of the play. (In the words of one authority, "The *climax* is usually defined as the point in the plot at which the protagonist's fortunes take a definite turn for the bettter or worse.")[3] After that remains the *resolution* of all drives, forces, conflicts, and problems which brings the play to an end. Each of these component parts of the rising and falling action is used to affect audience emotion.

Gustave Freytag, a German dramatist influenced by Aristotle's theory of complication and unraveling, wrote on *The Technique of Drama* in 1863 and visualized the graph of a play as a hill with both sides equal in length; one side was the rising action and the other the falling action. The rising action consisted of the exposition and complication leading to the climax or peak of action, and the falling action after the climax consisted of the resolution and conclusion. This concept of action was challenged by Brander Matthews in his *A Study of Drama*. He conceived the action as a gradually rising line. Applied to a three-act play, the first act began with the exposition and rose to the inciting action at the end of the first act; dropping a little lower than the end of the first act to reorient the audience, the second act consisted of the complication leading to the climax at the end of the act; and again dropping below the climax, the play rose to the resolution, which was not so high as the climax, and then receded to the conclusion.[4] The difference between these two points of view lies in the interpretation of the meaning of the rising action. Matthews maintained that in order to hold the attention and interest of the audience, the action may recede slightly after the climax but must rise again through the resolution. Certainly he is right. Freytag's diagram making the falling action equal in duration to the rising action is a mistake. On the other hand, if you interpret the action after the climax as less intense than that occurring before the climax, there is some validity to his concept. In this sense the action merely means a decrease of intensity. This can be exemplified by many plays. However, many modern plays continue to rise in intensity to the very end of the play. In fact, the climax does not always come at the end of the second act; it may come somewhere in the third and often near or at the end of the third act. (Tennessee Williams' *Death of a Salesman* and *Cat on a Hot Tin Roof* are examples of continuously rising intensity.)

Although the structure of each play has its own individuality, there is a fundamental structure for all plays. The main variations in the structures of plays lie in the length and duration of their parts. And, instead of seeing the action as a Freytag hill or a gradually rising line as described by Matthews, it is more accurate to see a play in terms of a series of peaks and valleys which builds to a climax and recedes to the resolution. (It must be noted that the valleys of the second act are never so low as those of the first, and the valleys of the third act, up to the climax, are never so low as those of the second.) This scheme is more practical for the director because the parts of the action must comprise a series of crises forming the smaller peaks leading to the climactic peak. The diagram of the action of a typical modern three-act play would in general look like this:

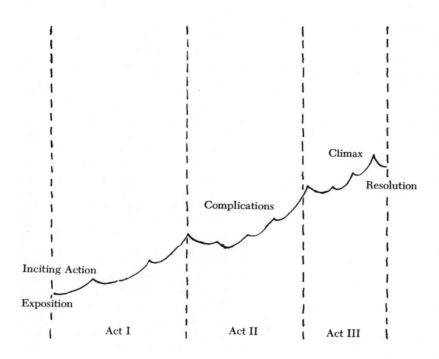

In act division this diagram approximates the relative playing time of each act of *Ghosts* and *All My Sons*, two plays of compact structure. The diagram also suggests the curve of intensity and rhythmic pattern of these plays, without reproducing exactly the peaks and valleys created by the emotional ebb and flow of the scenes. The modern two-act play like *Come Back, Little Sheba* has a similar curve of intensity, though it is divided into two scenes in the first act and three scenes in the last. The climax of this play is in the next-to-last scene and the resolution comprises the last scene. A graphic representation of this kind can be most helpful to the director in the actual rehearsals of a play.

With this view of the over-all structure or framework in mind, we can proceed to examine the organization of the elements of rising and falling action of plays. Organization will result in varying degrees of tightness and looseness of structure. From Greek classicism we have inherited a tight or compact structure, exemplified by *Oedipus Rex*. The "well-made" play, like Ibsen's *Ghosts*, is a lineal descendant. In contrast, we have the play of loose or diffuse structure, exemplified by such plays as Shakespeare's *Pericles*, Hugo's *Hernani*, Hauptmann's *The Weavers*, all the plays of Chekhov, Anderson's *Anne of the Thousand Days*, and McCullers' *The Member of the Wedding*. The authors of plays of loose structure seek freedom from the unities of time, place, and, to some degree, action. Theirs is a conscious or unconscious rebellion against the well-made play. However, much of modern drama has comparatively compact structure. Let us examine its characteristics first.

b.   Compact structure

The preparatory action of the first act consists of establishing time, place, each character, character relationships and involvements, and past events bearing on the present, and introducing the theme, a line-up of forces, and the inciting action. Aware of this pattern, the director will take special care to clarify and communicate these *dramatic facts* necessary for engaging and maintaining the audience's attention. We can demonstrate this by turning to Arthur Miller's *All My Sons*, an excellent example of post-Ibsen technique, and examining the structure of the first act. In this act, in the back yard of the Keller home somewhere in the middle west of the United States, early Sunday morning, we are introduced to Joe Keller, his wife, his son Chris, the girl Chris loves (Ann), and the neighbors of the Kellers. We learn that Ann used to live next door and was in love with Larry, Joe's son presumably lost in the war. Mrs. Keller thinks Larry is alive and that Ann still loves him and is waiting for him. Chris, Joe, and Ann believe Larry is dead. Chris has invited Ann to visit him so he may ask her to marry him. Mrs. Keller is opposed to the marriage because she thinks Ann is Larry's girl. We find out that Ann's father is in prison, convicted of failure to report defective airplane cylinder heads which later caused twenty-one P-40's to crash in Australia. Though Joe was accused of the same thing, since he and Ann's father were in business together, he was exonerated because he said he did not go to the office that day. When Ann and Chris are alone Chris talks about the necessity of man's love for man and man's kinship to man. Then Ann's brother George telephones long

distance to say he is coming to see Ann and the Kellers because
he has visited his father and his father has told him something
about the case. Mrs. Keller is upset, suspecting George is out to
stir up trouble, and she also implies that Joe knows more than
he has told. Joe says he doesn't care what Ann's father told George.
And Mrs. Keller (called Mother) says: "You're sure, Joe?"

KELLER (*frightened, but angry*). Yes, I'm sure.

MOTHER (*She sits stiffly in a chair*). Be smart now, Joe. The
boy is coming. Be smart.

KELLER (*Leans over her—into her face. Desperately*). Once
and for all, did you hear what I said? I said I'm sure!

MOTHER (*She nods weakly*). All right, Joe. (*He straightens
up*) Just . . . be smart. (KELLER, *in hopeless fury, looks at her, turns
around, goes up to porch and into the house, slamming the screen
door violently behind him.* MOTHER *sits in the chair downstage,
stiffly, staring, seeing.*)[5]

This act gives the audience all the preparatory exposition
needed for it to understand character and situation background
creating the main situation or plot premise which the audience is
asked to believe and accept. This situation finds the characters
in a state of delicate balance which involves a line-up of forces
waiting to be incited to action. George's telephone call foreshadows
him as the catalytic agent. (Ann's appearance in the first act is
used to upset the status quo. She is the catalyst of that act.) The
balance is in danger of being upset. The main action has begun.
It is to be noted that Miller creates tensions and conflicts, little
peaks and valleys, which gradually move forward in a rising action.
It is exposition with a double action and is highly dramatic. The
direction of the play is clear. The audience knows what it is about.
It knows what the dramatic problem is. The theme, expressed
by Chris in his talk with Ann, binds the elements of the act into a
cohesive whole. The audience, moreover, knows what its attitude
should be toward the entire play.

Analyzing the structure of the second act, we notice that the
tension prevailing at the end of the first act has receded slightly
to open this act. It begins at twilight that same Sunday evening;
the family are waiting for George. The tension heightens when he
arrives and tells Ann she can't marry Chris because Joe destroyed
their father. His father told him that Joe was at home when the
defective cylinder heads began to appear at the plant. He called
Joe and Joe told him to cover up the cracks and ship them out.
Joe said he would take the responsibility but didn't come to the
plant because he suddenly got sick. Later in court Joe denied

the phone call. He was exonerated and George's and Ann's father was convicted.

An argument ensues between George and Chris, George trying to convince Chris of Joe's guilt. This subsides when Mrs. Keller enters. The scene becomes peaceful and nostalgic as they talk over the past. Then the mood changes with the entrance of Joe. They begin to talk of George's father. This leads to the *inciting moment* when George traps Joe into admitting that he was not sick on the day he claimed he was—the day when the cracked cylinder heads were shipped out. Frank, one of the neighbors, enters and tells Mrs. Keller that he has worked out Larry's horoscope and that the day on which he was supposed to have died was his "favorable day" and that the odds are a million to one against a man's dying on his favorable day. George asks Ann to come home and Mrs. Keller tells her to go, that she has packed her bag. Chris says he's going to marry Ann and Mrs. Keller says he won't. Joe interferes and calls his wife a maniac for insisting these three years that Larry is still alive. She slaps his face and says that if Larry is dead Joe killed him. Joe says that Larry never flew a P-40 and therefore he didn't kill him. Chris says then Joe killed the others who crashed—twenty-one men. Joe explains that he was afraid of losing his business and took a chance on the defective parts; he did it for Chris. Chris tells him he has a duty to his country and the world. He shouldn't be thinking of business. This is a great disillusionment for Chris. In his anger and grief he pounds his father on the shoulder and stumbles away. The act moves from minor crises to this major crisis. The line-up of forces, represented by Chris and George on one side and Joe and Mrs. Keller on the other, becomes locked in a profoundly critical conflict. One side or the other must inevitably give in. Thus two points of view must be resolved to demonstrate the play's theme. We come to the end of Act II and move on to the last act.

Though the third-act opening relaxes the tension somewhat, Ann's insisting on Mrs. Keller's reading a letter from Larry which proved that he died heightens the tension again. Chris reads the letter to himself and then aloud to his father. The audience is informed that Larry committed suicide by crashing his plane when he learned that his father was responsible, because of the defective airplane parts, for the death of the twenty-one men. This is the *climax*—the turning point for Joe and "the moment of highest audience tension."[6] At this news Joe agrees to go to jail for his crime—to pay his debt to the world. He enters the house and a moment later shoots himself. Mrs. Keller turns to Chris and tells him: "Forget now. Live." Thus the crisis at the end of the second act leads to the climax and *resolution* of the third act. It will be noted that the action continues to rise from the curtain of the second act in the sense that from then on the action is forward moving rather than retrospective. The emphasis is on what the characters will do and not on what they have done. The action has declined in the sense that the play has led up to the main revelation of Joe's guilt—the crux of the dramatic problem. From then on the main knot is loosened, the threads of suspense become less taut and are unraveled with the revelation of Larry's death. When Joe commits suicide, the knot becomes untied. It must be pointed out, however, that though the rising action after the end of the second act has less accompanying suspense than the previous rising action, the emotional aftermath enhances all that comes afterward. Depth of emotion has been acquired with the loss of some of the tension of suspense.

The tragedy *Oedipus Rex* is structurally similar to *All My Sons* in that the climax comes with Oedipus' recognition scene, when he learns that he has killed his father and married his mother, though the rising action continues through Jocasta's death and his putting his eyes out. This physical action is a part of the resolution or, more properly, what Aristotle called the catastrophe. However, it might be claimed that the depth of emotion is greater after the climax of *Oedipus Rex* than after that of *All My Sons*. The reason lies in the intellectual and spiritual "size" of Oedipus in comparison with the "little man" Joe Keller. It might be pointed out that the director can direct the scenes after the climaxes so as to accelerate the pace and continue to heighten the intensity to an emotional crescendo which may surpass that of the climax. And, incidentally, the structure of the play will be a graph of the rhythmic pattern to be followed in the direction of the play. *Hamlet*, though not a "well-made" play, is a play of comparatively compact structure and has similar structural aspects. For example, if the play-within-the-play scene is the climax, we have action that continues to rise through the killing of Polonius, the burial of Ophelia, and the duel in which Laertes, Hamlet, and the King are killed. Certainly the tension should slacken only temporarily when Hamlet is sent off to England, but it gathers momentum in his fight with Laertes at the grave of Ophelia and continues to its inevitable catastrophe. Here, even more than in *Oedipus Rex*, the emotion progresses in depth at many levels.

To take one more example to test the theory of structure, we can analyze a two-act play, William Inge's *Come Back, Little Sheba*. The exposition and preparation set the plot premise and foreshadow the inciting action by the end of the first scene of Act I. The complication and struggle continue until Turk, the catalytic agent, creates the inciting moment when Doc sees him coming out of Marie's room and it is revealed that he has spent the night with her. This incites Doc to take the bottle of whisky and leave the house to return the next morning drunk. His attempt to kill Lola is the climax. He is then carried away to the hospital. This ends the second scene of Act II. Scene 3 of Act II is the resolution and is the falling action. The reconciliation of Doc and Lola and their realization that they must stop yearning for their past youth, symbolized by the lost Little Sheba, builds the play to a scene of great pathos and emotional intensity. Despite the structural traits of this play, the pattern of exposition, complication, inciting action, climax, and resolution can be applied.

c.   Diffuse structure

Inasmuch as Miller's *All My Sons* has served as an example of compact structure, it is interesting and profitable to turn to his next play, *Death of a Salesman,* because of its comparative looseness of structure. At the outset it is necessary to point out some organizational differences and similarities between the two.

All My Sons opens with an atmospheric scene in which the audience learns from the conversation of Joe, Jim, and Frank that the day is Sunday morning and there's not a cloud in the sky. Then there is some light, friendly talk about the want ads in the paper. This is a quiet, though interesting, scene of inconsequential talk among neighbors. Then there is a reference to the wind's blowing down a tree, which introduces the question of whether Kate, the mother, has seen it and the discussion of Larry's being lost in the war. Thus the play begins with a discussion which is expositional, and conflict is merely foreshadowed. Frank and Jim have a speech or two indicating a conflict in point of view. Then there is more exposition, this time about Ann's being at the Kellers'. The entrance of Jim's wife creates a good-natured tiff between her and Jim. The following short scene between Joe and Lydia, Frank's wife, tells the audience that Ann and Larry were engaged to be married. Then Frank and Lydia exit as Chris enters, and there is another reference to Ann and the question of Kate's reaction. This is a little transitional scene foreshadowing action. Bert, Jim's little boy, enters and has a conversation with Joe about playing detective and putting someone in jail. This is a light, playful scene with dramatic implications. When Bert exits, Joe returns to the subject of Kate. The audience learns that Kate insists that Larry is still alive, though Joe and Chris believe he is not. This suggests a problem and conflict leading to Chris' telling his father that he intends to ask Ann to marry him. It is assumed that Kate will object to this, and further conflict is assured. This develops into a crisis between Joe and Chris because Joe thinks it is not a good idea inasmuch as Kate thinks Larry will return. Chris insists he will marry Ann and leave his father's business. Joe is very upset because he has worked hard to leave the business to Chris. The entrance of Kate ends this conversation. From then on the conflict develops around the subject of Larry and the possible marriage between Chris and Ann. For approximately seven pages of dialogue this appears to be the main plot line of the play. When Kate tells Joe that he, above all others, must believe that Larry is still alive and will eventually return, another plot line is introduced. Gradually the play develops this second line, which by the end of the act is the dominant one. The expected arrival of Ann's brother George, Joe's business relations with their father, and the scandal of the faulty airplane engine heads complete the exposition which establishes the plot premise of the play.

In contrast, *Death of a Salesman* begins with a scene calculated to arouse suspense and tension. Linda's calling Willy "with trepidation" keys the audience to the mood. It soon learns of Willy's inner turmoil and his determination to ask his boss for work in the New York office. This scene presents Willy in a highly dramatic situation resulting from worry about his job and foreshadows the various conflicts to come. The talk that follows about the boys, Biff in particular, indicates the standing conflict between Willy and Biff, though Willy admires Biff enormously. Obviously there was once great love between father and son. The audience wants to know why their relationship has changed. And then it learns that Willy's mind is affected by his troubles because he gets the past entangled with the present and often does not know where he is.

The following scene between Biff and Happy establishes their characters and their conflicts. Suspense is heightened when, in talking about Biff's difficulties with his father, Biff says other problems are depressing to Willy. Then Biff decides to see his old employer Bill Oliver about a job the next morning. Willy reminisces about the past and in a flash-back we see him with Biff and Happy as boys and with the woman in Boston. Charley interrupts this scene from the past and has a game of cards with Willy. But Willy's mind goes back into his dream world again and brings forth Uncle Ben, Willy's ghostly symbol of success and the ideal way of life. Charley leaves Willy in disgust, and Willy continues with his thoughts of Uncle Ben and the boys, Charley, Bernard, and Linda. Linda momentarily breaks off this drama of the mind by coming to Willy, but he goes out of the house still in his memories as Biff and Happy enter.

Linda tells the boys about Willy's recent behavior, his now having a rubber hose behind the fuse box, and her fear that he is contemplating suicide. She blames the boys for not looking after him. Biff and Linda are seen in conflict about Willy. This comes to an end when Willy enters. The scene involving the four of them is one of excitement: Willy and Biff quarrel and then the boys present Biff's plan to see Oliver to borrow some money for setting Biff up in business. The scene ends with Willy's going to bed in comparative peace with Biff, and Biff goes to the basement to get the rubber hose. Thus the first-act curtain comes down with the audience looking forward to the result of Willy's seeing his boss and Biff's seeing Oliver. However, coupled with the suspense inherent in the question of the outcome of these future events is the audience's tension springing from the knowledge that the relationship between Willy and Biff is still unresolved.

We can compare the structural differences between the first acts of the two plays, starting with *All My Sons*.

1. It begins its main plot line after several pages of dialogue. The plot line initiated is about Larry's being missing in action and its effect upon the Kellers and Ann, his fiancée. This, however, might be a false lead for the audience.

2. Several pages later starts the plot line which develops into the main line of action.

3. This line of action concerns the father-son relationship, which is the dramatic problem and illustrates the theme of the play.

4. The plot unravels the past and shows the present simultaneously. The technique is Ibsenian and is quite similar to that employed in *Ghosts*. Plot sequence is based upon causal progression, which becomes increasingly tightened.

5. The action occurs in one place and during one morning.

Turning to *Death of a Salesman* we find that:

1. A state of imbalance exists at the outset of the play. Thus the plot begins immediately with conflict and there is no pure exposition. The exposition comes out of conflict.

2. Though in the opening scene between Willy and Linda the main plot line seems to concern Willy's relationship to his job, it is soon apparent that it concerns Willy's relationship to Biff. Thus the audience is not given a false start.

3. The father-son relationship is the subject of this play, just as it is in *All My Sons*.

4. The development of the plot line is based upon an expressionistic flash-back technique. The realistic and expressionistic scenes are intermingled and their cumulative effect, because it springs from inner as well as outer conflicts, creates an emotional intensification greater than that of tight causal progression founded on foreshadowed and actual outer conflicts.

5. Though this play and *All My Sons* both employ the Ibsenian retrospective action while simultaneously forwarding the action, the techniques are different. In the former the audience sees the past and in the latter it hears about it: One is demonstrative and the other is expositional. However, both result from conflict and emotion.

6. The action occurs in more than one place and over a period of years.

7. The organization of the scenes results in looser structure.

If we pursued the comparison of the structures of the two plays by studying the remaining scenes and acts, we would find other similarities and differences. In *Salesman* Miller divides the play into two acts, evidently trying to get away from the conventional three-act well-made play. His technique is suggestive of that used in the novel because of his full use of time and place. The fact that he meant the play to be novelistic may be inferred from Gassner's quotation from Miller: "the conventional play form forces the writer to siphon everything into a single place at a single time, and squeezes the humanity out of a play. Why shouldn't a play have the depth, the completeness and the diversity of a novel?"[7] Here there was an attempt to break from the bonds of tight structure and broaden the scope of the play. However, the search for freedom in structure does not mean that Miller desired diffusion of emotional effect. His starting both plays near their climaxes and going backward as well as forward indicated that he was working for depth and compactness of emotion. As has been suggested, he achieved greater suspense, tension, and general emotional intensification while exercising less rigid control of his material.

Another recent modern play is worthy of study because of its structure. This one, *The Member of the Wedding*, by Carson McCullers, is looser in structure than *Death of a Salesman*. In fact, it is so loose that it does not seem to be a play at all. It avoids being conventionally dramatic by its lack of plot. Instead it is "a triumph of feeling over plotting and of acute observation over the strenuous dramatics often supposed to be the secret of theatrical success."[8] Plot-wise, it starts off with the impending marriage between Frankie's brother Jarvis and Janice. By the end of the act the audience learns of Frankie's desire to go away with them and become a "member of the wedding." The main plot line is definitely established and so is the plot premise. Though the act demonstrates a series of minor outward conflicts among Frankie, Berenice, John Henry, and some little girl neighbors, the main conflict is inside Frankie. The second act shows Frankie after she has bought her wedding dress, and with the exception of the little scene of conflict between Honey and Mr. Adams, there is little overt action. The drama comes from Frankie's restive mind and spirit. Act III, scene 1, presents off stage the wedding and Frankie's attempt to go on the honeymoon with Jarvis and Janice. The audience sees the effect of these incidents. And again action gives way to reaction. However, the tension of this scene is jacked up considerably, first by the wedding and Frankie's attempt to go with the bride and groom and then by her running away. The references to Honey's being in trouble presage more trouble and add to the emotional atmosphere. Scene 2 shows Frankie returning home and the sudden arrival of Honey, who is running from the police after attacking a white man with a razor, and presents the news that John Henry is sick. The last scene of the act and play is essentially epilogue. The physical action of the play is over but Frankie has arrived at a new stage in her growth to maturity.

Carson McCullers wrote both the novel and the dramatic adaptation. It is natural that the technique of the novel would be transferred to the play since the author was experienced only as a writer of fiction. Though she restricts the action to one locale and the time to the space of a few days for all except the last scene, which came several months later, she does not restrict the emotional range of the play. By inlaying the varied mood patterns she creates a mosaic of feeling which gives the audience a sense of progression through sheer variety of emotion. To the audience little seems to be happening in the sense of outward action, but a great deal happens in the lives of the three central characters of the play. At the end of the second scene of the last act Frankie realizes this when she says: "The wedding—Honey—John Henry— so much has happened that my brain can't hardly gather it in. Now for the first time I realize that the world is certainly—a sudden place."[9] This is so like life that it hardly seems like a play.

In general structural organization, however, *The Member of the Wedding* is similar to all plays: It has a plot premise which the audience is asked to accept; Jarvis' proposed wedding incites the plot into action and the action develops to its climax and obligatory scene when Frankie attempts to go on the wedding trip and runs

away from home when she is prevented; and it moves to its
inevitable resolution and denouement when the last scene reveals
that she has taken one step in her growth and is about to take
another.

In *All My Sons, Death of a Salesman,* and *The Member of the
Wedding* we see structure in three degrees of compactness and
diffuseness, the first being the most compact and the last the
least. They have been selected because they represent the kinds
of structure most likely to be encountered in the modern conventional and commercial play.

To find plays with greater diffusion we must turn to the old
morality plays, Elizabethan plays, plays of the romantic school
of the nineteenth century, expressionistic and impressionistic plays.
They are characterized by many locales and characters and a broad
time spread. All except the expressionistic and impressionistic
plays have numerous subplots.

The structure of a play should be mirrored in the director's
choice of tempo and rhythmic beat for each scene and in the
pulse of the entire performance. Character tensions, their emotional
intensity, patterns and speed of movement, kind and amount of
movement and pantomimic detail, as well as the rhythmic qualities
of the dialogue will stem from the structure. If the director will
carry the rhythmic graph of the structure in his mind, he will
know how to relate the rhythm of each scene to those of the other
scenes while remembering the rhythmic shape necessary to the
whole performance. A play's structure is a vital factor in interpretation and should be reflected in the direction of the play. If the
director imposes upon a play of loose structure, *The Member of
the Wedding,* for instance, an intense and taut rhythm suitable for
a play of compact structure, the nature and style of the play will
be changed—and the play ruined. On the other hand, many plays
of loose structure, especially romantic period plays, require a
general tightening of pace for a modern audience conditioned to
sharp, climactic scene and act endings. Yet the director should
be ever perceptive of the structural qualities of a play to the extent
that they express the playwright's intentions. The rhythmic shape
of the performance must not warp the play's structure.

d.   Action in depth

The director will note that the pattern of plays of compact
or diffuse structure has been made by an over-all action which
stresses the progression of events and situations of plot. Though the
emphasis may be upon the movement of the plot, the development

and movement of other elements must be included. Structural action is action in depth.

The action of a play occurs on several levels and permeates the entire structure. As the plot moves, so do characters and theme, all propelled forward by dialogue. These elements express themselves in tributary actions feeding the main stream. We have already pointed out that plot is the interaction of character; plot and character are interdependent and cannot be separated. (They may be arbitrarily separated for purposes of discussion.) A character has will or desire causing him to act. When his action meets opposition he becomes involved with the source of the opposition. This involvement creates a *situation* and more action, resulting in more situations. A series of situations results in the *plot* of a play. Plot thus results from action and reaction or "the interplay of character and situation."[10] Obviously, action and movement operate on two levels simultaneously, in character and plot. This action is outward and inner. As a character acts outwardly, an inner action, which may be more important, is taking place inside him. This is important for the director and actor to remember. For example, Chris in *All My Sons* desires to marry Ann. As a result of this motivation Chris acts: He brings Ann home to ask her to marry him and to present to his mother their intention to be married. These actions meet opposition from his mother, and the involvement creates a situation. The creation of this situation results in a series of crises and conflicts which forward the outward action. Step by step the inner life of Chris is affected and he moves gradually to a realization that changes his whole life. Simultaneously with the outward action of the play and the inner action taking place in Chris, the characters of Mrs. Keller, Ann, Joe, and George experience inner change and movement. Coincident with the progression of outward and inner action, the theme of the play develops from the first thread revealed in the first-act conversation between Chris and Ann to a complete fabric of meaning which emerges from the play as a whole. This chain of actions and reactions forged simultaneously creates a depth and intensity of emotional response in the audience not possible from the single action of the individual elements of plot, character, or theme. Thus the tributary actions flow together in a powerful stream which generates the compulsion of the play.

COMPULSION

If the director, reading and visualizing the play as an audience of one, does not feel compelled to attend to the play, does not feel its pull in such a way as to be forced to continue to read from scene to scene and act to act to the end, the play may be judged to be deficient in the dynamics of drama. It lacks compulsion. Compulsion derives from the interaction of characters, their crises and conflicts which create a pervading suspense. This is not merely the suspense of what is going to happen next but that of how and why it is going to happen. The structure of the play defines and shapes it into the curve of intensity responsible for the general emotional impact on the audience. The directorial rhythm of the performance is the technical means of conveying it.

In *All My Sons* the author arouses our curiosity after only a few lines at the opening of the play by having Joe's neighbor Frank say, "Hey, what happened to your tree?"[11] Joe answers that last night's wind blew it down. This leads Frank to ask whether Kate knows about it. She's still asleep, Joe thinks, and he is waiting for her to see it. This makes the audience look forward to her entrance and sharpens their curiosity. When Frank says, "Larry was born in November. He'd been twenty-seven this fall. And his tree blows down,"[12] the curiosity of the audience is increased. The implications are tantalizing and the audience can hardly wait to find out the facts. It soon finds that Larry was reported missing on February 9 but Kate believes he is still alive and Frank is working on his horoscope to see whether February 9 was his favorable day; if it was, it's possible that Kate is right. Then Jim, another neighbor, appears and, on being asked by Joe whether Frank is right, Jim says he is out of his mind. This prompts Frank to say that Jim doesn't *believe* in anything. Jim's rejoinder is that Frank believes in *anything*. This little contretemps not only establishes the two characters but brings them into a conflict that adds to the tension and suspense. In fact, there is now a second line of suspense. The audience wants to know more about these two characters to test the evaluation made by each one about the other. As the scene proceeds more is revealed about Jim and Frank.

Then Jim asks where Ann is. Joe replies that she's sleeping upstairs and goes on to say that she left here a scrawny kid a couple of years ago and has returned a "regular woman." "That was a very happy family used to live in your house, Jim,"[13] concludes Joe. A third line of suspense is started. Who is Ann? Why is she here? What about her family? Is it not happy now? Miller diverts the audience's attention for a few moments by bringing on Jim's wife and then Frank's wife, thus delaying the answers to these questions and stretching the elastic of suspense. Jim's wife asks about the tree and then about Ann. What does Ann have to do with the tree? We find that she is unmarried and Frank's wife asks if she's going to get married and if there is anybody. We next learn she has been mourning the death of a boy for a couple of years. Is it Larry? Joe says he had two sons and now he has one. The war changes things. Then Chris, Joe's son, enters. There is some inconsequential talk between Frank and his wife as they exit. Joe and Chris, left alone, talk about reading the paper. This interval of dialogue relaxes the suspense only to increase it when Joe asks whether Kate and Ann are up. The author keeps the audience's attention focused on the plot line of the play and does not divert it for long. The audience is compelled to listen and to be involved. Chris says that his mother Kate and Ann are up. Joe asks Chris whether he has seen the tree and wonders what Kate will say. The entrance of Jim's little boy Bert prevents the pursuit of that subject and thwarts the audience's curiosity.

Joe's conversation with Bert about their game of playing policeman and jail appears to be for comic relief, but later on it will have symbolic value and will be seen to have foreshadowed coming events and to have revealed Joe's character, past and present. In this little scene with Bert the gun is "planted." It is the gun Joe uses to kill himself in the last act. This foreshadowing adds to the general compulsion of the play. The fact, too, that this scene is light and amusing intensifies the emotional impact of the scenes that follow. The intensification results because of the contrast of mood and because the apparent lightness of the scene with Bert is later revealed to be portentous. Its ironical value enhances the tension.

In outlining the act up to this point we see how the author, forwarding the play on several levels, selects and organizes his materials to engage the attention and curiosity of the audience and create suspense. In so doing he has created certain expectations which must lead to eventual gratification. They are aspects of compulsion. For example, in the very first act he raises the question of whether Larry is dead or alive. This line of suspense continues until near the end of the play. All along the audience expects an answer. At last it is gratified when Ann's letter from Larry is read by Chris. In addition to the expectation that questions be answered, the audience expects opposing forces to come together finally to fight out their differences. This expectation must be gratified, especially if the forces are central and are responsible for the main line of action of the play. Joe and Chris are central to the theme of the play and there must be a showdown between the two. It comes at the end of Act II; it is the *obligatory scene* of the play. There are minor obligatory scenes between Chris and Kate, Joe and Kate, Ann and Kate, Ann and Chris, and Joe and

George. Audience expectation leads to these scenes. Their gratification is the satisfying reward accruing from the compulsion of the play. The resolution of each conflict and of the web of conflicts leading to the climax is also the outcome of expectation and, as such, is gratifying. Gratification ensuing from the play's resolution cannot be complete, however, unless it is, in the opinion of the audience, logical and inevitable. Certainly the resolutions of the subsidiary conflicts in this play are logical and inevitable. The resolution of the entire play, insofar as it relates to Joe's suicide, has logic and some degree of inevitability. It is undeniable that his life has been a failure and that he has nothing to live for as he sees it. Yet it might be asked whether his going to jail in expiation of his crime might not be a stronger action than killing himself. This might give him spiritual stature which would add to the tragic tone of the play. His suicide may appear to some to be melodramatic—for sheer shock effect. Of course his suicide is consistent with the weakness of character he has shown in committing the crime of shipping the defective airplane parts, lying about it, and allowing his partner to be falsely convicted and imprisoned. His life has been a lie. Miller has been consistent and logical with his characters, who are not of the tragic but of the dramatic mold. (In view of his article in *The New York Times* about *Death of a Salesman* and the tragedy of the common man, he would not agree that his characters are not tragic.[14])

In speaking of consistency, logic, and inevitability we are concerned with the operation of motivation, which must be inherent in all drama.

MOTIVATION

The architecture of any particular play must be based on motivations individual to the characters, events, and theme selected by the playwright. They constitute the control to be exercised in the selection and use of the elements of drama. Audience belief and conviction are secured by motivations. Subconsciously the audience measures each moment by the questions: "Would he do that? Would he say that? Would he feel that way?" It answers them by saying, "I believe" or "I don't believe."

An audience, because of its willing suspension of disbelief, will accept motivations for theatrical or conventional reasons rather than psychological reasons if the kind and style of play—the frame of reference—demand such motivations. Nevertheless, the playwright must prepare the audience to accept the motivations. The foreshadowing of attitudes, actions, and reactions is the technique employed. A hint, an implication, a teasing question left unanswered for the time being are sufficient. For example, the audience is quite willing to accept and believe Jim's revelation about his disillusionment and his leaving his wife to seek spiritual freedom because Jim has been established previously as a skeptic. Frank's belief in horoscopes is equally acceptable because it is motivated by all his dialogue and previous actions. When Chris reacts so violently against his father at the end of Act II he is believable and convincing because we have been shown his idealism in the scene with Ann earlier. The closing lines of dialogue between Joe and Kate at the end of Act I foreshadow and motivate the revelation of Joe's guilt in Act II.

As an example of improper and unconvincing motivation, let us consider an unproduced play which presents an attractive, intelligent, and stable middleaged college professor, a man whose counsel his students and friends seek, apparently living in happiness with his wife. He cannot at the whim of the playwright, without sufficient foreshadowing preparation, suddenly fall violently in love with his son's fiancée simply because he sees her in a revealing negligee. The audience will not believe it. Nor will it believe that the girl, established as one in love and willing to marry his son, suddenly finds herself in love with the boy's father. There is not the proper motivation for such a turn of events. Underlying motivation is the law of cause and effect which is also related to consistency, logic, and inevitability.

CAUSAL PROGRESSION[15]

Action, reaction, and interaction progress in accordance with causality. In *All My Sons* Frank's working out Larry's horoscope to prove that February 9 was his favorable day leads him and Kate to believe that Larry is not dead. This belief causes Kate to say that Ann must not marry Chris. Only the disclosure of Larry's letter about his intended suicide convinces Kate of his death. George's coming to the Kellers' causes the family to learn the truth about Joe. The causal progression of plot must be reflected in the directing and acting of the play.

Character intention is the cause of a conflict with another character or with forces within or without the character. Director and actor awareness of a sequence of causality will help them to bring design to the play and the characters.

A plot is actually a design created by causal progression. It is an interconnecting chain of events occurring in a forward movement propelled by causality. E. M. Forster in his *Aspects of the*

Novel makes the distinction between story and plot by invoking the concept of cause and effect.[16] In story he says the king died and then the queen died. In plot, the king died and the queen died of grief. Here is causality. Which is the more dramatic? Plot. A play is more effective if it possesses a good plot, which is the result of selection, order, and organization, rather than story, which is unselected and disorganized. Plot has causal progression; story does not. Moreover, causal progression ensures direction, compression, intensification, and the resultant emotion and thought desired by the writer. This is the end result of all effective drama. If drama is to be not only effective but a work of art, it must achieve unity, an outgrowth of causal progression.

UNITY

There is a natural desire for unity. It is not surprising that an audience looks for it in a play or other work of art and is dissatisfied when it is lacking—whether or not it is consciously aware of its absence. Unity, balance, and form are associated with beauty. Unity is a part of aesthetic pleasure. An audience seeks it as the natural concomitant of the artistic experience to be found in the theatre. It, no less than motivation, consistency, cause and effect, and inevitability, brings gratification and satisfaction.

As critics have pointed out, Aristotle insisted only on the unity of action and not on the unity of time or place. His saying that tragedies usually consumed no more time than that measured by a single revolution of the sun is not tantamount to saying that more time could not be consumed. He merely stated the practice and not the rule. The critics of the Renaissance interpreted his remarks as a rule and also deduced that unity of place was necessary for verisimilitude and belief. Thus they, instead of Aristotle, are responsible for the so-called "Aristotelian unities." Though critics for many eras thereafter followed the injunction of the Renaissance, modern critics and playwrights feel compelled to give attention to none of the unities except that of the unity of action. This is indeed the most important unity in the architecture of drama. It, more than the other two, is essential to a play's structure.

Unity of action is a natural and logical result of the compression and concentration required of dramatic art. The requirements of time in the theatre necessitate control and concentration of action. What Shakespeare called the two hours' traffic of the stage will not permit multiple or meandering plots. It is true that Shakespeare, who continued in the traditions of the medieval drama rather than those of the Greek, used numerous subplots, but he eventually drew them together in a single line of action (*Henry IV, Part One, King Lear,* and *Twelfth Night,* for example). The length of his plays in the modern theatre is a vexing problem to many present-day theatregoers, who must get home soon after eleven o'clock in order to have enough sleep for the next day, which begins at eight or nine o'clock.

Even though the romanticists, under the aegis of Victor Hugo, revolted against the classicism of Corneille and Racine and their adherence to the unities, and indulged in unrestrained freedom of diverse action, the result dramatically was neither more realistic nor more effective. As a matter of fact, the realists like Ibsen and most modern playwrights have found unity of action an asset and a necessity. It has produced greater intensity and compulsion. It has sharpened the focus and heightened the emotional response of the audience. Notice the concentrated action of *A Doll's House, Ghosts, All My Sons, A Streetcar Named Desire, Death of a Salesman,* and numerous other examples of realistic theatre. A large share of the emotional effectiveness of these plays is dependent upon unity of action.

It is interesting to note too that these plays, except *Death of a Salesman,* adhere pretty much to the unities of place and time. And this play adheres to the unity resulting from a multiple-scened setting requiring no scene changes, which makes for concentration in effect. The economics of modern professional theatre demand a single setting and thereby affect the unity of the play's structure. Though the present-day playwright often writes effectively by eschewing the law of unity of place, he more often than not obeys it. (The musical and revue type of show can indulge in numerous and diverse settings because it aims for a chiroscuro and a non-concentrated theatrical effect. The more settings there are, the more spectacular they become; and spectacle is one of their characteristics.)

Unity of time is perhaps the least necessary of the unities. However, looseness and diversity of time can present definite problems to the playwright. They usually manifest themselves in a resultant looseness and diminution of tension and emotional effect. Even Shakespeare in a number of his chronicle plays has fallen victim to his use of disjointed time. Fortunately for him, the power of his poetry has sometimes compensated for the lack of this unity. On the other hand, a modern play like *All My Sons* is considerably more powerful because of its compression of time into "a single revolution of the sun."[17] Except for remembered time, the same is true of *Death of a Salesman,* another play with great emotional impact.

Unity resulting from the centrality of character is another aspect of structure. The hero of biographical and historical plays can, because of his dominance over diverse actions, locales, and extension of time, achieve unity of effect. *Abe Lincoln in Illinois, Victoria Regina,* and *Anne of the Thousand Days* are examples. The audience feels the unity because of the all-pervading attractiveness of the central character who so deeply involves their emotions. A play in which the playwright centers the audience's attention on a group of characters rather than on a single character can, through sheer richness of character, also give the impression of a work of unity. In such cases unity of time and place contribute to the sense of over-all unity. *The Cherry Orchard, The Sea Gull, The Three Sisters,* and *The Lower Depths* are examples.

Inasmuch as characters are so inextricably interwoven into a play's meaning, they project a theme which effects unity. This is true of *Abe Lincoln in Illinios* and the character-group plays just cited. They are the embodiment of the themes circumscribing the plays. The multiscened play about Lincoln is extended in time, but the man who fears his destiny and its incumbent responsibilities and obligations to his nation projects meaning and unity into a patchwork of events. The lives of Chekhov's and Gorki's characters are inseparable from the meaning which aids in bringing unity to the plays. No less important than their meanings and as adjuncts to them are the authors' guiding attitudes and philosophies of life which pervade their plays. The particular concepts of life seen by Chekhov and Gorki tend to give coherence to their seemingly directionless and static works. They are the core of the meanings of their plays.

Perhaps the most quickly felt and perceptible lack of unity occurs to the audience when the total emotional effect of the play seems chaotic and confusing. As we have pointed out before, the audience wants to know what its emotional response to a play should be. If the playwright has been successful in establishing unity of mood, the audience knows whether it is to laugh or cry or react in some other way. A mixture of moods can be confusing to the audience. No doubt some members of an audience watching Sean O'Casey's *Juno and the Paycock* are disturbed by his mixing the comic Joxer-Captain Boyle scenes with the serious scenes involving Johnny, Mary, and Mrs. Boyle. He establishes a comic point of view and then shifts to a serious one. By actual count of scenes and time duration of scenes, the comic ones occupy the stage more often and longer than the serious ones. Here is a lack of tonal unity. Yet the play achieves unity through its characters and theme, which are bound together by O'Casey's personal view of Irish life. There is unity of action too. Johnny Boyle's subplot line is only a minor thread but it contributes to what O'Casey intends the play to say. Too, the juxtaposition of the serious scenes with the comic enhances the serious ones. DeQuincy[18] pointed this out in the *London Magazine* in October, 1823, in his discussion of the porter's scene in *Macbeth*. The low comedy of the porter's speech by contrast with the terrifying discovery of Duncan's murder makes this event the more shocking. It creates an emotional response appropriate to the announcement that "Most sacrilegious murder hath broke ope/The Lord's annointed temple . . ."[19] Here is an act of sacrilege. More than a crime—a sin—has been committed. Shakespeare uses this same technique of contrast when he places the gravediggers' scene of macabre humor immediately before the Ophelia burial scene, in which Hamlet and Laertes fight around and over the dead body. Violent contrast of mood serves both to enhance the serious tone of the following scene and to underscore its intellectual values as well. The concept of the divinity of kings is given eloquent and moving meaning in the scenes from *Macbeth,* and the subject of death and the brevity of man's life is made sharply and shockingly meaningful in *Hamlet.* Similarly, O'Casey underscores poverty, ignorance, waste, and man's inhumanity to man by presenting the comic spectacle of the lazy, gossipy, lying, narrow-minded Captain Boyle and Joxer in contrast with the plight of Johnny, Mary, and Mrs. Boyle. Too, O'Casey is saying that Boyle and Joxer are typical Irish comic characters at whom the Irish and everybody else laugh, but he is saying too that they shouldn't be laughed at. The Irish and the world ought to point the finger of shame and scorn at their depravity and uselessness. They should be condemned and not made light of. Ireland is poor, sick, and illiterate, and something should be done about it. The world should sorrow for Cathleen Ni Houghlihan.

This technique of contrasting moods is used extensively in melodrama. It is part of the suspense pattern. A scene of great expectation, excitement, and suspense is broken by a comic line, piece of business, or scene. This is known as comic relief—relief from tension. Such relief heightens the tension that follows. This has become a classic device for writers and directors of mystery melodramas. American audiences have been thrilling to this emotional teasing ever since Zazu Pitts appeared as the jittery, screaming maid in Mary Roberts Rhinehart's *The Bat.* Alfred Hitchcock has used this device as his personal trademark in his direction of the films *The Lady Vanishes, The Forty-nine Steps, Foreign Correspondent, Rebecca, Rear Window,* and others. He builds up the suspense through silences, atmosphere, and music,

or relentlessly searching dialogue or taut action, and then he makes
the audience laugh by showing the trivial antics of a cocker
spaniel, the inane ditherings of two British soccer fans, or by
suddenly scaring the audience by some sharp and dry sound.
Sudden sharp changes of mood when used with sufficient fre-
quency create a pattern and a kind of tonal unity. (As has been
pointed out before, change and contrast in tempo are also a part
of Hitchcock's methods.)

The recent practice of mixing moods to create unconventional
types of plays presents an interesting problem in unity. *Arsenic
and Old Lace* makes fun of murder. Here is a farcical melodrama.
The laughable is mixed with the suspenseful. The comic mood
predominates, however, even during the scenes of suspense because
the audience laughs at itself for becoming tense when it knows
that the action on stage will resolve happily, that it is safely removed from the action. It is enjoying being teased. Thus there
is unity of feeling. Ionesco's *Rhinoceros,* however, is an example of
the ambivalence of mood. Its humor is underlined with or counter-
pointed by the mocking seriousness of its theme. In fact, it is a
frightening comedy. A number of other French *avant-garde* plays,
whose chief concern is the absurdity of life, present the director
with the problem of disunity of mood. Edward Albee's *The Zoo
Story* is an American representative of the same general subject
but the humor turns to shocking seriousness at the end and the
dichotomy of moods actually deepens the total emotional effect
of the play.

A great deal of critical ink has been spilled over the question
of the unity of Shakespeare's *Henry IV, Part One.* That old devil
Falstaff has been the chief source of trouble. First of all, in the
opinion of some the comedy of Falstaff has jarred the serious
tone of Hotspur's quarrel with King Henry. Again, however, it
can be argued that comic contrast can serve to heighten the serious.
The comedy is also relief from political tedium and furnishes
much-needed variety. As a matter of fact, the mood contrasts
make for interest. Several attempts have been made to separate
the comic plots and serious plots into two plays, but the results
have not been satisfactory. The Falstaff plays have failed because
of too much fat meat and the Prince Hal-Hotspur plays because
of too much lean. Brooks and Heilman make a good case for the
unity of the play by showing that Falstaff demonstrates another
aspect of the honor theme projected by Hotspur.[20] The disparity
of their points of view is necessary to the exposition of the theme.
Both Falstaff and Hotspur illustrate the extremes. Both are childish
and childlike in their attitudes. Here is unity by contrast. In addi-

tion, though the Falstaff-Hal plot line alternates with the Hotspur-Henry line, the two come together and are unified in Act III, scene 3. Unity of action is ultimately achieved. Many critics have called the play, composed of the central characters of Falstaff, Prince Hal, and Hotspur, three headed and thus lacking unity. Extending the argument of Brooks and Heilman about character constrasts and similarities, it might be said that each of the three constitutes an aspect of the same character. If the play can be said to be about training for kingship, the frivolity of Falstaff, the wild ways of Hal, and the pride of Hotspur serve to teach needful lessons in the schooling of a king. Prince Hal matures to his responsibilities. Though he does not reject Falstaff and his way of life until *Part Two* of the play, his speeches over the supposedly dead body of Falstaff and the corpse of Hotspur reveal development and growth toward eventual manhood. The character triad of Falstaff, Hal, and Hotspur demonstrates unity by contrast.

The question of the unity of a play is extremely important to the director. It is the key to the physical production of the play as it relates to time, place, and action, to the focus of the play in terms of dramatic values, and to the basic problem of audience attitude, orientation, and the control of its emotional response. Though this problem imposes a heavy burden upon the director's interpretive and directorial ability, structural unity accruing from the contrast of mood, character, and action multiplies the layers of emotions and enriches the texture of the play.

TEXTURE

The texture of a play might be described as its emotional stratification expressed vertically and horizontally. Stretching over the play horizontally is its all-encompassing style, which is a unifying agent. Beneath this upper horizontal emotional layer is that created by the mood and kind of play: tragedy, comedy, melodrama, drama, farce, etc. Vertically, numerous emotional layers can be found, the number varying with each particular play. One layer is created by the emotional qualities of the characters as individuals—their individual inner and outer tensions and involvements. Another results from the complexities of action made up of its own layers. The pattern of thematic threads forms another layer. The symbolic and metaphoric suggestiveness of the play might be said to form still another emotional layer. If the critic and director take them all together, horizontally and vertically, they can assess the play's texture by descriptive adjectives and similes. *All My Sons* is homespun, durable, rough cut, without gloss, dark brown streaked with black and green, with threads that, criss-crossing and intertwining in depth, form a pattern of meaning. Its fabric does not tear easily but once torn it unravels quickly and permanently. *Henry IV, Part One,* is a tapestry of rich and vibrant colors, with three main warm colors dominant. The design is Gothic in spirit: It soars and it moves leisurely but always with virile heartiness and swagger. It is not lacking in grace and wit, though the latter may be larded o'er with unblushing references to "country matters."[21] Here is little delicacy but a great deal of fiery feeling circumscribing duty and honor. It is a procession of banners flapping to the warm but fresh wind blowing off Elizabeth's England.

This purview of the nature and pattern of drama as a literary form is intended to equip the director with a fundamental grasp of what to expect in the play as a work designed for the theatre and to make him aware of certain interpretive and directorial problems inherent in drama.

4

tentials of Dramatic Values

IN THE ___ ter the director has been concerned with the general charac___ ics of drama unique to it as a literary form and with some of the special problems of dramatic writing. These problems exist for the playwright regardless of the type or style of play he may intend to write. Their solution depends on the use of certain working principles to which there is a basic adherence by all who write plays. A knowledge of these principles should help the director to a better understanding of the process of constructing and writing a play and this should facilitate his job of interpretation and direction. Up to this point he has tried to understand the totality of the play and those aspects which are all-pervasive. Now he is ready to investigate the playwright's technique as it affects the emotional climate of the play as a whole and the parts of a play to test them for their dramatic potentials and general stageworthiness.

Directorial interpretation in a general sense consists of finding any and all aspects of a play that can be considered potentially dramatic and therefore interesting to the audience. The greater the number and the finer the dramatic quality of such aspects, the richer the theatrical experience will be for the audience. Each aspect possesses its own dramatic traits and audience appeal and is of value dramatically. The playwright's treatment and the director's subsequent interpretation and direction give each its relative value. Although anything in a play that is emotionally and intellectually stimulating to an audience may be considered to have dramatic value, the main dramatic values come from the aspects of *mood, character, plot, dialogue,* and *theme* of the play. All except mood are the basic elements used by the playwright to compose a play, and the director is concerned with them in interpreting it. Certain plays, however, may possess special dramatic values peculiar to them by virtue of their type, style, novelty, singularity, or other individual qualities which will appeal to audiences. These special dramatic values will be considered when we discuss the focus of a play achieved by the relative dominance of its values. (See "Points of Focus.")

The director analyzes mood, character, plot, and theme values for the dramatic power of each and must also regulate and relate by techniques of directing the amount and kind of power inherent in a value to conform with the over-all interpretation of the play. Values will, of course, vary from play to play and from interpretation to interpretation. This variation comes from the kind, amount, and degree of drama emanating from each value and the amount of emphasis it receives.

For many years the accepted critical procedure was to give primary attention to the play's characters. In fact, character analysis formed the entire body of criticism and interpretation. (Coleridge, Hazlitt, Bradley, and other members of the romantic school of Shakespearean criticism followed this view and devoted all their work to character analysis. Moreover, the analyses were from a psychological point of view—just as though the characters were real people. Elmer Edgar Stoll and others have finally righted matters and have emphasized the fact that Shakespeare's plays are works of art and should not be considered life. This is true, of course, of all plays. They must be analyzed and criticized as art, with life as the reference point.) The characters are certainly of vital interest to the audience. Plays are about human conduct and, as we have already seen in our discussion of the audience, people go to the theatre to participate vicariously in the lives of others and learn more about them. However, the director must analyze and interpret the characters of a play in terms of that particular play. The play as a whole restricts, confines, and limits character behavior. Therefore, it must be approached as an entity and be so understood before the various parts—character, dialogue, plot, and theme—are analyzed. The star actor very often makes the mistake of judging the stageworthiness of a play entirely by its characters and/or its possibilities as a personal vehicle. The actor-director also frequently falls into this error by interpreting a play in terms of the characters to the exclusion of the other elements. Interpretation primarily through character is proper and effective if the play is a study of character and character is its point of focus. Even so, character emphasis implies a relation to other elements within a given framework. This means that the other elements must receive their share of attention and all must be in reference to the play as a whole.

Inasmuch as the anticipated response of the audience is the director's interpretive guide he must first think in terms of this response. In watching a play the audience receives impressions moment to moment, scene to scene, and ultimately organizes them into a single over-all impression of the play. This organized total impression is the one it will remember and refer to. The memory of this impression consists mostly of a feeling experienced from the play. Intellectual impressions are secondary in importance and are secondary in sequence of response. It is logical then that the emotional impact of the whole play should be the director's first consideration in interpretive procedure.

MOOD

The director reads the play and responds to it unconsciously as he imagines it on the stage. Afterward he becomes consciously aware of the emotional state resulting from the imagined performance. It is a kind of exhilaration, a heightening of feeling. Specifically, his emotional state is his mood. It must be pointed out at once that the word "mood" means more than the popular and loose conception which implies an emotional state of "moodiness" when one may be irritable, capricious, sad, serious, or off in another world. Mood here means a state or temper of mind which results from feeling and, as such, it includes the entire gamut of emotions possible to a human being.

The great difficulty in responding to the mood of a play as one reads it to one's self lies in the inability to hear the dialogue as spoken, to see the movement, pantomimic detail, and groupings of the characters together with their costumes and scenic background. The director must read to see the images the words make and to hear the sounds they make. He must learn to be so responsive to the visual and aural stimuli of the play that his imagined performance will be a picture of the actual performance. Although the student may learn to do this after many years of experience, the problem may be considerably lessened by a conscious effort to improve his capacity for responsiveness. Listening to music, likening it to a play, and analyzing his responses will be helpful.

1. Music and mood

Music has universal appeal. The response to it is immediate and usually effortless, perhaps because of its rhythmic and melodic nature. Music is an ideal aid for developing the director's sensitivity to the rhythmic and melodic qualities of the auditory and visual aspects of a theatrical production which create mood.

The late great teacher of play directing Alexander Dean recognized this and for years played for his classes recordings of Chopin's preludes to teach the similarity between the emotional qualities of music and the mood of a play. The interesting thing about this experiment was the general agreement among the students about the evocative and connotative qualities of particular preludes which suggested the moods of certain plays. For example, the tenth prelude has a playful, impish mood quality similar to that of Sherwood's *Reunion in Vienna*. For many students the eleventh prelude evokes a general feeling of physical activity and conflict of a melodramatic sort. Its mood seems like that of many early American melodramas, Gillette's *Secret Service*, for instance. The twelfth prelude has a sweet, sad, sentimental, and meditative quality reminiscent of *East Lynne*. (Of course, responses to music are associational. See Leonard Meyer's *Emotion and Meaning in Music*, Chicago, University of Chicago Press, 1956.)

Listening to music in this way develops not only responsiveness to mood but even the sensing of the necessary directorial treatment in terms of movement, business, pictorial dramatization, and rythm. Mr. Dean's classes and those taught in succession by the writer have demonstrated this. In fact, the process of analyzing the mood of music often becomes, in the minds of the students, inseparable from the technical approach to the staging of the plays. This is evidence that mood dictates specific technique.

2.   *Play elements creating mood*

The elements of a play which create mood include all those aspects that are of an emotionalizing nature. Dialogue is strong in its emotional quality: the sound, connotation, and imagery of words, their selection, emphasis, arrangement, and melody. The dialogue of Noel Coward's *Private Lives*, for example, is epigrammatic and witty, evoking laughter. That of Maxwell Anderson's *Winterset* creates a feeling of profound seriousness and tragedy underlined by the sharp bite of modern connotation and colloquialism. The emotional elasticity of plot is readily recognized in terms of suspense, complications, and surprise. *The Visit*, by Friedrich Duerrenmatt, demonstrates this. Character actions, reactions, and states of mind affect the tone of a play. The characters in Ustinov's *Romanoff and Juliet* possess a variety of tonal aspects quite different from those in Hellman's *The Little Foxes*, yet both sets of characters stimulate the audience's feelings. It must be pointed out that, although the characters of a play as a group create a dominant mood, each one brings variety to the over-all mood of the play through his own individual mood. The element of idea in a play is primarily intellectualizing, yet it usually has its emotional impact as well. The central idea of Odets' *Waiting for Lefty* is so emotionally stirring that the play, when originally produced, was one of the most electrifying experiences in the theatre. *Darkness at Noon, Time Limit,* and *The Skin of Our Teeth* are other examples of theme plays that strongly move the emotions.

In addition to the contributions made by dialogue, plot, character, and idea, there are the factors of locale, historical period, season of year, time of day, and social background that affect mood. The middle-class family with social ambitions in eighteenth-century England in *Pride and Prejudice* creates a strongly pervading flavor and spirit. Present-day, poverty-stricken, crime-breeding sections of New York City like the one in *Dead End* establish the entire emotional key of a play. The cold, barren, wintry plains of the countryside come on stage with each character in Susan Glaspell's *Trifles* and effect stark tragic implications.

3. *Analysis and description of mood*

Since mood is evanescent and becomes elusive with time and familiarity, the director must seek means of remembering his initial response and making it permanent. Mental pictures, emotionalizing symbols, descriptive words and phrases can serve as stimuli to the memory and fixatives for the mind. To illustrate, John Millington Synge's *Riders to the Sea* may be analyzed. (This is the play chosen to illustrate the entire procedure of creative interpretation at the end of this book.) On reading it and hearing it in the mind's ear, one may be moved by the undercurrent sound of the waves of the sea beating relentlessly against the rocks and by the low mournful keen of women whose voices seem half human and half animal. Furthermore, there is a simple straightforward, rugged, cosmic strength about the play which evokes beauty no less than soul-stirring sorrow—sorrow for the helplessness of mankind's futile struggle against the omnipotent forces of fate and nature. It is with the help of this descriptive and expository analysis that a director can stimulate the memory of an emotional experience which we call mood.

The analysis of a totally different and contrasting mood may further clarify the discussion. *The Constant Lover,* by St. John Hankin, is the antithesis in mood. It is fresh, pastoral, gay, bright, sparkling, and bubbling like a small, effervescent brook in springtime. Here is a carefree, Oscar Wildean game of hearts, punctuated by the flip, mechanical chirrups of the cuckoo, which touch off the mind to light laughter and the heart to faint nostalgia.

4. Mood variations

Monotony in a theatrical performance is one of the surest means to failure. An audience demands variety. Variety of mood is essential. In explaining how a playwright could write a successful play, Wilkie Collins once said, "Make 'em laugh, make 'em weep, make 'em wait." The director of *The Diary of Anne Frank*, for example, might make the mistake of continuously stressing the serious, melodramatic, and tragic from the beginning to the end of the play. Not only is comic relief necessary because of the emotional strain on the audience but it makes the serious scenes infinitely more effective through contrast. The director of the serious play needs a good sense of humor. The wise director of comedy is well aware of the fact that continuous laughter is tiring and monotonous, and needs the relief of seriousness. The productions of *The Male Animal* and *Life with Father* are excellent examples of playwriting and direction which capitalize on mood variety. The production of Dylan Thomas' *Under Milk Wood* demands a well-thought-out pattern of mood variations.

5. Mood units

The study of a play will show that it may be broken into units of mood. To refer again to *Riders to the Sea*, we will recall that it opens with Cathleen on stage finishing making a cake, which she puts down in the pot oven by the fire, and then she wipes her hands and sits down and begins to spin at the wheel. Nora enters and "in a low voice" asks, "Where is she?" There is a whispered conversation about clothes from a drowned man brought by a young priest who thinks they belong to Michael. During the middle of this conversation the door is blown open by a gust of wind. As the two girls continue speaking, they hear Maurya stirring in the next room and immediately hide the clothes in the turf-loft when the old woman enters. She, thinking that Cathleen is looking for turf, is totally unsuspecting, and with the mention of Bartley's going to Connemara, the subject changes to whether he will go, what with the wind and the tide. The entrance of Maurya marks the end of one mood unit and the beginning of another.

The emotional effect of this first unit comes from the quietness as Cathleen moves around doing her chores and the surprise of the sudden opening of the door, with the sound of the wind and the sea, as Nora whispers her opening lines and softly enters the room. Mystery, suspense, and excitement pervade the stage, causing a tension which increases when a gust of wind bangs the door, heightens with the entrance of Maurya, and is not relaxed and changed until she sits down and begins talking of Bartley. The scene up until Bartley's entrance comprises the second mood unit, which is transitional, a unit of comparative relaxation underlined with tension and foreboding, and blends into a third mood.

As Bartley makes a halter with a rope, then puts on another coat, Maurya pleads with him not to go to sea, but he does not answer, merely asking Cathleen to look after the sheep and try to sell the pig with the black feet. After Nora tells him that the ship is coming to the pier, he gets his purse and tobacco and goes out. Here we have a tension quite different from that of the first unit; there is no mystery and suspense but a feeling of deep sympathy with characters struggling against one another, themselves, and fate. Thus we could analyze each change of mood in the play and work out a series of mood or tonal units.

Because of the popular conception of mood which does not associate the word with lightness and gaiety, it is worth while to analyze a comedy for its mood variations. Recalling the brightly titillating quality of *The Constant Lover*, it is interesting to discover the changes and differences in tone. In his stage directions the author writes, "The orchestra will play the Woodland Music (cuckoo) from *Hansel and Gretel* and possibly some of the Grieg Pastoral Music from *Peer Gynt*, or some Gabriel Fauré"[1] before the curtain rises. The play opens with Cecil sitting under a tree, reading a book, with birds chattering and cooing all around. A cuckoo's call is heard above it all. The scenery and the sound effects set the mood for the entire play: Here is spring under a big green tree, with sunshine and gaiety everywhere. As Evelyn enters and Cecil reproaches her for being late, pastoral peace and calm are broken by the comic conflict between them. It all really seems like a gentle tennis match with the ball being hit back and forth. The bantering does not subside until Evelyn confesses that she is the one who should have thought of the roses and admits, "But this morning I forgot," and Cecil says, "I see." This marks the end of unit one.

On Cecil's invitation to sit down, Evelyn hesitates and then sits but begins to fear that she really shouldn't. The boy's epigrammatic rejoinders gradually allay her fears and she is completely convinced when he lays his hand on hers for a moment after saying he would always have regretted it if he hadn't spoken to her a week ago. The sudden loud call of the cuckoo breaks the spell and she draws her hand away. This is the end of the second tonal unit and the beginning of the third. Here is teasing suspense broken by chuckling laughter which eventually lapses into dreamy calmness. Talk of the cuckoo leads Cecil and Evelyn into the eternal quarrel between the male and female points of view and we are launched upon another mood. An examination of the entire play will help the director to evolve a tone pattern made up of great variety.

6. Graph of mood variations

For the sake of study and subsequent direction, the director might find it profitable to mark off each tonal unit in the script and even work out a graph of changes in order to fix each mood variation in mind and give the key to each scene as it is being directed.

Now let us turn to the dramatic potentials of a play's theme.

THEME

1. Definition and function

In one sense the theme of a play is its subject or topic—what it is about in terms of the composite elements of the play. A description of what happens often constitutes the theme in the minds of the audience. In another sense, theme is more precisely the overruling idea of the play which can be reduced to a simple declarative statement. This concept is associated with the drama of ideas. This is of course a limited use of the word "idea" which is usually associated with social, moral, or political reform. Plays of "idea" in the broad sense of the word certainly include all plays with meaning and cover the entire field of dramatic literature, beginning with the Greeks and including the latest play by any one of the French avant-garde playwrights.

Stemming specifically from the drama of ideas are the problem play, the thesis play, and the propaganda play. The problem play simply presents the problem without taking sides or offering a solution. Galsworthy's Strife is an example. The thesis play presents the problem and offers a solution or at least an interpretation, e.g., All My Sons. The propaganda play presents a problem, offers a solution, and urges definite action, as in Waiting for Lefty. In each of these three kinds of plays characters tend to be subordinated to idea.[2]

In our discussion of theme as a dramatic value the word will be understood to cover all the meanings cited above. It is a term to signify the dramatized thought of the play.

Mood, as we have emphasized, is the emotional climate enveloping the entire play. The theme or meaning of a play, though having an emotional effect upon the audience, is primarily intellectual in effect. In order to be all-encompassing in our definition, we might say that the theme is the total emotional and intellectual meaning of a play. Inasmuch as it emanates from the play as a whole, it is important for the director to consider it in connection with mood in analyzing a play for interpretation and direction.

Like the mood, the theme permeates a play and affects each element. Born out of creative emotion, it is the objectification of subjectivity. It is *conceptual*. It therefore is formative and sets limits for its component parts. We shall see later how characters, dialogue, and plot contribute to the theme and are restricted by it. By permeating a play and affecting its various parts, the theme organizes and unifies the play. It is the overruling rationale which gives it direction and shape.

A sermon, debate, essay, or other nondramatic writing can express theme in verbal explanations and arguments. A play cannot argue in words alone but must demonstrate in action and character. Brooks and Heilman make this quite clear in their discussion of the use of theme in *Everyman*.[3] The playwright asks the audience to comprehend his meaning through emotional response and the power of imagination. The audience is involved in the action of the play while it responds to meaning. The action of a play, generated by character, demonstrates its theme. This must be so because there is a reciprocal influence between plot, character, and theme. Looking at action more broadly, it is a property of a work of art which, as Jacques Maritain points out, not only exists, "it *acts*, it *does* . . . [It] is the formative principle of the dramatic work."[4] Therefore, he insists, "Theme is the term and *significance* of the *action* . . . [It] does not exist in the poem separately from the action (as a *thesis* does which is introduced into the poem from without); the theme is immanent in the life of the poem, because it is the meaning of the action."[5] Maritain draws his conclusion about action from Fergusson's definition in *The Idea of a Theatre* and applies it to poetry. It thus seems logical to apply his thoughts about theme to drama.

Harold Clurman speaks of "The Spine of the Play"—what we call theme—as "the *basic action of the play*"—what the play is about "from the standpoint of the characters' principal conflict." He goes on to say that to give a play "its specific meaning, the director must decide what fundamental desire does the plot of his play symbolize, what deep struggle gives it shape and direction? What is the play's *core?*" He illustrates by saying that *Hamlet* was for Gordon Craig "a story of a man's search for truth" and that

Saroyan's *My Heart's in the Highlands* was for Robert Lewis, the director, "the story of people eager to give things to one another." Clurman sums this up by following Richard Boleslavsky, his teacher, and calling the line of action of the play its "spine" or what Stanislavsky called the "superproblem."[6]

Here we have theme discussed from the point of view of the literary critic, the philosopher and aesthetician, and the director. Clurman's view is especially important for the director because it relates specifically to problems of acting and production.

From the standpoint of the characters' principal conflict and a symbolization of the plot or the significance of the action, the theme of *All My Sons* is expressed by Chris in the scene with Ann when he says, speaking of his company in the war: "They didn't die; they killed themselves for each other . . . And I got an idea . . . A kind of responsibility. Man for man."[7] And he makes the point specific when he learns that his father allowed the faulty airplane parts to be shipped out in order to protect his business and to save the business for him, Chris. He turns to his father and says: "For me! Where do you live, where have you come from? For me! . . . Is that as far as your mind can see, the business? . . . Don't you have a country? Don't you live in the world?"[8]

These speeches tell the audience why the playwright has selected these particular characters, has revealed their past—their desires and actions—and has brought them into a conflict which has a specific outcome. The playwright had something to say to a large group of people. Instead of writing an article, poem, novel, or speech which they might read, he wrote a play which they were to *see* and *hear*. He used graphic and illustrative *action* to convey his meaning. The characters and plot were so chosen and organized as to set forth a particular problem and give some answer to it. The characters in this play, like the audience, started out in ignorance and grew in knowledge. (In some plays the characters may not grow in knowledge and understanding. They may simply experience while the audience is enlightened.) The theme in *All My Sons* is demonstrated and not simply stated.

The director must see the importance of this principle in playwriting. An audience comes to the theatre and expects to gain meaning which is illustrated by action. It does not, as a group, react to a play or judge it the way it judges other literary and art forms. (Certain individuals in the audience may do so.) It applies the dramatic, not the literary or historical, approach. On the other hand, the director may use these two other approaches in his attempts to understand the play, since they possess great creative value for him, the actors, and other artists collaborating in the production. Let us consider some of the literary methods of finding meaning.

2. *Theme through symbolism*

We have stressed the fact that the audience tends to interpret a play dramatically, that is, in terms of the literal meaning of the characters and action. This is one level of meaning. Another is the symbolic. *All My Sons,* for example, can be interpreted in this way. Joe Keller's family might be seen both as an individual family with a father, mother, sons, and friends, and as a national unit, representing the people in the United States. Keller might even symbolize the president and his attitude toward his country and the rest of the world. His point of view might be considered nationalistic and isolationist. Chris might symbolize the opposite point of view. His is a world view. The meaning of the play could be that the United States must think not only of its own sons but of all the sons of the world, that we are part of the world and have an obligation to it. With this approach it is possible to see each one of the characters as a symbol and the action of this play as symbolic, thus pointing up a meaning on a second and more imaginative level. The plays of Shakespeare lend themselves quite easily to this method of interpretation. G. Wilson Knight's symbolic interpretation of *Measure for Measure* is typical. It is a kind of parable whose action is symbolic. The Duke is seen not in literal terms as "the old fantastical Duke of dark corners" but as "a power divine."[9] Here, of course, the poetry of the play is rich in allusions and connotations that key us to its meaning. We have a microcosm representing the macrocosm. Thus the symbolical reading of the play is possibly intrinsic. However, it is reasonable to ask whether Shakespeare had such a reading in mind when he wrote the play.

A play can be symbolic as an entity or in its structure and various parts. All contribute to the meaning of the play. In the case of Williams' *A Streetcar Named Desire* two worlds are symbolized. Stanley's and Stella's is the physical, hard, passionate, present-day world of reality. Blanche's is the world of illusion, dreams, romance, gentility, and pride of the past. Each character is a symbol of the world he or she represents. The environment in which Stanley, Stella, and their friends and neighbors live symbolizes the down-to-earth, hard present. "Belle Reve" is Blanche's dream world, as the translation of the words indicates. The language of the play is symbolic. Soon after Stanley enters in the first act he throws a bloody package of meat to Stella and says "Meat." This

is symbolic of the carnal, animal passion existing between them.
In the ninth scene the flower vendor's singsong words "Flores.
Flores. Flores para los muertos. Flores. Flores" are poignantly
symbolic of Blanche herself. Blanche's cry at the end of scene 9,
"Fire! Fire! Fire!"[10] symbolizes Mitch's lust and Blanche's inner
fiery torment. The action of the play symbolizes the triumph of
brute strength over the weak, and reality over weak dreams—the
power of the body over the mind. Blanche's ante-bellum world is
destroyed utterly by the twentieth-century modern world.

The storm scene in *King Lear* symbolizes the storm in Lear's
mind and feelings. The Fool is an aspect of the character of Lear
and symbolizes a part of him. Good and evil are symbolized by
Cordelia on the one hand and Regan and Goneril on the other.
Edgar and Edmund parallel the symbolism. The many references
to clothes in *Macbeth*, it has been pointed out by Shakespearean
critics, symbolize the smallness and falseness of the man who tries
to dress in a king's robes. Hamlet's inky cloak symbolizes his
mourning and his black thoughts. And thus symbols run throughout
plays of poetic feeling especially. The main value of dramatic
poetry is in its symbolic riches, which increase the scope of a
form of literary expression which by its nature is limited.

Often a playwright will deliberately make symbolism a part
of his basic concept, and the play must be interpreted with reference to the symbolism if it is to be understood in its full dimensions.
Ibsen utilized symbolism frequently. However, in some of his
plays his symbolism is confusing and actually stands in the way
of audience understanding. *The Master Builder* and *Rosmersholm*
are, from the point of view of general audiences, two examples of
obscure and confusing symbolism. Yet these plays cannot be interpreted in purely literal terms. *The Wild Duck*, on the other hand,
is perfectly clear symbolism, and Ibsen's meaning is satisfactory
if taken literally or symbolically. Chekhov is another playwright
who constructed his plays with symbolism as a basis. *The Cherry
Orchard* and *The Sea Gull* are two examples. Maeterlinck, like
Ibsen, in some instances used symbols that baffle rather than clarify.
The Blind and *Pelléas and Mélisande* are, as plays, victimized by
symbols, though the latter can be satisfactory to the purely romanti-
cally minded. Symbolism must have universally recognizable connotations if it is to convey meaning clearly and be most evocative
dramatically. Symbols should be used only when the playwright
wishes to elevate his drama to a higher aesthetic level. The widest
use of symbolism is found in literary expression other than prose
drama. The symbolic values of poetry and fiction can be realized
by the reader and can serve to enrich his understanding. The illus-

strative action of drama makes symbolism a dangerous instrument in hands other than those of the master playwright. Therefore, the utilization of it for the audience can be an aid or a hinderance.

Symbolic interpretation can be creatively suggestive to the director, the actor, and the designer (and to the playwright while he is conceiving and writing the play). Theatre artists can find stimulation in symbols if they are sensitive to them.

3. Theme through imagery

Another literary method of use to the director is the interpretation of the theme or meaning of a play through its word imagery. The "seeing" image has served Brooks and Heilman brilliantly in analyzing and finding the significance of *Oedipus Rex*.[11] As we have already seen, A. C. Bradley and Caroline Spurgeon have opened a provocative and imaginative field of Shakespearean criticism and interpretation. The many mentions of disease in *Hamlet* and the sky in *Romeo and Juliet* can be keys to entire productions of these plays. The imagery in the plays of Chekhov is useful for interpretive purposes. The recurrent references to birds in *The Three Sisters* are keys to the theme of the play. The imagistic use of time is significant thematically. Irina tells Chebutykin in the first act of her happiness, which makes her feel as though she were "sailing with the great blue sky above . . . and big white birds flying over it." Chebutykin replies by calling her "My white bird."[12] All three of the sisters might be seen as birds yearning to fly away to Moscow —to happiness. They are birds beating their wings against the cage shaped by their special circumstances. Their desire for freedom and a better life is given thematic importance when Vershinin recalls the story of the French minister who, in prison because of his participation in "the Panama affair," watched with delight the birds outside which he had never noticed when he was a free man. Vershinin then goes on to say: "In the same way, you won't notice Moscow when you live in it. We have no happiness and never do have, we only long for it."[13] The time image occurs in the first act when Olga refers to the clock's striking twelve. It occurs again strongly when Vershinin talks in each act about how life will be beautiful and better in two or three hundred years. The significance of time is pointed up in Chebutykin's smashing of the clock in Act III, in Fedotik's reference to time in the last act, and, of course, in Vershinin's references to it in the same act. Finally, Irina's last speech beginning with "A time will come . . ." and Olga's last speech which includes "Time will pass . . ."[14] tie in with the dominant theme of the play about happiness and a better life to come

with the passage of time. This theme expresses Chekhov's essentially
optimistic view of life which recurs in all his plays.

4. Historical themes

Interpreting the theme of a play in purely historical terms
is often more interesting and rewarding to the scholar and historian
than to the modern audience. The director who produces *Macbeth*,
for example, as a study in "kingship," following the studies of some
scholars, and tries to stress the dialogue emphasizing that point of
view only is likely to neglect the mad, headlong rush of the melodrama and the portrait of the poetic, conscience-stricken murderers.
This approach is theatrically shortsighted for two reasons. One is
that the audience to whom the play is presented is modern, not
Elizabethan, and only a small number of people are interested
enough in history to care about the point of view being emphasized. Scholars and students would be interested in this theme, but
their interest is that of specialists. The usual theatre audience is
not composed of specialists. The second reason why this purely
historical view of the play should not be emphasized is that a
theme supported by dialogue alone is not the theme that has been
communicated by demonstrative action and therefore is not dramatic. Shakespeare was a practical man of the theatre and wrote
for his audience. They, of course, needed no special lesson in the
concept of the divine right of kings; they accepted it automatically.
They doubtless saw Macbeth as a villain because he killed Duncan
and usurped his throne, and felt that his defeat and death were
therefore justified. To the Elizabethan audience the appeal lay in
the play's blood and thunder. Such an audience thrilled at the
bloody tale and the villain's high-sounding words as well as his
bold and horrible deeds. Excessive ambition and tyranny must, in
their opinion, ever end thus. The modern audience's view toward
ambition and tyranny is not different from that of the Elizabethan's.
The most successful recent productions of the play have proved
that it has not lost its power to shock and thrill—and that its appeal
lies in its sheer melodrama and poetry.

Even though it is impractical for a director to interpret the
theme of a play from a purely historical point of view, he nevertheless can point up such a theme as a thread of meaning rather
than the entire fabric of meaning. As such it can and should be
an enriching element—a kind of extra dividend for those few especially favored with historical knowledge. Furthermore, the director's
recognition of this thematic thread can enrich his interpretation of
the other elements of the play. This enrichment can shine through

and be felt if not entirely understood. It can add to the texture circumscribing the play. Furthermore, in the director's attempt to utilize the historicity of the play he can point up modern parallel themes, events, and characters. Are not Macbeth's rise to power and sequent blood purges repeated each time ambition and tyranny raise their ugly heads? Is there no history lesson here?

5. Title as key to meaning

The title of a play often sums up its meaning and offers a key for understanding it. *The Dark at the Top of the Stairs* exemplifies this. Sometimes the title states a course of action, as in Odets' *Awake and Sing!* More often the title indicates the theme by implication, as in Kingsley's *Darkness at Noon;* a knowledge of the life of the character Rubashov gives the title meaning. However, titles sometimes indicate not an intellectual point of view but merely what the play is about in terms of subject. *I Remember Mama, The Man Who Came to Dinner, The Cave Dwellers, Visit to a Small Planet, The Tenth Man, Beckett, Bus Stop, Berkeley Square,* and *Life with Father* are titles giving the subject more than the theme, though some of them have definite themes. Titles of many modern plays, though pertinent to the subject matter of the play, are chosen also for their publicity value. The title *The Seven Year Itch* exemplifies this. *Cat on a Hot Tin Roof* piques public curiosity. The title *Come Back, Little Sheba* is intriguing and is also the key to that play. The title of the play can give the audience and the director a key and sum up the meaning.

6. Direct and indirect presentation of theme

The techniques used by playwrights for presenting themes vary considerably. The two general methods are *direct* presentation and *indirect* presentation. Miller's technique in *All My Sons* is direct and Inge's in *Come Back, Little Sheba* is indirect. The former is direct because a character expresses it specifically. However, the expression of the theme by Chris is not incongruous with his idealistic character and is not obvious. There are more obvious methods. They include the use of the *raisonneur, narrator, chorus, prologue,* and *epilogue.*

Ibsen provides a number of examples of the direct presentation of theme through the raisonneur; Dr. Relling in *The Wild Duck* is one of the best. Though he speaks in character, he actually has no function except to act as the author's mouthpiece and express the meaning of the play. Except in the scene near the end of the

play when he, as physician, attends Little Hedvig, he stands aside
from the action; he never becomes involved in it. He doesn't enter
the play until the third act. He comments on what he sees and
hears. He sums up the action by saying: "Rob the average man of
his life-illusion, and you rob him of his happiness at the same
stroke . . ." and "Oh, life would be quite tolerable, after all, if
only we could be rid of the confounded duns that keep on pestering
us, in our poverty, with the claim of the ideal."[15] Other examples
are Judge Brack in *Hedda Gabler,* Ulric Brendel in *Rosmersholm,*
and Pastor Manders in *Ghosts.* Each of these characters is actually
the playwright's messenger who delivers the theme to the audience.
Each one involves himself in the action, but at the will of his
master Henrik Ibsen he stands to one side and lets the action
flow past him while he observes omnisciently, comments, and
interprets for the people out front, who are also onlookers. However, Ibsen is such a superb artist and craftsman that the audience
is seldom aware that he is the great puppeteer guiding the
raisonneur from back stage. The director must handle this character
with care to avoid his becoming an obvious mouthpiece. The
character must seem conversational and allow the theme to come
spontaneously out of emotion. He must apparently let it come out
almost reluctantly, even against his will. Hesitations or pauses and
changes in tempo, volume, and pitch resulting from the proper
emotional background will often give conviction to speeches which
are too intellectual or "sermonizing." A character like Dr. Relling
is, of course, intellectual, ascetic and philosophical, and needs to be
less emotional than some others. Even a philosopher, though, must
not appear to be detached and clairvoyant at the risk of de-
humanizing himself. In realistic plays like many of Ibsen's, the
director must give the actor carrying the theme a great deal of
realistic business and movement to increase his power of conviction.
During the thematic scenes he must focus on other characters or
objects and must never turn out to the audience to give the impression of speaking directly to them. He must at all times be
related to other characters and appear to be a part of the action.
In nonrealistic plays he may directly address the audience when
speaking thematic dialogue.

7. *The narrator*

In the case of the narrator like the stage manager of Wilder's
Our Town or the newspaperman Jack in Warren's *All the King's
Men,* the style allows them to stand aside literally and speak
directly to the audience as they explain the meaning of the play or

comment upon its action. However, the presentational style of the play is softened and made more realistic by the relaxed, conversational, and "folksy" manner of the narrator. Sometimes the narrator or commentator will speak to the audience over a loud-speaker system as he does in Cocteau's *The Infernal Machine*. He speaks personally and conversationally as he points up the theme of the play. Tom in Williams' *The Glass Menagerie*, like the narrators of Wilder's and Warren's plays, stands at one side of of the proscenium arch, talks to the audience, and participates in the action of the play as a character. He tells us the meaning of this "memory" play.

8. *The chorus*

Another device for presenting the theme of the play directly is the chorus. The raisonneur and the narrator are one-man versions of the Greek chorus. (You will remember that Shakespeare used one person and called him "The Chorus" in *Henry V,* thus antedating our present-day streamlined versions.) The Greek chorus and all classical choruses were, as we know, interruptions of the action of the principal characters which the playwright devised in order to communicate his own thoughts to the audience. The chorus, like their descendants, participated in the main action or stood apart from it as the playwright willed. The classical style of directing the chorus emphasizes its presentationalism and underscores its formal behavior. In movement and voice the chorus reacts to and comments upon the words and actions of the principals. It comprises a single character and should be used theatrically for its emotional effect to underscore and heighten as well as to communicate the meaning of the play. It is a mistake to use it as a declaiming statue in *Oedipus Rex,* for example. Neither should it be choreographed to trace a pretty mosaic of movement and composition. It should have strength, simplicity, and power and should avoid pose and artificiality. The Broadway performances by the Greek National Theatre proved how electrifyingly theatrical the chorus of *Oedipus Rex* and *Electra* could be while directly presenting the theme of the plays.

9. *The prologue and epilogue*

The prologue and epilogue are also devices for presenting the theme. The prologue presents the "argument" and sets the action; the epilogue draws the conclusions and points the moral. This technique amounts to a kind of conceit which the audience enjoys for its own sake as well as for its thematic function. As used in Molière's *The School for Husbands,* adapted by Arthur Guiterman and Lawrence Langner, the prologue and epilogue frame the play and emphasize the period charm for the modern audience which indulges itself in a theatrical whim. This method of direct presentation of theme is of theatrical value and should be exploited by the director. As a matter of fact, the other stylistic devices—those of the narrator and chorus—are not necessarily disadvantages for the director but are advantages in terms of the unusual, which is always a prized theatrical quality. The modern audience is often grateful for a style of production which deviates from the conventional, realistic, run-of-the-tread-mill kind.

10.   *Universality of theme*

After determining the meaning of the play and its manner of presentation, the director should be concerned with its timeliness and applicability or universality. Themes emanating from the subjects of man's relationship to God, to himself, and to others are likely to be timeless and of universal interest. *Oedipus Rex, Hamlet, King Lear,* and *Othello* have such universality. Plays written wholly for timeliness of the moment are in danger of being forgotten in later years. In the chapter on the audience it has already been pointed out that war plays, written with themes pertinent only to a specific period, environment, and type of character, have lost most of their appeal because they are dated. They are dated because our attitude toward the themes has changed. Plays of timely themes without solid, interesting, and universally appealing characterizations are likely to pass from the stage. The playwright intent on social issues to the exclusion of other values is in danger of being forsaken by the public. John Galsworthy and John Howard Lawson are two victims whose names come readily to mind. Will Arthur Miller, successor to Clifford Odets' social consciousness, also fall a victim in a few years? His penetrating character drawing will certainly give him a longer life span in the theatre than that of Galsworthy and Lawson.

Ibsen is alive today to the extent that his characters live. The themes of *A Doll's House* and *Ghosts* were controversial and even shocking when first presented to audiences. The social problems they epitomized were applicable and timely for Victorian audiences. Ibsen's suggested solutions were revolutionary and incendiary. Now that the western world, at least, is in agreement with his points of view, these plays are no longer controversial. Performances of these plays some years ago by such fine actresses as Miss Ruth Gordon and Madame Nazimova proved that human beings as such are always interesting. Nora became a fascinating and highly sympathetic person, and Mrs. Alving became a deeply moving tragic figure. *Ghosts*, dominated by Nazimova's Mrs. Alving, emerged as a play whose original social theme was secondary to the classic tragedy of a human being caught in a web of circumstances spun by the gods.

It is obvious, then, that the theme of a play is both its spine and its heart beat. Its life can depend upon it. Yet, as we have seen, the life of a play may continue in spite of its dated theme. Accordingly we see the importance of the director's interpretive powers. He must be able to evaluate the appeal of the theme for his audience and must be able to find compensating values in the play if need be.

11. *Plays without significant themes*

In our attempts to define theme we have used words to indicate a significant meaning for a play. But do *all* plays have significant meaning? Are there not plays which are merely diverting and entertaining? Does Plautus' *The Merchant* or *Menaechmi* have "meaning"? Do *Three Men on a Horse* and *My Three Angels?* What is the "significance of the action" of these plays? What are they about "from the standpoint of the characters' principal conflict"? It is obvious that the playwrights of these plays did not intend to emphasize a particular meaning, philosophy, or idea to their audiences. They wished to entertain them. There was no serious point of view here except to comment jokingly on some aspect of human conduct. None of the characters are involved in serious conflicts or troubled with more than trivial and transient social problems. Of course these plays are farces and are not to be taken seriously. They are *about something* in the sense that they have a *subject*, but they do not have thought-provoking meaning. In other words, you can say what they are about in terms of what the characters do and what happens to them, but what they are about does not add up to an overruling and important idea. (Some directors start their interpretive procedure by asking what the theme is. If their concept of theme is in terms of subject matter— what it is about—there can be no objection to their interpretive procedure. However, it must be emphasized that not all plays have significant themes and that the theatre is primarily emotional in its impact and import. Furthermore, as has been pointed out in our discussion of mood, the emotional climate of a play must be analyzed and interpreted first if the director is to understand the elements generating it.) In the four plays mentioned above the characters are acting and being acted upon with only one aim, and that is to be amusing. *Meaning* cannot be attached to their actions. They do not imply or symbolize more than they overtly say and do. There is no hidden significance.

Does this mean that all amusing plays are without meaning or theme? Surely Molière had themes in mind when he wrote *The Would-Be Gentleman* and *The Affected Ladies*. And so did Shakespeare in *Love's Labor's Lost*. Molière and Shakespeare wished the audience to see the implications of these comedies. They made intellectual but amusing comments upon the foibles and follies of the day. Congreve's *The Way of the World* and Wilde's *Lady Windermere's Fan* similarly commented upon their day. Claire Boothe's *The Women* is a lineal descendant of these satirical comedies of manners.

Up to this point we have investigated the two dramatic values, mood and theme, which circumscribe the play, so to speak. They are unifying values in the sense in which we have approached them. (Later we may see them as relative and subordinate values.) We have seen mood as the emotional aspect and theme as the intellectual. It must be emphasized, however, that this division has been made merely for the sake of discussion. In actuality no aspect of a play is purely emotional or intellectual but is a combination of both, with each dominant by turns. We can now turn to another dramatic value, character.

CHARACTER

1. *General problems*

a.   Selectivity

As we pointed out in the "Nature and Pattern of Drama," the number of characters in a play must be limited. Time does not permit the revelation and development of a large number. The playwright must concentrate upon one central character, two central characters, or a small group. The central or main characters will receive most attention from the playwright and will be presented in most detail and depth. However, in spite of the disparity in character depth, all characters must be presented according to the demands of the style or genre in which the play is written. For example, the card-playing friends of Stanley Kowalski in Williams' *Streetcar* are on the surface fully drawn characters like the principals, Stanley, Stella, Blanche, and Mitch. They speak, act, and react naturalistically, but the playwright does not have the time and space to present more than one or two recognizable and telling traits. They serve their purpose. They are purely peripheral characters. To spend time revealing them would distract the audience's attention from the important characters.

In addition to selectivity of number of characters, a play demands selectivity of character details. Too many details retard the progress of the play and confuse the audience. Selectivity also applies to motivations, actions, and reactions and results in aesthetic heightening as well as clarity of character.

b. Consistency

Characters in plays must not be contradictory but must be consistent. This is essential if the audience is to be able to assemble character details with clarity. Once again the director must be aware that the headlong rush of a performance does not permit the audience to pause, speculate, and sort out a superabundance of character data. Another aspect of character consistency is that dramatic characters may, in nonrealistic styles particularly, be inconsistent as to psychological behavior in contrast with realistic or lifelike behavior. We expect psychological consistency in life. But art is a reflection, a heightening, of life and thus demands only aesthetic consistency. This may be illustrated by the character of the Duke in Shakespeare's *Measure for Measure*. He is obviously a theatrical character and not a psychological one. (Some critics wrongly call him a puppet.) He thinks, feels, acts, and reacts in conformity with the demands of the organic structure of the play. He is utilized for theatrical purposes. The modern actor, trained in the psychological school of acting only, must realize this and justify the character's behavior in terms of theatricality. If he learns to play Shakespeare, he must learn to play for theatrical truth rather than psychological truth.

c. Typification

In the general necessity for rigorous selection and compression the drama loses scope when compared with poetry and fiction. Yet it is able to compensate for the loss. In character values the compensation is the heightening, the increase in "size," resulting from the characters' symbolizing more than themselves. They have greater symbolic and aesthetic weight. This operates in comedy as well as in tragedy. The essential nature of the character in

drama is his typification of a class or group. As such he achieves
not only easy identification with the audience but universality.

If we can visualize a play as a series of concentric circles,
the outer circle might be considered the emotional climate, mood,
or spirit of the play; the next circle, the theme; then the plot, then
the dialogue, and finally the center, basic to all the circles, would
be the characters. This center is the generating force creating the
circles. Such a force is so powerful, complex, and extensive that,
for study, it requires some simplification of approach. Therefore,
it would seem logical to attack the subject from two points of
view. First we shall look at character in terms of the director's
analysis of the group character values and their relationship to the
play as a whole. (The group character values influence the over-all
structure, kind of play, and style of play.) Then we shall examine
character in terms of the director's analysis of individual character
values and their relationship to the actor.

2.   Group character values

a.   Character introduction

If the director has analyzed a play for its mood and theme
values, he has read it a number of times and has learned a great
deal about other values, particularly character values. He now needs
to ask himself *who* the characters are. This is, of course, the first
question the audience asks. In the older plays the characters introduced themselves. In Plautus' *Menaechmi*, Act I, scene 1, starts
out with the entrance of Brush, who says, "my nickname is
Brush . . ."[16] In *Everyman* the Messenger enters and speaks a
prologue which introduces "our heaven King" and asks the audience
to "hear what he doth say"; then, after God speaks, Death is introduced by "Where art thou, Death, thou mighty messenger?" And
Death says, "Almighty God, I am here at your will . . ."[17]

Shakespeare starts off *King Lear* with the entrance of three
men. After two of them speak of the king's division of the kingdom
and the question of whether he favors the Duke of Albany more
than Cornwall, one turns to the other and asks, "Is not this your
son, my Lord?" The answer is that he is his illegitimate son. Then
the same lord turns to his son and says, "Do you know this noble
gentleman, Edmund?" Edmund: "No, my lord." The answer is
"My lord of Kent: remember him hereafter as my noble friend."
Now the audience knows Kent and Edmund but does not know
the third person. Then the third person says, "The king is coming."
And Lear enters with the Duke of Albany, Duke of Cornwall,

Goneril, Regan, Cordelia, and attendants. When Lear turns to the third person of the first group, not yet identified, he says "Attend the lords of France and Burgundy, Gloucester." And thus Gloucester is identified. Thereafter Lear introduces Cornwall and Albany, and his daughters Goneril and Regan, then Cordelia, the youngest and unmarried daughter.[18]

The modern author is a little more casual, even though he is direct. An entering character says, "Hiya." And a character on stage says, "Hello, Frank." In this way Frank is introduced directly and naturally. The conversation moves along and by implication the audience gathers that another character is a doctor. He is so identified by his asking, "You didn't see my kid this morning, did you?" Frank says, "No." And then the third character on stage says, "Imagine? He walked off with his thermometer. Right out of his bag." And when Frank says, "That boy's going to be a real doctor; he's smart," his father says, "Over my dead body he'll be a doctor." To clinch the fact that the character is a doctor Frank refers to him and says, "There was a doctor in that picture . . ."[19]

Whatever the technique used by the playwright to introduce and identify his characters, the director must be sure that the audience understands who the characters are and what their general relationships are. He can help the audience identify characters by placing them on stage in such a way as to use their body positions, movement, and business to show their relationships with each other. A passionate embrace, for example, will usually indicate without dialogue that the two people involved are deeply in love. The director faces a definite problem when the curtain rises on the first scene of a play and the audience sees a large number of people on stage. Shakespeare poses this problem in many of his plays. The director must use his ingenuity to point out the characters one by one through pictorial emphasis and action. The audience cannot even begin to be interested in the play until characters are identified. After that it will want to know the *what* and *why* of the characters: what they are and why they act as they do. This involves character revelation and motive, which we shall investigate later.

b. Character categories

After the director answers the question of who the individual characters are, he will relate them to the play in their degrees of importance. The degree of importance of each character can be determined by ascertaining the amount of dialogue he has, his contribution to the plot and theme of the play, and the amount of time he is on stage. The director will thus divide the characters into *principal, supporting,* and *subsidiary.* Sometimes the distinction between principal and supporting characters can be difficult to judge. It is important not so much for academic reasons as for reasons of understanding, interpretation, and direction of the play. The principal characters consist of those whose conflicts directly force an outcome and resolution of the central problem of the play. They create the main line of action; the supporting characters, the contributing but minor lines of action. The subsidiary characters are usually a part of the environment and atmosphere. Thus the division of the characters into these three categories will tell the director something about the structure of the play as an entity. Such knowledge will contribute not only to the interpretation of the play but to the information needed for rehearsal procedure and methods.

In *King Lear,* for example, Lear, Kent, Gloucester, Edmund, the Fool, Edgar, Goneril, Regan, and Cordelia may be said to be the principal characters because they contribute most to the action and theme of the play, regardless of the amount of time they spend on stage. It will be noted that Cordelia spends less time on stage than Cornwall and Albany, yet the latter two must be considered supporting characters insofar as the structure of the play is concerned. The remaining characters, Oswald, Burgundy, France, Doctor, Servants, Messengers, et al., are subsidiary. It is to be noted that the conflicts involving Gloucester, Edmund, and Edgar are secondary in one sense but in another are principal and contributory to the main action by virtue of their parallelism with the events involving Lear and his daughters. *King Lear* is a double-pronged tree with a single tap root.

In the case of *All My Sons,* Chris, Joe, and Mrs. Keller are the principal characters because of their contribution to the main action and theme of the play. Ann and George are the supporting characters. All the others are subsidiary.

c.   Protagonist and antagonist

In deciding which characters belong in the three categories just discussed, the director has also determined the central character, or protagonist, and the antagonist. The protagonist is the character whose conflict or problem motivates the main action of the play. Hamlet is the protagonist. The antagonist creates the force in opposition to the protagonist. Claudius is the antagonist. The antagonist can be another character or a force outside or inside the protagonist himself. Man can be in conflict with another man, a fate or a force, or himself. The sea is the antagonist in O'Neill's *Anna Christie*, for example. Most of the great plays have a central character or protagonist. *Hamlet, King Lear, Othello, Oedipus Rex, Macbeth, Faust,* and *Dr. Faustus* are examples of such centrality. Some plays are centered in two characters around whom the other characters revolve. *Menaechmi, The Taming of the Shrew, Come Back, Little Sheba,* and *All My Sons* are examples, with the twins, Petruchio and Katharina, Doc and Lola, and Chris and Joe as the paired central characters. Other plays have three or four central characters. *Henry IV, Part One,* has Falstaff, Hal, and Hotspur; *Measure for Measure,* the Duke, Angelo, and Isabella; *Twelfth Night,* Viola, Malvolio, Orsino, Olivia, Sir Toby, Sir Andrew, and Maria. In the case of these plays the paired or multiple characters are principals who oppose one another and are equally central. Their conflicts create separate streams of action which eventually merge and create unity of action.

d. Character recognition and sympathy

After the director has ascertained that the audience will understand who the characters are and the group categories to which they belong, he must determine the audience's degree of recognition of and sympathy with them. If members of an audience are to be interested, they must recognize the characters in a play as like themselves, people they know or have heard or read of. To become deeply interested in the characters, the audience must sympathize with them.

Audience recognition of characters comes from seeing believable actions and hearing believable speech on stage. The familiar is of course believable and will evoke attention and interest. The audience receives pleasure and becomes interested when it can say in reference to a character that he's just like his next-door neighbor, the guy he met in the army, his brother, or even himself. The factor in a play permitting the recognition of familiar people is a definite dramatic value. This recognition value of plays like *Mister Roberts, At War with the Army, Command Decision,* and other war plays is important to the degree of success achieved by them. *Life with Father* capitalized strongly on its recognition values. Pleasure and interest come from familiarity with human conduct.

Yet too much familiarity can breed boredom. Thus type characters whose behavior is completely predictable have dangerous limitations in terms of audience interest. An audience wants enough familiarity to recognize and believe but it wants a dash of the unfamiliar to engage its interest. Unfamiliar attitudes, customs, or environment make for unpredictability. Unpredictability, however, must be believable. The audience must be able to say of a character, "I didn't expect him to do that, but it seems right for him to do it." The recognizable and believable but unpredictable character is a theatrical character.

Unfamiliar attitudes make for the unpredictability of speech and action which accounts for the audience's interest in the characters in *You Can't Take It with You, Arsenic and Old Lace, The Time of Your Life, Waiting for Godot, The Man Who Came to Dinner,* and other comedies and farces, particularly. There is less unpredictability of character in serious plays like *Death of a Salesman, Look Homeward, Angel,* and *Picnic.* Psychopathic characters like Blanche DuBois in *A Streetcar Named Desire* are highly unpredictable and therefore theatrically effective. Leading characters in melodramas like *Ladies in Retirement, Anastasia, Uncle Harry,* and *Dial "M" for Murder* are also highly unpredictable. Yet all such characters must have traits that make them similar to other human beings in order to be recognizable and believable.

Strange customs and environments create a fascinating unpredictability in characters. The characters in *Porgy and Bess, Tobacco Road,* and *The Rainmaker,* though living in the United States, have environments, customs, and attitudes unfamiliar to most audiences, but they are recognizable because we have read or heard about them and because they demonstrate basic emotions and actions common to all mankind. They are, therefore, believable too.

Audience recognition of characters can come from both the familiar and the unfamiliar but believable. Audience recognition is the process of identifying itself and mankind with the characters on stage. An audience will not respond with interest and understanding to the inhuman. It must see in the characters of the play certain similarities with itself. There must be a bond of kinship between the characters and the audience. This kinship arouses sympathy.

Closely allied to the importance of recognition values is sympathy with characters. The audience must sympathize with characters if it is to empathize with them. The more tragically serious the play, the more important it is for the audience to sympathize deeply at least with the central characters. Sympathy with characters has a great deal to do with the success of a play. The director must beware of plays whose characters the audience will not like, since audiences must like the characters if they are to care about what they do and what happens to them. It will be noted that the word "like" has come into the discussion. It indicates some degree of sympathy. An audience may be sympathetic with comic characters but it must not be so deeply sympathetic that it becomes emotional about them and is unable to laugh. Laughter is, after all, the aim of comedy. Perhaps it will be better to say that the audience must *like* comic characters and be *sympathetic* with serious ones.

Audiences like characters for reasons other than that they are comic. For instance, wicked characters can be likable in a play. Mephistopheles is a character the audience has liked ever since he appeared in the medieval drama as the devil. He is liked because he is so cleverly wicked. In *Faust* he is liked not only for his clever wickedness but because he is amusing. Regina and the Hubbard brothers in *The Little Foxes* are liked by the audience for the same reasons: They are clever and funny. The success of this latter play is partly due to the fact that the wicked are pitted against the good and sympathetic, and the audience has someone to root for. Too, the wicked triumph of Regina, the central character, at the end of the play is empty and ironical. Danny in *Night Must Fall* and Jack Manningham in *Angel Street* are likable and fascinating, though unsympathetic, because of their diabolical cleverness—a trait that we admire in spite of ourselves. Again, though, the audience has sympathetic characters to root for, and the wicked characters are apprehended.

Unsympathetic or unlikable characters are a liability to a play and will usually cause it to fail. The characters in Lillian Hellman's *The Autumn Garden* are either so petty, immoral, negativistic, or downright unlikable and unsympathetic that the audience simply did not care what they did or what happened to them. The play was consequently a failure in spite of some good qualities of writing. A play by Roald Dahl, called *The Honeys,* tried to make the audience laugh at the murder of unlikable characters but failed, probably because the so-called likable characters were not likable enough in spite of the two ingratiating actresses who played them.

e.   Character causation

The audience's sympathy with a character is partly due to how much the character cares about something. If he cares, the audience will care—out of understanding and sympathy. To care, a character must have the drive and the will to do something, to be something, to escape something, etc. A character is continually showing his will. The director must constantly seek for demonstrations of this. The character's will is the cause of his action, internal or external. To be dramatic a character must demonstrate that he has a will.

In analyzing the play for its general or group character values the director must look for characters with will power; the stronger the will, the greater the possibilities of drama and the more believable the play. A play with wishy-washy characters will be of little interest to an audience. The plays that have proved their audience appeal through the test of time are those of strong characters, who are strong because of their wills, convictions, and passions. Strength of will may be demonstrated by inner anguish as well as outer physical action. Hamlet illustrates the former and Tamburlaine the latter. Often the exercise of the will can result in a combination of inner and outer action, as in *Othello*. Lear's will is illustrated almost entirely by inner stress and action. The power of his thoughts and emotions compensates for his lack of physical action.

The will of the protagonist can incite an entire play into action. It can create imbalance out of balance. The playwright must select the kind and amount of exercise of the protagonist's will needed to do this. Characters and events must be so situated and organized as to be potentially combustible and waiting to be touched off by a willful act of the protagonist. This discussion implies that the characters surrounding the principal character must have wills too. In order to exercise their wills, characters must be related to other characters. They cannot be in isolation. Relationships usually result from desire and will. Hamlet's desire for education prompted him to go to the university at Wittenburg, where he established a relationship with Rosencrantz and Guildenstern who were at the university for a similar reason. Their later wish to spy upon Hamlet for Claudius created another relationship. This resulted in a conflict of wills between them and Hamlet when Hamlet suspected them and resisted their desire to gain information for the king. This conflict of wills was between characters. There are two other sources of conflict: the will exercised against itself and the will exercised against an outside force like fate, law, conventions, and environment.

In Hamlet's "To be or not to be" soliloquy we have an example of will exercised against itself. In *Winterset* we have numerous examples of Mio struggling with parts of his personality—his conscience, his love for Miriamne, his love for his father, etc. The heart of *King Lear* is Lear's struggle with himself. Macbeth is constantly in conflict with his sense of duty to Duncan before he is persuaded to murder the king. Doc in *Come Back, Little Sheba* shows an inner conflict as a result of his wanting to take the bottle of whisky and his resisting the temptation momentarily. Mrs. Keller has many moments of willing herself to believe that Larry is alive even though part of her tells her that he is not. Willy Loman in *Death of a Salesman* shows his inner struggle to live instead of die when he insists on planting seeds in his yard at night.

Oedipus is the classic example of a will in conflict with fate or the gods. Prometheus in *Prometheus Bound* is a similar example. Bartley in *Riders to the Sea* fights against the fatal power of the sea when he wills to go to the fair. Gimpy in *Dead End* wages a fight against his environment.

In most cases of the clash of will the character is in conflict with more than one opposing force at a time. He may be in conflict with himself and with another character at the same time. Hamlet illustrates this when he struggles against his past love for Ophelia while he accuses her of being false to him in the "get thee to a nunnery" scene. Gloucester also demonstrates this kind of double conflict when Edmund tells him of Edgar's supposed treachery to his father. While Oedipus quarrels with the blind Teiresias he is clashing with another character and fate simultaneously.

It must be clear by now that characters have *relationships, wills, opposition,* and *conflicts,* in that order. This is the process of creating drama. The director must search for these elements in his interpretation of the play and must establish them in performance.

f. The active and the passive protagonist

The amount of will determines whether or not a character is active or passive. Speaking relatively, it is not so bad to have weak-willed supporting and subsidiary characters, but it is fatal if the protagonist is also will-less. The passive protagonist prohibits the possibilities of dramatic conflicts. Things may happen to him, but he is never the cause of things' happening to anyone else. He becomes the victim of other characters and events, but he never puts up a fight and therefore does not create a dramatic situation. Such a character is seldom interesting or sympathetic to an audience. If, however, this lack of will can be compensated for by inner torment and sensitivity, he may gain sympathy. It is probably impossible for a dramatist to create a character who is completely devoid of some manifestations of will. Even when the physical actions of a character consist merely of going from one sitting place to another, some will has been shown. The protagonist of H. R. Lenormand's *Time Is a Dream* is an example of an almost totally will-less character. He sees very little in life worth living for. He spends his time gazing into the depths of a lake and apostrophizing upon the futility of it all. Even the people around him seem

equally passive to life. He eventually commits suicide. Needless
to say, the audience does not care. Most of them will fall asleep
before the end comes.

There are two interesting examples of comparatively weak-
willed or passive protagonists in plays by Maxwell Anderson and
Robert Sherwood. In Anderson's *Key Largo* we have King McCloud,
who volunteers to lead some men to fight in the Spanish civil war.
In the prologue of the play he sees that their number will be
overwhelmed and he leaves them to their fate when they refuse
to give up. This showed a weakness of will and possibly cowardice.
His exercise of will was negative and not positive. Afterward his
conscience pricks him and he returns to the United States where
he searches for the family of each of the men whom he left behind
to die. With these families he hopes to salve his conscience by
telling them their sons died bravely. The second scene of the play
finds him at Key Largo in Florida where he locates the last family,
the D'Alcalos. Here he meets his friend's sister and blind father.
The sister, influenced by her brother's worship of his hero King
McCloud, falls in love with him. When King finds the D'Alcalo
family in the hands of a gangster and his mob, he makes a feeble
attempt to defend them but is cowed into submission and gives
himself up to the gang. While King watches and philosophizes,
most of the play is devoted to the efforts of the blind father and
the girl to defeat the gangster's plans. Finally King makes one
supreme effort, though it means his own death, and kills the
gangster to free the D'Alcalos. Though the conflict of the wills
of the D'Alcalos and the gang makes for some drama, the play
lacks tension because of the cowardice and weakness of will of its
central character. *Key Largo* is one of the few unsuccessful plays
written by Maxwell Anderson. The reason lies primarily in his
generally passive and weak protagonist.

The other example of a predominantly passive central character
is Alan Squire in *The Petrified Forest*. He comes, disillusioned and
without hope, to a roadside filling station-café. Here he becomes
interested in a young girl who has ambitions to paint. When he is
on the point of leaving to continue his aimless journey, he is
forced back into the café by Duke Mantee and his gang, who have
escaped after the robbery of a bank. The gang hold the young
girl, her grandfather, the station attendant, and Alan captive while
they wait to make contact with another of their members. Considerable suspense and tension are engendered after this because
the attendant momentarily overpowers the gang leader and because
Alan shows no fear of the gangsters. Alan is not a coward, though

he is completely fatalistic and relatively inactive. As a matter of fact, because of his fatalistic philosophy he fears nothing and seems capable of doing anything, however wild and reckless. This makes him in the eyes of the audience potentially active, and there is the resultant expectation that he will do something. In order to give the girl a chance to leave this petrified forest for Paris where she can study painting and have a chance in life, he makes her the beneficiary of his life insurance policy and then deliberately makes Duke Mantee kill him.

This play of Sherwood's, unlike Anderson's, enjoyed quite a bit of success in spite of its relatively passive protagonist. The reasons stem from certain compensating elements in the play which generated interest and excitement. First of all, Alan Squire, though weak in will, is an attractive and likable personality. (Leslie Howard, who played Squire originally, brought his own charm to the part, and this helped.) He has a sense of humor though he is fatalistic. He is not cowardly but is foolhardily brave. Second, the young station attendant, a football player and in love with the girl, is an active character who threatens the gang. His activity is a substitute for that of the protagonist. In addition, the leader of this gang is an interesting character in himself. These factors, coupled with the intermittent comedy provided by the grandfather, the football player, and other characters, give the play variety of mood, excitement, and suspense. *Key Largo*, conversely, lacks comedy, variety of mood, and interesting characters to compensate for its weak-willed and passive protagonist. Its prologue premise is not exactly an asset either.

In assessing the several character values of a play, the director is cautioned to test the characters, especially the central character or characters, for strength of will. The director must ask himself specifically whether the protagonist is an active or a passive character. The answer will do much to tell him of the play's stageworthiness. Active and opposing wills are needed to generate conflicts between the characters. Whenever possible the director must so interpret a line of dialogue, an action, or bit of business as to indicate a positive and active will. The director is constantly faced with choices of meaning and interpretation. He should select the positive and active rather than the negative and inactive. While being mindful of the over-all values, he must squeeze every drop of drama from every moment in a play. Constant exploration of character is needed to find possible sources of the activity of the will. The actor, feeling and thinking in character, will sometimes see such sources more quickly than the director. The actor can be helpful in another way. His apparent personal strength and will can make the character's lack of will and activity seem less obvious to the audience. Thus, if desirable, casting can compensate for the loss of a character value. As a matter of fact, the casting of a strong-appearing actor who seems to possess great personal will power can, by contrast, make the weak-willed character more tragic or comic, as the case may be. If the actor possesses great personal charm and wit as well as strength of appearance, still other values are added. The director must not compound weakness of character with weakness of appearance of the actor.

g.   The main relationship[20]

The conflict of the central character or protagonist of a play is with the antagonist. Such a conflict creates a main relationship which forms the main action. Hamlet vs. Claudius is an example of a main relationship which is maintained throughout the play. Doc and Lola in *Come Back, Little Sheba* also establish such a main relationship. So do Chris and Joe in *All My Sons*. A central character can be involved with characters other than the antagonist, yet such involvements are a part of the main relationship. For example, Hamlet becomes involved with Polonius, Laertes, Ophelia, his mother, and Rosencrantz and Guildenstern, but these conflicts are related to his involvement with Claudius. Lola and Doc as paired central characters become involved with both Turk and Marie, and such involvements affect their relationship. Chris and Joe become similarly involved with Mrs. Keller, Ann, and George and still maintain their own relationship, which is central. (These relationships will be dealt with from the standpoint of the supporting and subsidiary characters and will be called secondary relationships.) The histories and chronicles of Shakespeare have multiple relationships which can be considered main ones. A biographical play like *Victoria Regina* and *Abe Lincoln in Illinois* presents the central characters in conflicts with numerous characters in multiple scenes, but such conflicts relate to a main action that holds the play together and gives it unity. The unity of action, whether from a main relationship or a multiple relationship, makes for tightness and tension not possible otherwise. The director should be careful to avoid a play of diffuse relationships and actions. He must establish, point up, and emphasize the main relationship and the unity of action. The principal characters who maintain the main relationship must not be allowed to drop out of a play for any considerable length of time. The central character who is off stage a great deal loses the focus of the audience's attention and thus weakens the play. If he must be off stage, then the action on stage should relate to him. The maintenance of a central relationship assures audience attention, interest, and tension. The audience is confused by disorganized and diffuse involvements.

h.   Secondary relationships

The principal characters create the main relationship of the play, and the secondary characters, with supporting and subsidiary ones, contribute to it. They contribute to it by becoming involved with the principal characters or by becoming involved with one another in such a way as to relate to the principal characters and the main relationship. In *All My Sons* the main relationship is that between Joe and Chris, as pointed out. George's entrance in the second act and his subsequent involvement with Joe and Mrs. Keller cause a revelation that strongly affects the main relationship. George, in the analysis above, has been considered a supporting character and his secondary relationships are vital. Frank, a subsidiary character, affects the course of action relating to the main relationship when he enters with Larry's horoscope just after the scene between George, Joe, and Mrs. Keller. Later on in the play the doctor living next door, another subsidiary character, has some little involvements with Mrs. Keller about Joe and Chris which also contribute to the main relationship. In *King Lear* Oswald, though a subsidiary character and a representative of Goneril, engages in several skirmishes with Lear and Kent and thus contributes to the main relationship.

Not all subsidiary characters have important relationships and involvements. Some are merely atmospheric and environmental or serve as attendants and messengers but do not have conflicts as a result of their relationships with other characters. Their function is often technical rather than dramatic. The attendant in *King Lear,* who in Act I, scene 4, is told by Lear to go and tell his daughter that he would speak to her, has such a technical function.

The importance of secondary relationships and involvements lies in their dramatic qualities. The director must constantly seek such involvements because they keep the play alive. He must be cautioned against those plays which have a main relationship that fades out in certain scenes and is not supplemented by secondary relationships. A play of large conflicts with smaller ones in between is in danger of lulling the audience to sleep between the big scenes. Without the secondary involvements the play will lose tension and even directionality.

i. Character contrasts

Contrast implies difference and difference usually implies opposition and conflict. And, as we have said, conflict is drama. The director in analyzing a play must always be alert to and looking for the dramatic. As he explores the totality of the play he may, if he is visually minded, see it as a design of colors. The characters as a group and as individuals contribute their coloration to the design and structure. As the director thinks of each individual he must see him in color contrast with the other characters. (He may see the sympathetic principal character as a design of varying tones of certain of the warm primary colors and the opposing principal characters in tones of the cool colors, with the supporting and subsidiary characters in tones of warm and cool colors in accordance with their relationships to the main characters.)

Contrast individualizes characters and sets them in opposition to one another. If the director cannot see his characters in contrast, either they are unclearly and weakly drawn or he has failed to grasp their differences. If after repeated study of the script he still fails to see the contrasts, he must advise the playwright to create them and he must cast, interpret, and direct the actors to achieve contrasts. If these things are not possible it would be advisable not to produce the play.

Every successful drama, whether it be a serious or a comic play, possesses characters in contrast to one another. Macbeth gains a great deal of his effectiveness because he is seen in relief against Lady Macbeth, Duncan, and Macduff. Hamlet similarly gains by comparison with Claudius, Horatio, Laertes, and Rosencrantz and Guildenstern. Oedipus and Creon are presented in sharp contrast. Nora, the doll wife, is shown in opposition to Torvald. Lola and Doc, though both yearning for their lost youth, are more dramatic because of their differences. Othello, Iago, and Cassio are other studies in contrast.

Character contrasts must be apparent between individual characters, and there must be constrasts within each character. Iago, though in contrast to other characters in the play, is also a character of contrasting moods. He is characteristically sardonic, but he is not always seen in the same degree of that mood. Humor, though ascerbic, and infinite shades of feeling are in his make-up. The great interpreters of Iago have shown the many tones of his character. An audience tires of a character who is continually in one mood. Such a character is of limited interest and restricts the dramatic potentials of a play. In seeking mood variations the director must seek tonal variations within each character. Many inexperienced playwrights think they have drawn interesting characters and consider their plays character plays when, as a matter of fact, they don't give their characters scenes in which they can be seen in more than one light. If a character is to reveal more than one or two facets, he must be placed in enough different situations to allow him to show other facets. The director may test the dimensionality of a character by determining whether he reacts to different situations in different ways. The character who acts the same way under all circumstances is a one-sided, type character. Unless a director distorts or changes the meaning of scenes he cannot show him otherwise.

j. Growth in character

Of great structural value to a play is growth in the characters. This is demonstrated by the characters' progression from ignorance to knowledge. Their achievement of new insight into their problems and an enlightened attitude toward them materially enriches the entire play. In some plays, of course, such growth in the characters would be contrary to the author's over-all intention. His point might be that they should have grown but have failed to do so. They have remained blind to their errors and weaknesses and have been overcome by disaster. Coriolanus is an example of a character who becomes progressively more embittered and hardened but does not become enlightened. (Coriolanus exemplifies *progression* of character but not *change* and *growth*.) In plays in which characters struggle with fundamental human problems, like a father's relationship to his children as exemplified by both Lear and Gloucester in *King Lear,* character development to a recognition of their tragic errors not only enriches the audience's emotional experience but lifts the human spirit. These values are to a large extent responsible for the worthwhileness of a play. They add to human knowledge and deepen man's understanding of man.

We find such growth in the character of Hamlet in the scene with Horatio after Hamlet's return from England. Othello, blind to the perfidy of Iago and to Desdemona's love, at last opens his eyes. Willy Loman and Joe Keller at last see themselves in a different light and destroy themselves. The young boy in Odets' *Awake and Sing!* awakens to a mature and hopeful point of view after the death of his grandfather. Doc and Lola are also enlightened to a new hope and a new way of life at the end of *Come Back, Little Sheba.* The girl in Richard Nash's *The Rainmaker* progresses through various stages to a realization of a richer life. This occurs in a serio-comic play. Lady Windermere in Wilde's *Lady Winder-*

mere's Fan, a comedy drama, achieves wisdom through the example of Mrs. Erlynne. *Everyman* is entirely devoted to the discovery of Everyman's relationship to life and death. Even Kate and Petruchio in *The Taming of the Shrew* achieve a new wisdom. Petruchio is tamed to a wife just as Kate is tamed to a husband.

Character change and growth create the curve of meaning of many plays. They may be the cornerstone of the structure of a play, and the director must sense them when he analyzes the over-all design. He must look for them first in the protagonist and then in the characters surrounding him.

An important part of the growth of the protagonist is his ultimate climactic behavior. Worthington Minor points out that the director must check this fundamental aspect of a play to test its logic and structure. He suggests reading the last act first to be assured that the play develops lucidly and believably to the climax. He even advises the playwright to write the last act first in order to build his play soundly.[21]

When O'Neill ends his trilogy *Mourning Becomes Electra* by having Lavinia Manon go into the house to be forever entombed there, the audience is satisfied that her ultimate action is consistent with her previous behavior. Tom in *The Glass Menagerie* cannot do otherwise when, at the end of the play, he must leave his mother and sister. The climactic behavior of the young doctor and Alma Winemiller in *Summer and Smoke* may possibly raise a doubt in the minds of some members of the audience because of the characters' sudden change of attitude. Yet such a change has been found satisfactory to others. It is no surprise to the audience when Treplev in Chekhov's *The Sea Gull* commits suicide. Nor is it surprising that Father is finally persuaded to be baptized in *Life with Father.* Burns, the editor in *The Front Page,* acts with complete logic when, at the end of the play, he wins the fight for possession of Hildy Johnson by telephoning the police to arrest Hildy for stealing his watch.

k.   Dimensionality of character

Finally, the director, in studying the play for character group values, must determine the degree of completeness or dimensionality of the characters as a group.

We have already seen that the special nature of drama demands selectivity, compression, and heightening of character. We also know that theatrical characters must have a consistency which is not to be found in people in life. Actually, definition and clarity of character amount to what we have called the *typification* of all characters found in drama. The convention of the theatre demands it. The director must always bear this fact in mind regardless of the degree of reality achieved by the play as a whole. Every style of playwriting, from naturalism to expressionism, is governed by the restraining boundaries of art, and the theatre must not be confused with life. Both directors and actors, when analyzing characters and attempting to create them in performance, sometimes forget this basic principle underlying their work.

Within the restrictions of the conventions of drama, however, a scale measuring the degree of fullness of character can be used by the director. In making his analysis of the play as a whole it is necessary for him to determine where the members of his group of characters belong on the scale. In our discussion we might start with examples of the least fully developed characters and move to examples of the most fully developed. It must be pointed out at once that this is a comparative study for interpretive purposes and is not concerned with the stageworthiness of any example. The expressionistic drama makes little attempt at character completeness. The characters are *ciphers* and nothing more. They don't even have names but are referred to as "The Man," "The Woman," or even "Mr. One," "Mr. Two," etc. They are abstractions. They have no life of their own but dangle on the strings of the puppeteer playwright. Mr. and Mrs. Zero, Mr. One, and Mr. Two in Rice's *The Adding Machine* exemplify this degree of character completeness. More fully drawn are the *allegorical* characters in the morality plays: "Gluttony," "Good Deeds," and "Lust," which at least have down-to-earth, recognizable, everyday traits. They are more than mere automata signifying ideas. There is a reality about them that expressionistic characters never achieve. Next in our scale we find the *type* character. Type or stock characters are found throughout the range of drama. They are expected in comedy, farce, and melodrama. They are easily recognizable and believable. The Roman comedies first established them; Kaufman and Hart have perpetuated them. The crafty and suave servant, the lecherous father, the lady of easy virtue, the young man with free-wheeling ideas, the bloated businessman are all familiar figures upon our stage. They may speak the latest jargon and talk about the most up-to-date gossip of Washington or Wall Street but they are usually just types. Examples are Erwin and Mabel in *Three Men on a Horse,* the milkman in *Come Back, Little Sheba,* the football player Joe and the dean in *The Male Animal,* the colonel in *The Hasty Heart,* and the "drummer" who appears in the barroom scene in *Ah,*

Wilderness. These characters are types, and as such the audience sees only one side of them. It learns little or nothing about their pasts. They are often in the grip of a single attitude and exercise their wills within the range of that attitude. Their moods are unvarying and their reactions can usually be anticipated.

Coming up the scale a few degrees we find the *conventionally realistic* character. The conventionally complete character is actually only two dimensional. It is more than a type, yet it is not many faceted and fully developed. The principal characters in *They Knew What They Wanted, State of the Union, Bell, Book and Candle,* and *The Reluctant Debutante* are examples. Even Mrs. Phelps in *The Silver Cord* is hardly more than two dimensional, although when the play was first seen she probably appeared to be fully drawn. Her impersonation by Laura Hope Crewes must have increased the impression. The personality of the actor often adds a dimension to the character as written. Rex Harrison and Lilli Palmer enhanced the characters they played in *Bell, Book and Candle.*

The supporting characters in naturalistic plays are often only two dimensional, for example, Turk and Marie in *Come Back, Little Sheba.* It has already been pointed out that a playwright must concentrate upon his principal characters and does not have the time and scope in a play to devote much more than cursory attention to the others. Actually, he grades them from principal characters to subsidiary ones, the details thinning as he descends. In a highly lifelike play like Odets' *Golden Boy* we find a number of supporting characters who are only two dimensional or even types. Nevertheless, these characters must be played as though they were fully developed.

The three-dimensional character more often than not is the protagonist. The author concentrates on him, shows him in many lights, reveals his past, and lays open to view his innermost thoughts and feelings. He exists only in the serious plays or the serio-comic plays. Only Rubashov, for example, can be called a fully developed character in *Darkness at Noon.* The others around him are two dimensional or types. This is also true of Detective McLeod in *Detective Story.* Van Horn in *High Tor* is the only completely drawn character in the play.

In some plays we have more than one three-dimensional character. Blanche and Stanley certainly are in *Streetcar.* Frankie and Berenice in *The Member of the Wedding* also belong in this category. All the characters in *The Sea Gull* except Shamreyev are complete; so are the father, his son, and his daughter-in-law in *Cat on a Hot Tin Roof.*

The director must assess the relative degrees of completeness of the characters in a group because this consideration involves their appeal and potentialities for drama.

3. *Individual character values*

The director's study of the group character values has inevitably resulted in his forming opinions about certain individual character values. These opinions were general and formed in reference to the play as a whole and to the structure of the play. Now, in reference to the actor, each individual character must be investigated for the particular dramatic dynamics which are peculiar to him alone. No attempt should be made to see a character in complete isolation, cut off from relationships with other characters. A character to be potentially dramatic must, as we have already seen, be in relation to something, some other character or force. However, it is necessary for the director to analyze his make-up, which separates him from other individuals and results in certain kinds of relationships and behavior rather than in other kinds.

a. Identification and recognition traits

The playwright presents a character at a certain time of his life, in a particular environment, with special relationships, in a particular state of mind and health, and with a personal history. These critical facts tell the audience who he is. The first step in the study of a character is to identify him by finding out those details that make him different from anyone else in the play. In the study of *All My Sons* we found that Joe Keller had two sons, Chris who is alive and with him in business and Larry who is presumed dead, lost in the war. We also know that Kate is Joe's wife and his sons' mother. We know that Ann and George are the children of Joe's former business partner and that Frank and his wife live next door, as do Dr. Bayliss and his wife and son Bert. We know too that Chris is in love with Ann and intends to marry her. The characters are thus generally identified, but we don't yet know a great deal about each individual.

Let's take Joe Keller and analyze him. Who is he? At the opening of Act I the playwright describes him as follows: "*Keller is nearing sixty. A heavy man of stolid mind and build, a business man these many years, but with the imprint of the machine-shop worker and boss still upon him. When he reads, when he speaks, when he listens it is with the terrible concentration of the uneducated man for whom there is still wonder in many commonly*

*known things, a man whose judgments must be dredged out of
experience and a peasant-like common sense. A man among men.*"[22]
We learn his age, his physical characteristics, his education, his
economic position, his social level and background, and something
of his psychology. Thus the director knows these identifying
factors. The audience on seeing him will learn some of them. When
he speaks and as the play develops it will learn all these things.
The facts that he is *"A heavy man . . . with the imprint of the
machine-shop worker and boss still upon him"* will dictate his
physical habits, movement, and gestures. His manner of speech
will also be influenced by these specific descriptive words. *" . . .
of stolid mind"* will be other key words. Now let us see whether
his manner of expression is appropriate for such a man. Joe's habit
of leaving off the "-ings" of his words and his speaking ungram-
matically indicate something about his education: "Askin' is all
right but don't beat her over the head. You're beatin' her, you're
beatin' her."[23] Contrast Dr. Bayliss' speech and we see a difference
in education and habit: "I've only met you, Ann, but if I may offer
you a piece of advice . . ."[24] The formality and preciseness of Jim's
speech seem appropriate for an educated man with his somewhat
embittered outlook. Joe's manner of expression tells something not
only of his background and environment but of his way of looking
at things. For example: ". . . You should've been here, Annie, and
you too, Chris; you'd a seen something. Everybody knew I was
getting out that day; the porches were loaded. Picture it now; none
of them believed I was really innocent. . . . So I get out of my car,
and I walk down the street. But very slow. And with a smile . . .
Kid, walkin' down the street that day I was guilty as hell. Except
I wasn't . . . and I walked . . . past . . . the porches. Result?"[25]
No one else in the play speaks in this way. His speeches completely
individualize him. His choice of words and their order and rhythm
seem right for Joe. As a matter of fact, no character other than
Joe and the doctor has a completely characteristic way of expressing
himself. The author uses individualizing thoughts and emotions
rather than language itself to characterize the others, whose dialogue
is more revealing psychologically than otherwise.

    Stage directions are helpful to the director but they are not
helpful to those members of the audience who have not read them.
The director must take note of this and remember that the audience
must be told and shown. Sometimes a playwright describes a
character exceedingly well and writes revealing stage directions,
but this is to no avail if the character does not have the characterizing action and dialogue which can be communicated to
the audience.

Miller, an excellent craftsman, dramatizes his character descriptions and stage directions. Joe Keller's dialogue says something about him: ". . . I don't read the news part any more. It's more interesting in the want ads."[26] We learn from this speech that he is an escapist and is disinterested in world issues and society in general. He is interested in things that concern himself. He is a businessman and is interested in what people want and will buy. When he expresses wonder at people's wanting Newfoundland dogs and old dictionaries he reveals his limited knowledge of people. "All the kinds of business goin' on. In my day, either you were a lawyer, or a doctor, or you worked in a shop" tells the audience that he obviously worked in a shop. He even admits that he is an ignorant man with: "You look at a page like this you realize how ignorant you are."[27] His simplicity and naivete are continually revealed, but so are his sense of humor and feeling of kindliness. Joe is a sympathetic character and an average guy. The audience knows who he is, likes him, and satisfies itself that he is like a lot of people it knows. His recognition value is an important part of his dramatic potential.

b.   Character objective and units of objective

Now that we know who Joe Keller is we need to find out *why* he behaves as he does—his motivation or causation. How active is his will? Stanislavsky referred to this aspect of a character as his "objective." Boleslavsky and the Group Theatre and their descendants the Actors' Studio call it his "spine." The spine should be expressed as a transitive verb. We must find that Joe wants *to do something*. In Act I Ann says, ". . . He just wants everybody happy." And Joe answers: "That's my sentiments."[28] Later on in the act he says to Chris, ". . . I want a clean start for you, Chris. I want a new sign over the plant—Christopher Keller, Incorporated. . . . I'm going to build you a house . . . I want you to spread out, Chris, I want you to use what I made for you . . . (*He is close to him now.*) . . . I mean, with joy, Chris, without shame . . . with joy."[29] From these lines and other indications in the play we might say that Joe's spine is *to make everybody happy*, particularly Chris, and he wishes *to forget the past* involving his business scandal and *to avoid* any unpleasantness. This wish is obsessive and pervades his every thought and act.

After establishing the character's spine or objective, the director must divide his over-all objective into units or "beats." Each moment on stage and off stage he is motivated by his objective, and each such moment is a unit. Joe's first unit is to be friendly with Dr. Jim Bayliss. Later we see him wanting to joke and be neighborly with Frank and Jim's wife. Then he has a unit or beat with Chris which shows his desire to talk and be close to his son. The scene with Bert which follows shows his good-natured friendliness with children. He seeks to avoid a difference of opinion with Kate and tries to keep the conversation light and happy when Ann and Mrs. Keller come close to a disagreement.

c. Sources of opposition

Now we know who Joe Keller is and why he behaves as he does. What are the sources of opposition to his overruling desire? First there is Chris, who in the first scene with his father accuses him of trying to evade the issue when Chris tells him of the problem of his mother caused by his desire to marry Ann. The further point is made that Joe and Chris have fundamentally opposed philosophies of life. As we have already determined, this opposition creates the main relationship of the play. Another source of opposition is Mrs. Keller. The little contretemps between the two the moment she makes her first entrance is indicative of a fundamental difference in point of view. Incidentally, could Joe's obsession about wanting to remove what he considers "the garbage" be symbolic of his desire to clean up his life? Of course, George is the active force of opposition that destroys Joe.

Joe's conscience is another source of his conflict. When Chris says, "You have such a talent for ignoring things . . ." Joe replies, "I ignore what I gotta ignore."[30] He refuses to read things in the newspapers that would make him think and feel, and this exchange of conversation with Chris implies a deeper refusal to face his past. When he worries about the news of George's coming to see them his conscience is again gnawing at him. He seeks too actively for happiness and peace for himself and everybody else. He is worried about happiness and peace. He wishes to compensate for his lack of them; he wishes to atone.

The author implies that Joe is also in conflict with his environment or was in conflict with his environment when he, like so many other businessmen during wartime, became the victim of an emotional and intellectual climate which encourages the attitude: Get rich while the getting is good; think only of yourself and your family; the devil take the rest of the world. Joe certainly indicates that he has adopted this attitude. Wartime profiteering at any cost is a thematic thread of the play. Chris explains the society the author is blaming for having that philosophy of life when he says, ". . . This is the land of the great *big* dogs, you don't love a man

here, you eat him. *That's* the principle; the only one we live by—
It just happened to kill a few people this time, that's all. The
world's that way, [Joe is even partly excused and certainly sympa-
thized with when Chris continues with] how can I take it out on
him [Joe]? What sense does that make? This is a zoo, a zoo!"[31]
(Edward Albee has the same concept of the world in *The Zoo
Story*.) Joe, when speaking to Chris, Kate, and Ann, is actually
speaking to the audience and saying he is no more guilty than the
rest of the country in the speech:

> What should I want to do? (*Chris is silent.*) Jail? You want me
> to go to jail? . . . Is that where I belong?—Then tell me so!
> . . . I'll tell you why you can't say it. Because you know I don't
> belong there. . . . Who worked for nothin' in that war? When
> they work for nothin', I'll work for nothin'. Did they ship a
> gun or a truck outa Detroit before they got their price? Is
> that clean? . . . It's dollars and cents, nickels and dimes; war
> and peace, it's nickels and dimes, what's clean? The whole
> goddam country is gotta go if I go! That's why you can't
> tell me.[32]

We, of course, do not see Joe struggling against the forces that
brought about his attitude, but his inherent decent instincts for the
right moral values are apparent throughout the play. His speech
explaining his attitude and actions about the pressures of carrying
out his war contracts is a rationalization about his conscious
wrongdoing.

d.   Tonality of character

From the character's identification, spine, and sources of opposition emerges his tone. Primarily this means his emotional effect
upon the audience. Joe generates warm sympathy and because of
his problems and his attitude toward them the audience takes him
seriously. He sometimes evokes laughter because of his sense of
humor, but all in all he is a serious and, tonally, a heavy character.
He is pitiable and emotionally affective. His words, actions, and
problems make him so. He is a "little man," down to earth, tough
fibered but disturbed, trying to cope with a serious, fundamental,
and human predicament. In contrast with him, Jim Bayliss is
serious too but of a different tone. His wry, sardonic way of
speaking and his joshing with his wife make him more humorous
and crisp than Joe. He has an objectivity toward life that involves
him less emotionally with the other characters and the audience.
Frank and Lydia are primarily comic characters and serve to

relieve the serious mood of the play. Bert serves the same purpose
and, too, is sympathetically humorous. Sue is sharp tongued but
with a sense of humor and is the source of chuckles for the audience.
She is tough and resilient, a mixture of sharpness and bitterness
in tone. Kate is a serious character constantly hovering between
anger, tears, and frustration. She is strong willed but on the verge
of seeming to break under varying pressures. Yet at the end she
proves stronger than Joe. She is essentially vibrant and strong
in tone.

The tonality of a character is a vital key to casting the actor
to play it. An actor's personal quality—his physical appearance,
voice, manner of speaking and moving, and his total personality—
should support and confirm the character's tonality. (By casting
"against type"—against an actor's personal qualities—the director
may achieve very interesting and novel dramatic values.)

e.   Dimensionality and growth

Joe is not a complex character but he is a complete one. He
is three dimensional. The audience learns many things about him.
His every speech and action are revealing. We see his varied traits
and moods. As the play progresses we see that part of the past
which is vital to the theme of the play. As he is revealed step by
step to the audience he is forced to stop evading the past and is
compelled to look at himself in the clear and scorching light which
Chris turns on him. Up until this time his course of action in life
was certain and definite. Now he does not know what to do. He
refuses to believe that he has been wrong. He blames the rest of the
world. His code of life has failed him, and he is not strong enough
to try to live by another. His world collapses around him. He does
not have the intelligence, spiritual insight, or strength to reorganize
his life, and he takes the only way out—suicide. There is a progression from ignorance to a new point of view, but there is not
progression to knowledge with understanding. He does not achieve
a new insight; he is incapable of it. This is part of his pitiful plight.

f.   Contribution to theme

Joe's life as we see it in the play is the demonstration of the
theme—the meaning of the play. His contribution to the meaning
is greater than that of any other character. He is the protagonist
in a sense. But he is an incomplete one. He needs Chris' intelligence
to make him complete and give him enlightenment. If he were a

complete protagonist he would be a tragic one. Chris' contribution to the play's meaning is secondary only to Joe's. Chris is a symbolic aspect of Joe, his father, in that he too has evaded the past and has closed his eyes to his worst suspicions about his father. His guilt lies in not facing facts. In addition to pointing out the crime committed by people like Joe Keller, indicting the country for encouraging such a crime, Miller is saying that we must take action against it and punish the guilty. Chris illustrates this latter point by his insistent desire to take his father to jail. Kate's contribution to the theme lies in her insistence upon Joe's facing the truth at last. She, like Joe, is guilty of hiding the truth. Her punishment will be to live on—without Larry and without Joe. In descending order from George to Ann to Jim to Frank and so on to little Bert, the rest of the characters contribute to the theme. In order to stress it the director must determine the amount of contribution each character makes.

In analyzing individual character values the director applies some of the same tests used for group values, but this is a necessary repetition because he must always have the whole play in mind in order to control the dramatic values to achieve his and the playwright's particular balance. Every playwright deals with the same media of expression, but the individuality of a play results from his particular treatment of these media. Emphasis and balance therefore vary from play to play to project different intentions. (This will be discussed further under "Points of Focus.")

Thus, seeing character values in terms of the individual, in terms of the individual's relationship to others, and in terms of the characters' contribution to the meaning of the play as a whole, the director has formulated a characterization for each actor. He has learned the physical, mental, emotional, psychological, and sociological *facts of identification,* the character's *spine, forces of opposition, tonality of character, dimensionality* and *progression,* and *contribution to the play's theme.* These aspects of character form its anatomy. From it the actor should be able to evolve a pattern of stimuli and responses which will create a fictional and dramatic life.

In the discussion of the director's problems with character it must be obvious that this element of a play does not exist as a separate entity but is inseparable from and dependent upon situation. A character creates situations which are the result of character motivation, will, and opposition. These situations result in plot. Therefore, as we saw in the discussion of *Action in Depth,* "Plot is never simply a series of situations but *the interplay of character and situation.*"[33]

PLOT

The director must not underestimate the appeal of what the layman calls a "good story." A provocative theme, interesting characters, and amusing or deftly moving dialogue are indeed assets to a play, but it is the story or plot which most members of the audience find most absorbing. Its power lies in its ability to involve the feelings of the audience in vicarious experiences. A good story line ensures deep absorption, pleasurable tension, surprise, suspense, and personal identification.

1.   *Plot units*

In the study of plot values the director first takes care to understand the story-telling parts of the play and to memorize them in sequence. He will find it helpful to break them down into scene units and commit to memory their salient points. A careful underscoring of all plot lines in the script will facilitate this and will be of great value during the rehearsal of the play. The scene-unit division is necessary for detailed analysis and rehearsal organization. The entrance or exit of a character marks the beginning and ending of the so-called "French" scene. This can be designated as a scene unit. However, an entrance or exit may not necessarily mean the start of a new scene in terms of mood, plot, or subject. In the first scene between Willy and Charley in *Death of a Salesman*, Ben enters, but the unit obviously continues in terms of a particular mood which pervades it. The exit of Charley might be considered the beginning of a new unit.

A play usually divides itself into scenes when the dialogue is concentrated entirely between certain characters. There will be scenes between two characters ("twosome scenes") or scenes between three characters ("threesome scenes"), and there will be group scenes, etc. While analyzing or directing these scenes the director must constantly remember their relationship to the entire plot line. The whole must be indelibly impressed upon his consciousness and never separated from its parts. Writing out the broad outline of the plot will assure the director's learning the main line of action. Then he may find it helpful to write it out in scenario form. Finally he may reduce this to sequential units and number each one.

The director may determine the unit limits by a change of mood, the beginning of a new step in the development of the plot, or a change of subject. For example, the opening scene between Linda and Willy could very well be considered one unit until the focus of attention shifts to the boys' room. Yet there is a change of mood, plot, and subject when (1) Willy asks about the boys, another change when (2) Linda says she got a "new kind of American-type cheese," another when (3) Willy asks why she doesn't open a window, another when (4) he asks whether she is worried about him, and again when (5) she suggests their taking a ride on Sunday. Each of these smaller units has definite dramatic values of mood, character, plot, and theme.

2. *Clarity of plot*

Clarity of plot is an elementary and basic problem for the playwright and director. The death knell is sounded for a play and its production when members of the audience querulously demand of one another in reference to the plot: "What's it all about?"

Miller's slow and careful expositional preparation in the first act of *All My Sons* informs the audience of the necessary facts that build up the plot premise. Notice how many times one of the characters refers to the tree which has blown down in order to explain the background of Larry's story and its relationship to certain characters. The audience's ability to see the tree when the characters see it makes the references natural. The motivations for seeing it and remarking about it and Larry would not be nearly so convincing if the tree were off stage. It is a visual stimulus and a symbol. It is what we might call a "conversation piece." The placement of the tree is therefore important in the ground plan for the setting. It must be in a prominent position on stage and yet must not impede the movement of the actors. The repeated allusions to the tree emphasize the plot factors and also build up suspense regarding Kate's possible reactions to it. The fact that the audience sees the tree and the reactions of other characters to it helps to clarify, support, and point up the dialogue. This visual means of conveying plot must also be utilized by the director in placing his characters on the stage and so grouping them that each step of the plot progression is dramatized. An important factor in building up the plot premise is the necessity of demonstrating the characters' belief in each moment. Belief is essential to all truthful acting, but illustrative belief is projected strongly when pictorial dramatizations, actions, and reactions have story-telling values. The director can check this by shutting out the dialogue of a scene or even an act and simply watching the groupings, pantomime, and movement to determine the clarity of the plot without the help of dialogue.

Earlier it was urged that the director underscore the plot lines in his script to ensure their emphasis in performance. The director will then be reminded that these lines must be protected from distracting movement and the audience's mind must be focused upon them. In addition, the actors must emphasize them by various oral means. In naturalistic plays actors must of course sound conversational while speaking. However, dialogue must be *dramatically* conversational and not merely lifelike. In life we fail to emphasize words or phrases or we place the emphasis upon the wrong words. The actors must exercise sufficient conscious control to make certain aspects of the dialogue emphatic. During performances they must believe so that they can justify points of emphasis through truthful emotion. If the actors will use a pencil or pen to underscore these points in their dialogue during the rehearsal periods they will, through practice, form the mental, emotional, and vocal habits necessary to convey them spontaneously but with clarity and emphasis to the audience.

3.   *Plot motivation*

Motivation and conviction are as important as clarity. They have already been mentioned in connection with the tree in the Miller play. Their use as stimuli for thought and conversation is of great value. External and internal stimuli—visual, auditory, sensory—affect human behavior, and it is the job of the playwright and the director to find them in order to motivate the thoughts and actions of the characters. And such motivating stimuli must be revealed to the audience. They must have psychological conviction and appear appropriate to the characters and situations. When the storm came the night before, Kate was dreaming of Larry and when she awoke the wind was blowing—"like the roaring of his engine"— and she came out to the yard and the tree broke right in front of her. She took this as an omen. She says, ". . . there are meanings in such things." This statement appears to be in character for Kate to believe. Frank has previously said that Kate wanted him to make a horoscope for Larry. Chris tells the audience Kate still believes Larry will return. Her seeing the tree blown down is the stimulus for her reaction. It is psychologically convincing.

Motivation is based both on stimuli and on other causes convincing to the audience. The development of a scene can be motivated by the causality of foreshadowing in the dialogue. Such foreshadowing can be seen in Kate's line, "Everything that happened seems to be coming back."[34] This, together with other foreshadowing dialogue, is sufficient to make the audience expect and believe in the essential unraveling of the entire past of the characters. Kate's saying that Joe above all others must believe that Larry did not die, her turning on him and saying furiously that she wants him to stop playing jail with little Bert, and her lines at the end of Act I that he must be "smart" when George comes are sufficient causal motivation for the revelation of Joe's guilt and possible imprisonment.

The characters are revealed to the audience in such a way that their speech and actions which create the plot are convincingly motivated. Chris' idealism leads him to strike his father at the end of Act II and in Act III makes him insist on his going to jail for his crime. Such shocking behavior on the part of a son would be unbelievable if his particular attitude toward society and his father were not properly dramatized in his scenes with his father and Ann in Act I. Ann's refusal to marry after Larry was reported missing, her coming to visit the Kellers, her attitude toward her father, and her forcing Kate to read Larry's letter are all plot actions which are believable and convincing because they are motivated.

4. *Audience acceptance of plot premise*

If the audience is to participate in the play as it progresses, it must understand and believe the background and steps leading to the basic situation upon which the action of the play is founded. The basic situation, it is well to remember, is the result of a catalytic agent which has upset the equilibrium—the peace and adjustment previously achieved by the characters of the play. And it is this imbalance or maladjustment of forces and characters in the basic situation from which the rest of the play will spring. While becoming oriented to the environment, the characters, their desires, the forces opposing them, and their consequent problems, the audience is in effect hearing and seeing the rules of the game. The principal players have been introduced, the goal has been established, and the limits of the playing area have been set. Having learned the rules of the game of watching and taking part in a play—and believing them—the audience is willing to take the imaginary journey implicit in the theatrical experience. Their thoughts and emotions have become conditioned to the given circumstances of the world of fiction which the play creates. They are then mentally and emotionally geared to the characters and their actions; they will move along with the stream of dramatic incidents. They have accepted the basic situation which is the plot premise of the play.

The audience's acceptance of the plot premise of all plays is

essential, but certain types of plays have premises that are more
difficult to accept than others. Farces, melodramas, and fantasies
are based upon factors which, compared with those of other plays,
stretch the elastic of credibility. The burden placed upon the audience's "willing suspension of disbelief" is indeed heavy. It is therefore commensurably heavy for the director. He must work pains-
takingly and slowly to induct the audience into the play. He must
present the characters ingratiatingly and convincingly to interest
the audience in them as people and to make it care about their
problems and their solutions. Once this is accomplished the audience
can be guided the rest of the way. However, the director must not
at any time along the way thereafter break audience illusion and
belief. The rules of the game have been established and accepted
by the audience, and the director, like the audience, must adhere
to them.

5.   Conflict and crisis

The characters are seen in various degrees of serious opposition
to one another during the process of building the play's basic
situation. In addition to the series of conflicts engaged in by the
principal characters, there are minor conflicts among the supporting
characters. The director must control the amount of emphasis given
to each. He must not overly stage a subplot conflict between supporting characters for fear of distracting the audience from the
problems of the main characters; keeping in mind the play as a
whole, he must remember the elements in their proper proportion.
Conflicts, large and small, important and minor, are the lifeblood
of a play, and the director must seek them out like the prospector
seeking uranium with his geiger counter. His choices of interpretation of a line of dialogue will often determine its generative
force for creating conflict. Whenever possible and not contrary
to the author's intention, as we have previously pointed out, a
line of dialogue should be interpreted for its emotional, positive,
and active values which foreshadow and underlie conflict. An
audience is soon surfeited with the even calm of speech and action.
It seeks change and conflict. It is like a hunting dog: It is constantly
looking for game and is quick to pick up its scent. The author's
foreshadowing by means of dialogue or situation gives the audience
the scent of impending conflict. When Joe Keller's next-door neighbor Frank says in the opening of Miller's play "Hey, what happened
to your tree?" the question is inherently suspenseful and portentous
because of the importance of the tree. The director's interpretation
and the actor's vocalization of the words will alert the audience

to its importance. If the question is asked too casually the audience will not take any more notice of it than of the preceding chit-chat. If asked with sufficient emotion and concern the audience tends to sit up and lean forward. And when Frank asks "What'd Kate say?" and Joe answers "I'm just waiting for her to see it," the audience gets the scent of conflict. The even calm has been disturbed. The plot is in motion, implied though not overt.

The director must develop a sense for *implied* conflict as well well as *actual*. The lines just referred to lead to actual conflict very shortly when Joe and Chris talk about Kate's reaction to the fallen tree and her insistence upon believing that Larry is still alive. The conflict is in the open when Chris says he and Joe have been dishonest with Kate in pretending to agree with her that there is a chance of Larry's returning. The word "dishonest" disturbs Joe deeply; when the audience is able to look back upon the incidents of the play it will realize that this reference to dishonesty casts a dark shadow over Joe and the rest of the play. His sense of guilt is a dormant flame which the word "dishonesty" ignites. The opposition here established between these two characters develops into the main plot line—the backbone of the play. The director must realize this, though the audience may not as it watches the scene. The point of difference between Joe's meaning of honesty and Chris' meaning is the introduction of the principal theme to be dramatized by the play. The attention it receives from the playwright in the first act is in proportion to the other elements and gives a pattern to the basic situation.

In so controlling the emphasis on given moments of conflict the director makes clear to the audience their degree of importance. Only the important conflicts will lead to one or more culminating crises. A crisis is significant plot-wise because it presents a moment of choice of decision and action for the characters. The decision made by the characters involved will change the course of action of the play. A classic example is Hamlet's happening upon the king praying, seeing his opportunity to kill him, but deciding to spare his life. This decision leads to his later mistaking Polonius for the king and killing him instead. The chain reaction to this act is well known.

In *All My Sons* Chris faces a crisis when Jim urges him to prevent George's coming in from the car waiting in the driveway. Ann starts to go to the car to drive George away but Chris stops her and goes out to get George. If George had been prevented from coming in or if he had been persuaded to go away before Kate and Joe entered, the whole course of the play would have been altered. Ann's decision to stay when George urged her to go was also responsible for changing the action. Later Chris and Ann had an opportunity to allow George to leave, but they urged him to stay. These crises led to the scene in which George forced Joe into a revelation of his wrongdoing and ultimately to the climax of the play.

Directorially, conflicts lead to crises and crises to the climax, and thus greater and greater suspense is created for the audience. This emotionalizing quality is established and maintained through the rhythm of performance. In the section on structure we have already seen what it looks like in diagram. The peaks made by the conflicts and crises are relative and the director must control the rhythm to keep them in relation and proportion to one another. He must hold down the peaks of emotional intensity and grade them upward to the climax. The flow must not be broken and it must gather momentum and intensity to its crest. Here is the pulse of the play and the director must keep one hand on it to test it and the other hand to regulate it.

6.   Obligatory scene, climax, and resolution

Every play, as we know, builds to a definite peak of emotional intensity which dominates all other peaks and is the ultimate and decisive emotional eruption of the play. This emotional and rhythmical development comes about when the opposing forces become locked in the decisive combat to which the action has been leading. The struggle is the main one to which the audience looks forward and is the *obligatory scene* necessary to gratify their expectations. After this comes the turning point or climax, which is followed by a gradual quiescence or a sudden calm and equilibrium or adjustment of the combustible elements which caused the momentous eruption. Some plays may achieve not an equilibrium but an adjustment. An equilibrium can be achieved only when the problem or issue can be solved. An adjustment is necessary if it is unsolvable. The process of reaching an equilibrium or adjustment consists of unraveling and disengaging the forces, and is the resolution of the play. The resolution often takes place simultaneously with the climax. It is therefore practical to treat these two plot values, climax and resolution, together as connecting units or as a single unit. We can see this in the obligatory scene of *All My Sons* which comes in the third act. It is a multiple obligatory scene inasmuch as Ann, Mrs. Keller, Joe, and Chris face one another and have it out. This is the turning point or climax. Joe's shooting himself and the rest of the act are the resolution.

A play can be likened to a symphony and divided into movements. In construction, *All My Sons* has some similarity to Beethoven's Fifth Symphony. This similarity lies in the fact that both are dominated by the presence of fate which moves inexorably and inevitably along its predestined course. Its infernal machine has been set in motion and nothing will turn it aside to avoid its ultimate catastrophe. Both the symphony and the play are divided into movements. Instead of being in four movements the play is in three. For the moment we are concerned with its third movement, for it contains the climax. The director cannot cope with the climax without carefully analyzing and directing the scenes preceding it. Though the entire third act is in itself a build, the climactic surge commences at the point in the act when a perceptible rhythmical change occurs, and it is at this point that the director must change the pace and tighten the action. This change starts with Joe's second entrance. For purposes of interpretation and direction it is convenient to divide the climactic surge into two steps. The first is the scene between Chris and Joe; the second begins when Ann takes the letter from Mrs. Keller and gives it to Chris and continues through Chris' reading of it to his line, "Do you understand that letter?"

These two steps must be made clear in development, and the dramatic values of each must be fully exploited. They should be rehearsed separately and then continuously. The director must be sensitive to the tonality of each step and must seek variety of mood without destroying the underlying portentous mood that binds together the two steps. He must also gauge each step for its relative intensification to assure a gradual acceleration and increase in tension. In rehearsing the climactic surge actors tend to force the pace and emotional intensity. This becomes apparent through shouting, vocal tension, rapid speech, and a general forcing of the emotions. If the actors play truthfully, they will try to restrain their emotions, which will erupt spontaneously. Such playing will result in the pattern of tension and relaxation which creates the suspense felt by the audience. Continuous playing of the two steps without interruption for a number of rehearsals will give the steps continuity and will help to relax the actors and set the pitch of their performance.

The climax in modern plays is at varying distances from the last curtain. In *Death of a Salesman* it is in the final scene between Biff and Willy, and the resolution requires only about a page of dialogue. *Come Back, Little Sheba* is so organized that its climax occurs near the end of the next-to-last scene, and the last scene is given over to the resolution. In *A Streetcar Named Desire* the climax comes with the end of the next-to-last scene, and the resolution occurs in the very last scene. All these are serious plays. It might be well to look at some less serious ones. The climax of the comedy *Bell, Book and Candle* comes at the end of Act II. It is the showdown between Gillian and Shep and the highest point of emotional intensity in the play. Act III is comprised of two scenes. The first works up to a sort of secondary climax when Gillian finds she can no longer cast spells and has turned into a human being. The last scene is the resolution. *State of the Union,* which is a comedy with a theme, has its climax very near the end of the play. The resolution is short and somewhat perfunctory, but it is sufficient for a comedy of this nature. The examples chosen are fairly typical for plays of compact structure.

Plays of loose structure show more freedom in the placement of climax and resolution. *Macbeth,* though a play of considerable compactness of structure, has two climaxes. One occurs at the murder of Duncan and the other at the banquet when Macbeth sees Banquo's ghost. Macbeth's fortunes decline thereafter. *Othello* combines the climax with the resolution. The death of Desdemona marks the peak of pity and fear of the play, but the subsequent death of Emilia, the momentary escape of Iago, and the death of Othello continue the intensification of the scene. The last knot of the thread is not unraveled until then. The arrival of Lodovico and the carrying off of Iago to prison bring the play to a close.

DIALOGUE

"*. . . the special power of the drama is its unrivaled use of the spoken word.*"[35] Dialogue is the main characteristic of drama. It may be, then, a key to drama. However, dialogue is more than a key, it is the heart; character is the hands and arms; plot and action, the feet and legs; and theme, the head in the "anatomy of drama." As the heart, dialogue is responsible for the life and vitality of the other organs. Character, plot, and theme come into existence only through dialogue. It is the playwright's only creative medium.

All dramatic dialogue is characterized by its inherent movement and progression, expository powers, emotion, credibility, intensity, and heightening. The dialogue of all plays must possess these general characteristics. Each individual play, however, varies in its particular dialogue characteristics and distinctive dramatic dynamics. The director must learn to look for them and be aware of them. This is most important in his work with the actors.

The interpretation of the dialogue in a play starts with the understanding that the word is "the spoken symbol of an idea."[36]

As such, however, it may not communicate the same meaning to each member of the audience. Meaning varies according to the knowledge and experience of the hearer. Memories, connotations, and feelings color words. The director's job in his directorial use of words is to make their meaning precise and specific for purposes of communicating the facts of plot and character to the audience as a whole in order to ensure common understanding and response. On the other hand, it is also the director's job to convey the overtones, ambiguities, and ambivalences of meaning to each individual member of the audience as a matter of personal interpretation and enrichment.

In interpreting dialogue the director must understand that the face value of words and sentences is not their only possible value. Their outward meaning often covers an inner meaning. The director must look between and under the lines to seek other meanings. The subtext of a play provides the actor with rich sources of character behavior. When in Chekhov's *The Three Sisters* Irina repeats Chebutykin's statement in Act II that "Balzac was married in Berditchev," the audience must gain a meaning quite different from that conveyed the first time the words are uttered. When Chebutykin says the words, he reads them from the newspaper, and they shed light on the life of Balzac for both Chebutykin and the audience. Repeating the words, Irina is thinking of herself in contrast to Balzac: Though he was married in an unimportant place he was nevertheless married and she is not. The director and the actress playing Irina must find the subtextual meaning and make it clear to the audience by intonation, rhythm, gesture, and look.

Dialogue is the element of a play that is most indicative of its literary quality. If it is distinguished the entire body of work is elevated in quality. However, the high quality of the dialogue can sometimes blind the director and critic to the stageworthiness of the play. Many so-called plays with fine literary dialogue are published but never produced because they have no claim to being drama other than the possession of beautiful words. Beautiful words must create characterization, plot, and theme which are dramatic.

1. General characteristics

a. Movement and progression

First of all, dialogue has the difficult job of revealing character, establishing the present situation, clarifying past action, and forwarding action, while pointing to the future. An example of this may be cited from *All My Sons*.

KELLER: Say, I ain't got time to get sick.

MOTHER: He hasn't been laid up in fifteen years . . .

KELLER: (*quickly*) Except my 'flu during the war.

MOTHER: Heh?

KELLER: My flu, when I was sick during . . .

MOTHER: (*quickly*) Well, sure . . . (*to George*) except for that 'flu, I mean. (*Pause. George stands perfectly still.*)

MOTHER: (*a little desperately*) I just forgot it, George. (*George doesn't move.*)

MOTHER: I mean he's so rarely sick it slipped my mind. I thought he had pneumonia, he couldn't get off the bed.

GEORGE: Why did you say he's never . . .?

KELLER: I know how you feel, kid, but I couldn't help it; I'll never forgive myself, because if I could've gone in that day I'd never allow Dad to touch those heads.

GEORGE: She said you'd never been sick.

MOTHER: I said he *was* sick!

GEORGE: (*to Ann*) Didn't you hear her say . . .?[37]

This dialogue certainly tells us who the characters are and the present situation, uncovers past action, and points to the future in its probable effect on Keller, his wife, his son, Ann, and George. Possibly the prime requisite of dialogue is that movement and progression be inherent in it. At the same time it should imply and reveal character. In other words, it must combine exposition with action. This is dialogue at its most dramatic.

b. Exposition

Exposition in a play is usually referred to as those sections of dialogue which explain to the audience facts they should know about characters, plot, and theme—whether past or present. It is used especially in reference to the past. We get this kind of information when the two servants in *The Wild Duck* discuss old Mr. Werle, the party then in progress, Werle's son Gregers, and Werle's friend Mrs. Sörby. This is the dialogue.

PETTERSEN: (*Lights a lamp on the chimney-place and places a shade over it.*) Hark to them, Jensen! Now the old man's on his legs holding a long palaver about Mrs. Sörby.

JENSEN: (*Pushing forward an arm-chair.*) Is it true, what folks say, that they're—very good friends, eh?

PETTERSEN: Lord knows.

JENSEN: I've heard tell as he's been a lively customer in his day.

PETTERSEN: May be.

JENSEN: And he's giving this spread in honour of his son, they say.

PETTERSEN: Yes. His son came home yesterday.

JENSEN: This is the first time I ever heard as Mr. Werle had a son.

PETTERSEN: Oh yes, he has a son, right enough. But he's a fixture, as you might say, up at the Höidal works. He's never once come to town all the years I've been in service here.[38]

This is obvious exposition to the trained critic and director. It might not be obvious to most of the audience. Ibsen tries to give it a semblance of reality by having this dialogue take place between the old servant employed in Werle's household and a new one hired for the occasion; thus the exposition seems motivated. In addition, Ibsen depends upon the audience's expectation that servants will gossip. Ibsen uses gossiping servants for expositional purposes in a number of his plays.

The soliloquy and the aside are two other well-known devices for conveying information to the audience. The soliloquy, when employed by a great dramatist like Shakespeare, not only is informative as to character and plot but is motivated and has great emotional power and beauty. The aside used characteristically by writers of the eighteenth and nineteenth centuries is informative but has a minimum of motivation or emotional conviction. Solitary dialogue, however, is seldom employed by the modern dramatist unless it is motivated by the character's being old and/or lacking in mental powers. People don't ordinarily talk to themselves at length. They may exclaim and utter words and short phrases to reveal their thoughts and emotions. Thus we see that these three expositional devices are conventions of the past.

The Greek and Elizabethan drama are notable examples of the use of the messenger to inform the audience of past events or to describe off-stage actions. We can cite the messenger in *Oedipus Rex* and *Antigone* for the Greek drama. Shakespeare uses messengers in countless instances in his chronicle plays when they enter and announce that a war has ended, a hill has been taken by the enemy, or that Lord So-and-So has been killed. The "bloody sergeant" in *Macbeth* is not called a messenger but his function in the play is that of one. The chorus in Greek and Elizabethan drama was also a means of telling the audience whatever was needful. It revealed individual character and past events, forwarded

the action, and pointed a moral. Its use in Greek drama is characteristic. Thornton Wilder's stage manager in *Our Town* and the
narrator in Robert Penn Warren's *All the King's Men* are modern
versions of the chorus.

A common device for exposition used by the twentieth-century
playwright is the telephone. It gives the character speaking on
stage to the character at the other end of the line a plausible reason
for explaining something not only to the character off stage but
to the audience. The telephone also gives the character on stage
who answers the phone a plausible reason to relay his information
to those on stage and to the audience. Examples of the use of
this device are familiar to us all. Confidants have been of great
use to the playwright ever since the sixteenth century. Shakespeare
and Molière used them extensively. Ibsen and later playwrights
have also found them convenient. The dialogue merely needs to
begin: "Did you know, my dear . . .?" And the playwright is off.
The inquiring stranger is also a helpful device. (George is not
a stranger in *All My Sons* but he is inquiring and motivates the
question-and-answer technique used by Miller. The seeking and
inquiring character is classic and can be found exemplified by no
less famous characters than Oedipus and Hamlet.) The stranger
gives the author the motivation for having the other characters
tell him things that they otherwise would not talk about since
they already possess this knowledge.

The playwright today may employ various expositional means,
but he is considered inept and obvious if they are purely expositional and do not combine information with action. Furthermore,
as has been previously pointed out, the characters in a play must
speak in character and not just for the author, who may wish to
convey information about something more than character. Characters cannot speak of things they as particular characters would
not naturally know about. Dialogue must imply information without conveying it directly, and such information must point to the
future even when revealing the present and the past.

Obvious exposition in a scene can be camouflaged in a number
of ways by the director. One way is to motivate the character
to reveal it emotionally: That is, he may reveal it against his will,
in anger, etc. Another is to find something for the character to
do while he speaks—anything to avoid the appearance of a set
speech given more for the audience's benefit than for the sake
of character or situation. Movement with speech, however, presents
the technical problem of the need to protect the words from distracting action. The director must keep the audience's primary
attention upon the meaning of the words. In the opening scene

quoted above from *The Wild Duck,* for example, Ibsen's stage directions give the director the movement needed to hide the exposition somewhat. If the director and actors can give Pettersen and Jensen definite attitudes toward the characters they speak of, the exposition will be less obvious. If these attitudes could be presented as *conflicting* attitudes the scene would be more dramatic.

c. Emotion

The most dramatic dialogue is emotional—not emotion for its own sake but emotion wrung out of the characters in spite of themselves. It is the expression of the character's will and is the outcome of conflict between the rational and the emotional, with the emotional breaking through and predominating. This kind of struggle keeps the dialogue from being incoherent emotional outpourings which will be unaffective. The question of control over emotional dialogue is important. Often when a playwright wishes to hammer home his theme he will place a character in an emotional crisis and then have him deliver a peroration carefully calculated to say exactly what the playwright wishes to say. It therefore becomes obvious and unconvincing. It is unnatural because a person under such emotional stress could not speak with so much rationality. Such dialogue is out of character; the character becomes a mouthpiece for the author. Propaganda plays like John Howard Lawson's *Marching Song* will yield many examples of this. (In high comedy where the mind controls and epigrams roll from the mouth, a character, even in a crisis, can speak with great intellectual perception and wit without seeming, in the flow of the performance, to be out of character. George Bernard Shaw's plays are filled with characters who are never expected to speak for themselves alone; they speak for and like Shaw.) Dialogue, like the other elements of drama, is subject to the law of dramatic economy and heightening. The playwright must allow his character to speak emotionally and discursively when the situation warrants but must select, order, and control the dialogue to give it point and ensure its dramatic effectiveness.

d. Credibility

Words no less than actions must be believable and logical. The question of credibility must not interpose itself between the dialogue and the hearers. Dialogue must seem natural to character, situation, and style of the play. It must be easy and yet without irrelevancies, and to the point without seeming to be selective and controlled. *What* is said and *how* it is said will thus influence the naturalness of speech. The playwright must have an ear for speech, its idioms, its color, and its rhythms, if he is to achieve naturalness in his dialogue. An actor's speaking in a hesitant, improvisatory manner emanating from thought will add an appearance of naturalness.

Dialogue must be appropriate to the character speaking. It must individualize. Often a big fault or weakness in playwriting is the failure of the dialogue to emanate from an individual. It is so nondescript and noncharacterizing that it could be spoken by any of the characters in the play. Interchangeable dialogue lacks color, is dry and undramatic. Dialogue must be suitable to the character and also to the situation, mood, kind of play, and style of play. The perceptive director checks this aspect of dialogue in analyzing a play.

The director and actor, when rehearsing a play, particularly an original one, should constantly subject a character's dialogue to the testing question: "Why would he say that?" Dialogue must be motivated. And behind motivation lie purpose and function. While appearing to be natural and appropriate, a word or a phrase, when selected, ordered, and pointed, can be by implication revelatory and portentous. Take the one speech from *A Streetcar Named Desire* in which Stanley Kowalski says to Blanche soon after meeting her: "You going to shack up here?"[39] This question meets all the demands of plausibility. The use of the two words "shack up" is natural and appropriate to the kind of character Stanley is. They have special dramatic force because of their connotation and foreshadowing of the relationship between Stanley and Blanche. In view of the sexuality of the two, the line of dialogue is more than a question; it is a proposition. It is also evocative of mood or tone. This is not idle questioning. It serves a dramatic purpose.

e.   Intensity

Dialogue charged with the same degree of emotion throughout a scene can be monotonous. (It is conceivable that such monotony could be used to create mood and suspense. For example, a group of gangsters who speak with deadpan understatement of highly sensational and emotionalizing topics could create great ominous tension.) Contrast of emotional intensity will break the monotony and give dialogue a sense of movement and progression. The dialogue of a relaxed, informal scene followed by a sudden moment of intensity just as sharply broken will, through its variety of intensity, create a dynamic pattern of drama.

f. Heightening

Like character and plot, dialogue in drama must be heightened. Through selection, compression, and arrangement it must achieve a clarity and pointedness greater than life, reflective of it but not duplicating it. The kind, amount, and degree of selection, order, and arrangement of dialogue will depend upon the style of the play. The further removed from life, the greater the heightening. From expressionism to naturalism we get a wide range, from the greatest heightening to the least. It is that characteristic of dialogue which gives it the stature of art.

2. *Special characteristics*

Words, individually and collectively, can take on different meanings and create different emotional effects when vocalized in varying ways. For example, the phrase "Oh, yeah" can take on different meanings according to the vowel emphasis, intonation, and rhythm of two different speakers. Varying the time interval between their saying these words can give the words different meanings. They may mean "Now I see" or "I don't believe that" or any emotional variation of these two meanings or many other different meanings. This is true regardless of the intentions of the writer. A word or line of dialogue is subject to many interpretations. They do not have absolute and unmistakable values. The point has already been strongly made that interpretation is bound to be individual. One proof of this is to be found in the fact that even the great master dramatists with their technical skill have not in their most glorious work been able to convey the same detailed meanings to every man who reads, studies, and sees them. However, in spite of individual variations in interpretation, the fundamental meaning of a play is not altered. In the plays that have endured, their significance cannot be extinguished. Their greatness lies in their communicable universalities. Dialogue, perhaps more than any other element of a play, can be varied in interpretation without a disturbance of the basic values. Yet the clearer the motivations and the more exact the meanings of the individual words and their organization, the more clearly will the playwright's intended meanings be conveyed to the interpreter.

a. Implication of character action

Possibly the first value for the director to seek in words and their use is their inherent suggestion of *action*, physical or mental.

We know this to be the basic ingredient of drama and an expression of a character's will. Let us take this speech: ". . . At one time I had a passionate desire for two things: I wanted to get married, and I wanted to become an author; but I did not succeed in doing either."[40]

There is certainly no physical action implied in these words and there is very little mental action. The words themselves have only slight emotionalizing values. They are negative, inactive, and suggest very little will power in the speaker. The degree of expression of the will of the character strongly affects word values. Let us contrast this speech with:

> . . . Don't ever talk that way to me! "Pig—Polack—disgusting —vulgar—greasy!"—Them kind of words have been on your tongue and your sister's too much around here! What do you two think you are? A pair of queens? Remember what Huey Long said—"Every Man Is a King!" And I am the king around here, so don't forget it![41]

There is active expression of a strong will apparent in these words. Notice that the use of the imperative adds strength of will and emotion to a speech. The questions also allow for emotional expression. The first speech consists entirely of simple declarative sentences and the words are, unlike those in the second speech, not only negative but colorless.

The identification of the two characters speaking thus and a knowledge of their motivations will, of course, indicate how appropriate the speeches are and will influence our reaction to the dialogue. Sorin, the sixty-year-old, chronically ill brother of Madame Arkadin of *The Sea Gull*, says the first speech; Stanley Kowalski of *A Streetcar Named Desire* the second. Here are, of course, two utterly different characters, one old, one young, one defeated and the other vigorously aggressive.

In these two examples we see the emotional and mental effect of the choice of words in terms of *action* and *inaction*. We also see the effect of grammatical construction in terms of the simple declarative sentence, the question, and the use of the imperative. It might be mentioned that punctuation plays its part in conveying meaning. (Richard Flatter, in *Shakepeare's Producing Hand,* has made some interesting discoveries about the meanings of some of the dialogue of *Hamlet* by comparing and studying the punctuation of the various editions of the play.) In Stanley's speech, for instance, the use of exclamation points is meaningful. The director must remember that the playwright signals his meaning by punctuation.

In discussing Stanley's speech we mentioned his use of colorful words in contrast to the colorless ones of Sorin. The words "a pair of queens" have an emotional and intellectual effect. Of course, Stanley is being ironical and he causes the audience to make a quick comparison between its conventional images of royal queens and Blanche and Stella. The effect is very telling.

b.   Connotative words

When the gaunt, emaciated mother of Baby Face Martin in *Dead End* sees her son after his years of crime, she walks silently to him and slaps his face. This is unexpected and shocking after his cocky and cheerful greeting. But it is even more shocking and unforgettable when she says in a flat, unemotional, and nasal voice: "Yuh dog! Yuh stinkin' yeller dog, yuh!"[42] These words brilliantly illustrate the power of speech. They are cryptic, stinging, and emotionally assaulting in their suggestiveness. How simply but eloquently they express the thoughts and feelings of the speaker and how clearly, sharply, and unmistakably they communicate themselves to the audience. This is dramatic dialogue of great brilliance, though it exemplifies the naturalistic mode of expression which is not the highest level available to the dramatist.

Realism is the style of playwriting in which the modern director works the most. It is therefore best that we investigate first the dramatic potentials of this kind of dialogue. It is supposed to be purely conversational and for this reason the average person does not think of its being in itself very dramatic. In his mind only high-flown language is dramatic. Yet everyone finds some conversations interesting and even exciting without knowing or asking why. The director should be sensitive to interesting, colorful, stimulating speech and he must be alert to its stageworthiness. His awareness and response to it will help him judge the possible audience response to it. The line of dialogue from Sidney Kingsley's play has been cited as an example of dramatic speech not only because the words are carefully selected and ordered, and economically used, but because they are *connotative*. They have an added richness and depth because they convey more than their literal meaning and they stimulate the emotions. A mother calling her son a "yeller dog" is surprising and lacerates the emotions by the horrible suggestiveness of the words. Of course, these same words uttered under different circumstances, by a different character, and at a different moment might not be so effective. The choice of the character to speak the words and the moment to have them spoken are almost as important as the choice of the words. Appropriateness to character and situation will be discussed in detail later, but it must be pointed out now that this is a factor in considering the dramatic values of a speech.

c.   Imagery

Another enriching value to conversational speech is its *imagery*. (It exists in prose as well as in poetry and that is one reason why prose can be poetic.) Blanche DuBois' speech in *Streetcar* often possesses this value. For an example we can take the long speech she makes to Stella in the first scene of the play. She is explaining why their old home Belle Reve has been lost. One big reason, according to Blanche, was the expense of so many funerals for members of the family. She talks of "The long parade to the grave-yard!" Here is an image whose irony stimulates the mind and emotions. A funeral cortege called a parade creates images of opposites which communicate horror and terribleness. Later on in the speech she says, "Why, the Grim Reaper has put up his tent on our doorstep! . . . Belle Reve was his headquarters!"[43] The image is simple, but clear and grimly vivid.

d.   Metaphor

In addition to *connotative* words and *images, metaphors* make dialogue colorful and thus affective. For the sake of simplicity, we might take metaphor to mean "any kind of comparison, implied or stated, simile, personification, hyperbole or any other type of figurative language" and it can include a single word or whole statement.[44] Masha's line from *The Sea Gull*, ". . . I trail my life along like an endless train . . ."[45] is beautifully metaphorical.

It is to be noted that connotative words, images, and metaphors can make prose poetic. Tennessee Williams has proved this in all his plays and in the short ones particularly. His dialogue is sensory and imaginative to a high degree even while he creates the general impression of everyday conversational speech. These poetic values in realistic plays are the dividends of dialogue and should be properly appreciated by the director.

e.   Poetic folk expressions

Closely akin to these qualities of prose dialogue are folk expressions which are characteristic of certain regions of the country. They appeal to the imagination of the hearer and make the speakers more interesting. The plays of Paul Green abound in these expressions and are often sheer poetry in spirit. *Green Pastures* is full of poetry. Frankie, Berenice, and John Henry endeared themselves as characters and created a kind of poetic expression each time they spoke in *The Member of the Wedding*. The philosophical tramp in Robert E. McEnroe's *The Silver Whistle* was possessed of such an imaginative mind that he too spoke a kind of folk poetry at times. Lynn Riggs' *Green Grow the Lilacs* is full of poetic prose. William Saroyan's *My Heart's in the Highlands* is a sheer delight to the ear. The dialogue of these plays creates an emotional climate which strongly affects the sensibilities of the audience and enkindles its imagination.

f.   Idiomatic and slang expressions

Idiomatic expressions and slang are aurally appealing to an audience because of their turn of phrase and general color. Their recognition value is also worthy of note. These qualities are as important as their ability to lend verisimilitude to speech. Plays about army or navy life gain a great deal from the audience's pleasure at recognition of words and expressions peculiar to these services. *At War with the Army, Command Decision, Home of the Brave,* and *Mister Roberts* are examples of such plays. Plays about baseball, the racetrack, football, college life, show business, newspaper life, and gangsters capitalize on dialogue expressive of these facets of American life. The jargon peculiar to each has become a part of our culture. The audience has actually heard it on radio, television, or in films, or has read about it and is thus familiar with it. Its colorfulness, tempo, turn of phrase, and personal appeal make it irresistible.

g.   Dialects

American dialects have a similar audience appeal. New Yorkese, Brooklynese, Southern, Western, and Down East dialects are particularly attractive and pleasure giving. Usually the audience finds them amusing—and the author so uses them. Americanized Irish, Italian, Jewish, and Swedish are also affectively heartwarming or amusing. Theatrical values come from audience recognition and appreciation of a character's imaginative use of words. Odets, Saroyan, Kingsley, Williams, O'Neill, and others have shown gifts for using American and Americanized dialects. Dialect in plays enhances their realism and creates an emotional texture denied plays with conventional straight speech.

h. Period speech

Still another dialogue value is that of period speech. This flavoring is emotionally and intellectually affective partly because of audience superiority. They tend to say, "How quaint and charming!" Or "That's interesting, isn't it?" "So this is how they talked in the fifteenth century!" Here strangeness of choice of words, construction, and rhythm have a fascination for the hearer. This is true when Fellowship says to Everyman:

> Everyman, good morrow! By this day,
> Sir, why lookest thou so piteously?
> If any thing be amiss, I pray thee me say,
> That I may help to remedy.[46]

The actor must exploit the naive rhythm because it is an important part of the charm of the dialogue.

If we jump into the first half of the eighteenth century and take an example of dialogue from George Lillo's *The London Merchant*, we in the audience find pleasure again in our sense of superiority to the language, though we may be fascinated by its formal expression and its aphorisms.

BARNWELL: [*Aside.*] This goodness has o'ercome me.—O sir! You know not the nature and extent of my offence; and I should abuse your mistaken bounty to receive 'em. Though I had rather die than speak my shame; though racks could not have forced the guilty secret from my breast, your kindness has.

THOROWGOOD: Enough, enough! Whate'er it be, this concern shows you're convinced, and I am satisfied. How painful is the sense of guilt to an ingenuous mind!—some youthful folly, which it were prudent not to enquire into. When we consider the frail condition of humanity, it may raise our pity, not our wonder, that youth should go astray; when reason, weak at the best when opposed to inclination, scarce formed, and wholly unassisted by experience, faintly contends, or willingly becomes the slave of sense. The state of youth is much to be deplored, and the more so because they see it not; they being then to danger most exposed, when they are least prepared for their defense.[47]

Period slang is particularly appealing. *The School for Scandal* furnishes some amusing examples: "Nay, egad, it's true." "O, lud! You are going to be moral and forget that you are among friends." "Oons, madam!" " 'Slife, madam, I say." "Bags and bouquets! Halters and bastinadoes!"[48]

Mid-nineteenth-century speech, early twentieth-century speech, and even that of the 'twenties, because of their comparative closeness to our day, have special dramatic values. They are quaint, amusing, and old-fashioned. It is important to note that old-fashioned is different from the old or period speech in that, like anything old-fashioned—clothes, manners, ideas, etc.—people laugh at it with a combination of good-natured contempt and a feeling of superiority of knowledge. Audiences feel an emotional and intellectual kinship but have the pleasure of knowing that they are more enlightened and advanced in outlook, manners, speech, and customs. This explains, to some extent at least, audience attitudes toward the dialogue of such plays as *East Lynne, Camille, The Octoroon, Hazel Kirke, The Cricket on the Hearth, Pride and Prejudice, The Pursuit of Happiness, Clarence,* and *Adam and Eva.* All except the last three plays were written with serious plots and meanings but their melodramatic frames have diminished their believability considerably since they were first performed. Therefore laughter at the dialogue is only part of the humor for modern audiences. (*Pride and Prejudice* was of course written by a modern playwright who adapted it from the novel written in the early part of the nineteenth century. Also, its dialogue is intentionally humorous at times.)

Many period studies written by modern playwrights have exploited the speech peculiarities not only for their charm but for purposes of engendering sympathy and authenticity for the era. Biographical plays like *Abe Lincoln in Illinois* and *Victoria Regina* are two examples. *Ethan Frome, Angel Street,* and *The Old Maid* are serious plays whose period dialogue contributes strong emotional qualities. A recent example is that of the stream-lined Puritan language of *The Crucible,* which was an important factor in its emotional impact on the audience.

i.   Surprise of utterance

All the emotionalizing qualities of dialogue we have discussed make demands upon what Shakespeare called our "imaginary forces." This inner appeal stirs the mind and emotions either by the unexpected or the fanciful use of words. The audience is encouraged and led into an expansion of its ability to imagine, and gains an aesthetically pleasurable experience. The more poetic use of language is likely to appeal to the imagination, the surprising to our sense of humor. The element of the unexpected or what we might call the *surprise of utterance* accounts for the turn of phrase. It means that the audience is surprised at the turn of thought: It expected one thing and was pleasantly fooled. This is the source of the comic pleasure of an epigram. Oscar Wilde created an entire style of writing based upon this technique. George Bernard Shaw and lesser lights have done the same. Lord Darlington in *Lady Windermere's Fan* delights us with this sample of Wildean dialogue:

> Oh, nowadays so many conceited people go about Society pretending to be good, that I think it shows rather a sweet and modest disposition to pretend to be bad. Besides, there is this to be said. If you pretend to be good, the world takes you very seriously. If you pretend to be bad, it doesn't. Such is the astounding stupidity of optimism.

The fun to be gained from this speech lies entirely in its surprise qualities. Wit is suspenseful. The speech must be read by the actor in such a way as to create the suspense. The character establishes himself quickly as a person of imaginative and facile mind and speech when he says, "I wish I had known it was your birthday, Lady Windermere. I would have covered the whole street in front of your house with flowers for you to walk on. They are made for you." And particularly when he says, "Ah, nowadays we are all of us so hard up, that the only pleasant things to pay *are* compliments. They're the only things we *can* pay."[49] These two speeches prepare the audience to *expect* his succeeding remarks to be witty. The moment he opens his mouth he creates suspense, yet the actor must not in any way show that the character is aware of this. His entire manner must be serious, though his way of speaking must be casual. His tempo must establish a continuity of thought and then he must break the continuity by a change of tempo or some other vocal change. The key words are, of course, "good" and "bad." And the last sentence requires special pointing. Now, for the first time, we are coupling interpretation with voice because sense and sound are here so inextricably interdependent.

j. Rhythm

Up to this point we have considered the dramatic values of dialogue which have stemmed primarily from the choice of words used by the playwright, though word order has received some consideration. Now we can examine the values deriving from the rhythm of the dialogue. These are almost wholly emotional in their effect on the audience. They are a strong determinant of the rhythm of the play and its performance and, as such, strongly affect the compulsion and general moving power of the play.

If we can posit that the rhythm of prose dialogue is chiefly concerned with the selection and pattern of words and emphasis, we can examine some of the characteristics of sentence construction. Let us contrast these two examples of the use of word order and the long and complex sentence with the short and simple. First we have a speech from *The School for Scandal*. Snake is speaking.

> Here are two young men to whom Sir Peter has acted as a kind of guardian since their father's death, the eldest possessing the most amiable character and universally well spoken of, the youngest, the most dissipated and extravagant young fellow in the kingdom, without friends or character; the former an avowed admirer of your ladyship and apparently your favorite; the latter attached to Maria, Sir Peter's ward, and confessedly beloved by her. Now, on the face of these circumstances, it is utterly unaccountable to me why you, the widow of a city knight, with a good jointure, should not close with the passion of a man of such character and expectations as Mr. Surface; and more so, why you should be so uncommonly earnest to destroy the mutual attachment subsisting between his brother Charles and Maria.[50]

And here is a speech of almost equal length on the printed page but quite differently constructed. It is from *Death of a Salesman*. Bernard is speaking.

> Well, just that when he came back—I'll never forget this, it always mystifies me. Because I'd thought so well of Biff, even though he'd always taken advantage of me. I loved him, Willy, y'know? And he came back after that month and took his sneakers—remember those sneakers with "University of Virginia" printed on them? He was so proud of those, wore them every day. And he took them down in the cellar, and burned them up in the furnace. We had a fist fight. It lasted at least half an hour. Just the two of us, punching each other down the cellar, and crying right through it. I've often thought of how strange it was that I knew he'd given up his life. What happened in Boston, Willy?[51]

In the first speech we have words of a literary flavor, often of several syllables, in long sentences with many parenthetical phrases and word stresses. The result is a heavy, formal, and slow rhythm, without much variety. The tongue, voice, and breath respond to it with some difficulty. In the second speech the words are more conversational; there are elisions and the sentences are short, with few parenthetical phrases or dependent clauses or word stresses.

The rhythm is staccatto, light, and generally fast, with considerable variety. The speech fits easily into the mouth, and the breathing spaces are frequent. The controlled, rational manner of speaking indicated by Snake's speech projects a character of cold reserve with an analytical, precise mind. The effect on the audience is more intellectual than emotional. Bernard's speech, on the contrary, is spontaneous, warm, friendly, genuine, and emotional.

It will be noted that the word order of both these speeches is generally direct and simple. Let us take a speech from a play whose dialogue has a poetic quality of a formal or heightened kind: Captain Vere's speech in *Billy Budd*.

> That is possible. Whatever step we take, the risk is great; but it is ours. That is what makes us officers. Yet if in fear of what our office demands we shirk our duty, we only play at war, at being men. If by our lawful rigor mutiny comes, there is no blame for us. But if in fear, miscalled a kind of mercy, we pardon Budd against specific order, and then the crew revolts, how culpable and weak our verdict would appear! The men on board know what our case is, how we are haunted by the Spithead risings. Have they forgotten how the panic spread through England? No. Your clemency would be accounted fear, and they would say we flinch from practising a lawful rigor lest new outbreaks be provoked. What a shame to us! And what a deadly blow to discipline![52]

Here the choice of words and the word order create a rhythmic beat quite different from that of the two other speeches. Though Vere's speech has some of the formality of Snake's, it flows more easily and gracefully. It is more closely reasoned than Snake's rational speech, yet it is syllabically simpler and more economical in the use of adverbial and adjectival words and phrases. Here too is a regularly measured and formal rhythm, but the emotional effect is considerably greater. It must, of course, be read more slowly by the actor than the speech from *Death of a Salesman*.

In order to see more pronounced effects of dialogue treatment on the tempo of the scenes of plays we need only to compare the long speeches in the Hicky scene of the first act of O'Neill's *The Iceman Cometh*[53] with the Act I scene between McLeod and Kurt in Kingsley's *Detective Story*.[54]

The reading aloud of these two scenes will make it quite apparent that the length of the speeches of the first makes it a considerably slower scene than the second. In addition to the speed, the second scene also possesses a gradual emotional intensification which is climactic.

These two scenes are characteristic of the dialogue of these two plays. *Detective Story* moves faster and is, by its selectivity and brevity of dialogue, more suspenseful than *The Iceman Cometh*. The very dramatic nature of the two plays is thus affected by their dialogue.

In discussing the fact that the scene in the Kingsley play builds to a climax we have hit upon another aspect of rhythm which is important as a dialogue value. Heretofore we have been discussing the order of words, the length of sentences, and the length of speeches as they affect tempo. Now we can examine the emotionalizing powers of sentences, their organization to effect a climax in a speech, and the sequence of speeches to effect a climax in a scene. We can therefore profitably reexamine the scene from *Detective Story* for this technique and its resultant dramatic values. First let us examine in this scene the author's method for constructing a speech toward a climax.

To build an individual speech to a climax he arranges sentences in an ascending order of emotional power. As McLeod divulges more damning information about Kurt, each succeeding sentence becomes more emotionally evocative for the audience. The longest speech in the scene illustrates this technique. The italicized lines are the ones which gradually intensify the speech.

> Hold your hats, boys, here we go again. (*Looking down on Kurt from behind him, murmurs softly*) You're lucky, Kurt. You got away with it once. But the postman rings twice. *And this time we've got you.* Why don't you cop a plea? *Miss Harris is waiting for you. We're going to visit her in the hospital. She's anxious to see you. And what you don't know is . . . There was a corroborating witness, and she's downstairs ready to identify you, right now. . . .*[55]

Now we can turn to the technique used for building a scene to a climax. Before we analyze the scene itself we must point out that the author has skillfully built up a background of information through the earlier scene between the detective and Kurt's lawyer, the scene after Kurt's entrance, and the scene between McLeod and the Lieutenant. Thus the emotions of the audience have been primed for the meeting between Kurt and McLeod. It will be noticed that the suspense has been created in two ways. One is by a gradual revelation of information and the other is by delaying the blocks of information by interpolating other scenes among the three involving Kurt Schneider.

Let us turn to the scene. Reading the dialogue line by line up to the question about Kurt's income from the farm, no single line of itself affects our emotions greatly. But we know that the surface casualness of the talk is but a blind for some deeper motives in McLeod's questioning. It is, therefore, the cumulative quantity of lines which plays upon the audience's emotions. When McLeod asks, "And you average two thousand a year?" and he stops typing, the tension increases. After this each succeeding question and answer becomes more emotional in effect. The emotion does not ebb from the dialogue until McLeod says: "You should have been a lawyer, Kurt. A Philadelphia lawyer."

This technique of question and answer is typical of courtroom trial scenes and all kinds of scenes of inquiries. In this scene the witness, so to speak, refuses to divulge much information by answering questions, and the detective must accelerate the tension by asking questions and giving revealing answers.

Thus the method used for building a speech is used for building the entire scene: Each succeeding question and answer contains new and more intensifying material. It should be noticed that the general pattern effecting the growing emotion of the scene includes questions, answers, and comments which reduce the tension at intervals. As the scene progresses toward its climax the nonintensifying dialogue diminishes. Thus we have tension and relaxation followed by more and more tension and less and less relaxation until the climax is reached.

Inasmuch as the scene we have chosen to illustrate the techniques of writing toward a climax is a "question and answer" scene and therefore special, it will be helpful to use another scene which builds to a climax and demonstrates a different technique. Let us select one from the same play. The last scene in Act III between McLeod and his wife Mary will suit our purpose.

Prior to this we have had a reconciliation between the two. We suspected, though, that the reconciliation was merely temporary, and there is a residual tension which leads us into the last and climactic scene. Here we find Jim striving with great effort to control his emotions at the beginning of the scene. Mary, as a matter of fact, is still thinking of their talk before Jim sees Sims and feels relieved and fairly relaxed, but there is left over in her enough emotion to be triggered into action and intensified. Therefore, as Jim's emotion shows itself, it ignites Mary's. Each succeeding speech adds fuel to the flame. As the flame rises, Jim and Mary hurl more and more fiery speeches at one another. Finally their hot argument turns their love to hate.

Obviously these examples of the use of words and their organization to effect certain rhythms and tempos can be multiplied many times. Variations occur from play to play in accordance with the playwright's intention to write plays of different types and styles. (The diction of the play does indeed characterize the dramatist's style as well. Dramatists of distinction have recognizable styles of writing no less than artists in other fields—painting, music, etc. The director must be sensitive to this interpretive factor.) The practical value of this study must be seen in terms of character and the rhythmic shaping of scenes by the director.

For the most part we have been dealing with dialogue technique and dramatic values in relation to examples of prose. Much of this applies equally to poetry. Poetry, more than prose, is consistent with that heightened level of drama achieved by the Golden Age of the art. Of late there have been numerous attempts to write poetry for the theatre. Robinson Jeffers and Maxwell Anderson in America and T. S. Eliot and Christopher Fry in England have achieved varying degrees of success with such plays as *Medea, Winterset, Murder in the Cathedral, The Cocktail Party,* and *The Lady's Not for Burning,* to name some of their outstanding contributions. The works of the Spanish playwright Federico Garcia Lorca, as translated by Richard O'Connell and James Luhan, have brought a wealth of poetry to our university and off-Broadway theatres. The theatre of today, however, is a prose—if not a prosaic —theatre. Audiences have adapted themselves to and even demand the prevailing convention. Poetry scares them. Plays in verse are at a disadvantage. The general public has its guard up against them; it is afraid it will not understand them and, if it did, it would be bored.

The public is not entirely to blame for its attitude. The poet-dramatist is partly responsible. Too often he falls in love with his words and forgets about the play. He fails to create drama while busying himself with his attempts to write poetry. To get down to cases, the most influential poet we have, T. S. Eliot, though having given significant evidence in a number of his plays of his abilities as a playwright as well as a poet, nevertheless has failed to reach a wide public. *The Confidential Clerk* had more snob appeal than theatrical appeal. It was a great disappointment to those who put so much faith in his *Murder in the Cathedral,* a really fine literary work in play form. *The Cocktail Party* has been his most popular play, and it is interesting to note that, though it was written in verse form, the audience hearing the dialogue was not aware of it because it sounded conversational. Before the production of *The Confidential Clerk* Eliot seemed to understand his failures to communicate with his audience when he wrote of his experiences in *Poetry and Drama.* Moreover, he seemed determined to correct his mistakes. He failed to do so in *The Confidential Clerk.* When it was feared that the audience would fail to perceive the meaning intended by Eliot, it was revealed by E. Martin Browne, the master's officially designated interpreter and director, that it was derived from *Ion*, an obscure play by Euripides. However, it is probable that even if a copy of this Greek minor work were presented to each member of the audience before he attended the play, the reaction of the audience would still be unfavorable. Thornton Wilder, it is said, based *The Skin of Our Teeth* on Joyce's *Finnegan's Wake*, but it is not necessary for the audience to know this in order to understand the play. The point is that though both writers were asking the audience not to take the surface appearance of their plays as their real meaning, Wilder made his play stageworthy through interesting, amusing, and moving, though symbolic, characters and dramatic action. Wilder's second level of meaning was clear without benefit of the knowledge of the play's derivation.

The case of Christopher Fry is an example of a poet writing for the theatre and often giving his audience verbal indigestion. His most popular play in this country, *The Lady's Not for Burning*, found a special audience on Broadway and in college communities. One reason for its success, though limited, is its humor. The romantic story and its raffish characters also possess audience appeal and offset the rather esoteric meaning of the play. *Venus Observed* and *Sleep of Prisoners* proved that indigestion is caused by serious internal disorders—even dramatic ones—and their theatrical lives were short.

Robinson Jeffers' *Medea* proved a brilliant marriage of drama and poetry and moved audiences deeply. His *Tower beyond Tragedy* was less successful. Both plays proved that audience tolerance of the heavy gloom of Greek tragedy has its limitations. Lorca's plays possess great beauty and power but their dark emotional climate, unfamiliar Spanish characters, customs, and tales of sadness seem to appeal to a very special part of the public.

Maxwell Anderson has used the poetic form with the most popular success. His *Elizabeth the Queen, Winterset,* and *Anne of the Thousand Days* have been outstanding. Whereas the critics and literary ladies and gentlemen have found his poetry weak, the public has been generally approving of his dramatic accomplishments. Anderson has managed, in spite of his obvious borrowings from Shakespeare in these plays, to create illustrative dramatic characters and action.

In these capsule discussions it must be apparent that these playwrights fail to combine equal talent for writing poetry with the talent for writing plays, a rare combination. Shakespeare is the only genuine example in the English language. The only outstanding modern example of a poet-dramatist is Tennessee Williams, and he, paradoxically enough, writes his plays not in verse but in prose. Nevertheless, his poetic prose is genuine poetry and genuinely dramatic. The meaning of all this for the director is that he must be aware of the great emotional and intellectual force of the poetic gained by the choice of words, construction, and rhythm, but he must also be aware of the problems of communicating to the audience and making it understand. He must not forget that language is only one element in a play and that when it is turned into poetry it may achieve grandeur from the beauty of words and fail because of its absence of dramatic action and obscurity of meaning.

The director who falls in love with a sea of words will drown with his audience. Even *Murder in the Cathedral,* an outstanding example of poetic drama, has, for example, proved the undoing of more than one director. A mere recitation, however beautiful, whether in a church or on a stage, conceived simply as ritual and procession, is not theatre. There is no reason why it cannot be—and it should be—ritualistic and processional, but it can also be theatrical. The director must give attention to movement, music, lighting, and pictorial dramatiziation if the play is to be dramatized. And these theatrical elements can be most effectively utilized by simple though humanizing characterizations. The tendency to stress the symbolism of the Tempters and Knights and the symbolic mass of women making up the chorus intellectualizes an already heavily cerebral play. Though most members of the audience fail to grasp the meaning of many of the words and speeches, the director must use his imagination and ingenuity to enhance the other dramatic values which can be found in character conflicts and suspense. He can even bolster up and invest with drama certain scenes which as written are low in dramatic effectiveness. The passion and psychological drive of the actors can generate considerable emotion to humanize metaphysical speech. Too, the director must use the visual resources of the theatre to complement and even clarify the aural eloquence of the play. In sum, he must remember that the poet must be a dramatist first and a poet second. Poetry as a medium of expression is not so important in the theatre as the thing it expresses. The thing it expresses is the *play!*

In pointing out the problems of poetic drama the intention has not been to take a negative and discouraging attitude toward it. Any director serious about his obligations to the theatre and the cultural welfare of the audience cannot help being interested in the contributions poetry can make. The director no less than the playwright and actor must deal in words to interpret, communicate, and stimulate. The love and appreciation of words must be a part of his equipment for his work. Surely the works of Eliot, Fry, Jeffers, Anderson, Lorca, and all the others using the poetic medium must be produced regardless of their weaknesses as either poetry or drama. Audiences should know them and learn to appreciate them for those qualities of excellence which can enrich their emotional and intellectual experiences.

k.   Emotional vs. intellectual dialogue

All along we have been stressing the importance of dialogue that has the power to create action, to change character relationships, and to affect the emotions of the audience through its use of words and structure. This dominant function of stirring the emotions through dialogue is a special trait of drama in contrast with other literary writing. Yet drama also uses words to appeal to the intellect. The pure thought content of dialogue varies from play to play. Plays of exposition and commentary rather than illustrative action are likely to possess considerable philosophical, ideational, or intellectual dialogue. Plays which are classical in structure, epic in style, or propagandistic in purpose often bear the heavy freight of such dialogue. (Poetic dialogue is of course underlined with thought, but its dominating effect is emotional.)

The professional theatre on Broadway is not well disposed toward any of these kinds of plays. Producers of entertainment are not impressed with the members of an audience as thinkers. The off-Broadway, educational, and community theatres have been more tolerant of the playwright as a thinker who is seeking an audience willing to think. There is one thinking playwright who has found acceptance on and off Broadway: George Bernard Shaw. The reason for this is that he is a better salesman of ideas than other playwrights. The experienced playgoer who knows his Shaw recognizes the tricks of such salesmanship but he is nevertheless willing to listen to the spiel. He knows that he will hear a lot of good jokes even if he has to think. Shaw sugar-coats the pill. The phenomenal success of Shaw's *Don Juan in Hell* à la "The First Drama Quartette," with actors standing in front of microphones making only the slightest effort to create characters, proved the appeal of good talk. However, even Mr. Shaw can be tiresome with his talk. The last acts of *Major Barbara* and *Too True To Be Good* are ready examples though there are others, especially among his later plays. Garrulity and unprovocative ideas—unprovocative because the world has already accepted them and sees no need to argue—have, of late, prompted members of the audience to pick up their hats and exit from the theatre with mutterings of "Oh, pShaw!"

A number of French playwrights have made oblique assaults on the present theatre of the world with dialogue bristling with ideas. Giraudoux's *The Madwoman of Chaillot* and *The Enchanted* had charm, wit, and striking thought in their speech. The first, especially, found audiences willing to listen. Jean Paul Sartre's *Red Gloves* had moments of rare brilliance of ideological talk. Anouilh's *Ring round the Moon*, rendered into English by Christopher Fry's facile and graceful hand, proved sharp and penetrating as well as whimsically comic in its language.

These are some of the rare examples from the modern theatre which possess dialogue of intellectual values. The director in the educational theatre will find audiences in the school or college community who are hungry for good talk and literate language in the theatre. The theatre can be and should be intellectually stimulating as well as emotionally evocative. However, better than average actors of style, excellent speech, lightness, and agility of tongue are needed for the Messrs. Shaw, Giraudoux, Anouilh, et al. Intellectual comprehension is needed by the director and the performers.

1. Speakability

From a purely practical point of view, the first questions a director should ask about the dialogue of a play are: Can the actors speak it? Does it fit into their mouths? Does it sound natural? Speakability depends upon the number of syllables in the words of a speech, the fall of the emphases, and the general cadence. These factors affect vocal production in terms of the use of the tongue, vocal placement, breathing, and vocal color. The test of all dialogue is made by the actor speaking it. In the rehearsals of new plays each line must be so tested.

Inasmuch as most modern drama is written in prose dialogue, it must be conversational if it is to seem natural. It must not sound "stagey" or literary. An experienced director and actor, with ears attuned to everyday speech, can easily detect such faults. In the case of questionable dialogue, the actor can say it in many different ways until the author and the director are satisfied. Sometimes it is necessary for the actor to memorize the speech and act it with the proper given circumstances of the scene before the speech can be judged for its naturalness. It is often helpful to the playwright and director if the actors will improvise the situation involved and make up the dialogue as they play it out. If the actors are playing truthfully, the dialogue is likely to be speakable and natural. This improvised dialogue, with some editing, can be set in the script. However, the real test of dialogue is the performance and audience reaction—not one audience reaction but several. Thus the playwright may continue to change the dialogue during the run of a play.

The speakability of dialogue is, of course, directly related to character motivation and individuality. The comparatively emotional character, for example, will speak impulsively, even explosively and jerkily. His thoughts may not be sequential. Thus his sentences will be short and staccatto in rhythm. The more intellectual character will tend to choose his words, speak more slowly, and construct his sentences more carefully. His thoughts will probably be sequential and his sentences will be long and flowing in rhythm. This has been demonstrated by the speeches of Joe Keller and Captain Vere quoted from *All My Sons* and *Billy Budd*.

It will be noticed too that the more unrestrainedly emotional a character becomes, the more voluble he becomes, and his speeches become longer and longer until his emotion is spent. (This is the pattern, of course, for climactic scenes as exemplified by that between Mary and McLeod in *Detective Story*, already discussed.) Emotionalism increases not only volubility but also the use of more imaginative language. Emotion stimulates creativity of speech and the character tends to use figurative and aphoristic language. We have seen this in Mary McLeod's climactic speech when she says "You think you're on the side of the angels?" Her language also becomes a little more formal. Of course Blanche DuBois is an emotional character and is highly romantic, and her speech is characteristically colorful. Yet in her most emotional moments her speech becomes both more colorful and even poetic. It is indeed a truism that poetry is the language of the emotions.

The poetic heightening of speech is convincing to the audience because it is clothed in emotion. Such heightening is usually accompanied by speed of speaking. In a realistic play such speed might stand out and jar the audience's sensibilities, but it is necessary in a nonrealistic play with poetic dialogue. Shakespeare, for instance, must be spoken rapidly in order to give it conviction and brilliance. Words may be savored by the actor but they must not be said at a funereal pace and with sepulchral tones. This attack for Shakespeare and all poetic drama is fatal. Sir John Gielgud and Sir Laurence Olivier have demonstrated on the American stage and in films a rapidity of speaking Shakespeare which has given it vitality and rare beauty. Christopher Fry and T. S. Eliot demand the same kind of quick-tongued utterance.

The difficulty of speaking poetry with speed involves enunciation and meaning. Slipshod enunciation is characteristic of naturalistic speech, and the audience can fill in sounds left out by the actor when the words are familiar. This is not possible in poetry because of the importance of the choice of words and the rhythmic beat. Clear enunciation, proper emphasis, and the beat will generally project the meaning. The music of poetry usually accompanies the words when the meaning is clear. If the director must make a choice between the music and the meaning, he must choose in favor of the latter. An audience demands that sounds signify something. Audience pleasure is of course greater when beauty of sound is combined with clarity of meaning.

5

Points of Focus

In the analysis of how the playwright has created a particular mood in a play and how he has treated the elements of theme, character, plot, and dialogue the director has become aware of the creative techniques of playwriting, the dramatic possibilities of the various elements of a play and its distinguishing traits. Moreover, he has become alerted to the interpretive and directorial problems arising out of these playwriting techniques. In learning how the playwright works he sees the relation between the play as written and the possible and necessary directorial techniques.

He is now ready to organize his findings into points of focus for interpretation and direction.

Special Appeal of Play to Director and Audience

In play selection, which is, of course, based on analysis, evaluation, and interpretation, certain dramatic potentials of a script come into focus and assume importance. They jump out at the director, strike a sympathetic and appealing chord. They appeal to him and are thought by him to be appealing to an audience. The director may say to himself, "I like this play because it has something to say to present-day America." In other words, its theme is a dominant dramatic value. This may be the reason for the choice of a play like Miller's *The Crucible*. The director may say, "I like this script because it appeals to my imagination." Thus the fantasy or mood of Giraudoux's *Ondine* may be the focal point of his interest. Another director may say, "The beauty and poetry of O'Casey's dialogue in *Red Roses for Me* appeals to me and I am determined to direct it." Still another may say, "The character of the lovely young girl is so touching," and he refers to *The Diary of Anne Frank*. "How like my own father. Why, I remember . . ." and the director becomes nostalgic—if he is old enough—about the horse and buggy days of *Life with Father*. He will produce the play because he thinks there are enough people like himself to enjoy the trials and tribulations of the Day family and the atmosphere of the "good old days." Here the period and the comedy are dominant.

At first glance Father Day might be considered a character study and the focal point of the script, but this is not so. He is the cause of a great deal of the comedy of the play, but he is not a completely drawn character whose facets deeply interest the audience. His appeal actually derives from the recognition of his stock character, and the fun for the audience comes from its ability to anticipate his every action and reaction as emanating from a person Bergson describes in his essay on laughter as one in whom ". . . there is a sort of rigidity."[1] These aspects of a play are what we might call its *points of focus*. They are determined from an analysis of the relative dominance of each dramatic value.

Now that we come to the study of the relative dominance of dramatic values, we may include values other than those of mood, character, plot, dialogue, and theme. In the plays mentioned in the preceding paragraph we have pointed to *special values* like fantasy, poetry, period, and kind of play. At the beginning of our discussion of dramatic values we pointed out that these special values are to be found in particular plays and are not present in all plays. These special values are those accruing from the author's general attitude and approach to his subject and his technique in writing the play. They are inherent in the kind and style of play. Williams' subjective approach to capture and convey the importance of memory in his *The Glass Menagerie*, Wilder's use of the stage manager or chorus to emphasize the narrational and thematic values in *Our Town*, and his use of a vaudeville-expressionistic technique and structure in *The Skin of Our Teeth* are examples. These technical and structural deviations from the conventional realism of our modern theatre are stylistic values no less than those aspects of dramatic values emanating from the varied experiments O'Neill used in such plays as *The Great God Brown*, *Days without End*, *Strange Interlude*, and *Lazarus Laughed*, Bertolt Brecht's "epic drama," the "living newspaper," Pirandello's technique for *Six Characters in Search of an Author*, Cocteau's surrealistic *Orphée*, and Sartre's existentialist drama *No Exit*. These special values in style are sometimes baffling to the general public but help to satisfy their desire for novelty and even sensationalism. They often serve to seduce audiences into the theatre and just as often propel them through the nearest exit. Nevertheless they must be considered in examining a play for its audience appeal.

We shall discuss the main dominant dramatic values first and then proceed to the special ones later. Let us consider the relative dominance of values as an indication of the focus and purpose of the play.

KEY TO PURPOSE OF PLAY

A playwright uses words to propagate characters, plot, dialogue, and a theme. His words are the seeds that produce the roots, stalk, leaves, and flowers of a plant—the characters, plot, dialogue, and theme of a play. The kind of plant or the kind of play and the distinctive characteristic of the plant or the style of the play are the aesthetic side effects or concomitants. The origin, the main products, and the by-products of a play are potentially dramatic; that is, they are capable of engaging the attention, interest, emotions, and minds of the audience.

Assuming that the playwright is an artist who knows how to use his means of expression to achieve the effects he desires, his purpose in writing a play is the factor governing the use of his media. This purpose is conditioned by his observation of human behavior and life. He accordingly controls his characters, plot, dialogue, and theme to give focus to his work. Focus is obtained by using certain elements to point to or emphasize something. These elements are thus contributory and subsidiary. In order to interpret a play, then, the director must analyze it to determine which are the subsidiary and which are the dominant dramatic values.

In works of some playwrights it is comparatively easy to determine the aspect emphasized. Take, for example, Lillo's *George Barnwell* or *The London Merchant,* and it is readily apparent that the plot is calculated to work strongly on the emotions of the audience to make plain the moral or theme of the play—the evils of London life. His characters, plot, and dialogue are maneuvered for this sole reason. The heavy and arresting hand of the author can be felt on each of these elements. The characters have little will of their own and make decisions conforming to their creator's will rather than theirs; and their conversation and actions result in a sequence of events purposefully planned rather than spontaneously and inevitably brought about.

If we study a modern melodrama for comparison we can see a similar exercise of control of play elements for the purpose of giving one more dominance than the other. Frederick Knott's *Dial "M" for Murder* exemplifies a central character who willfully catapults the play into action and is mainly responsible for all subsequent action. He is indeed the master of his will and is not subject to that of his creator to the same degree as is George Barnwell. However, Knott does control his central character indirectly and less obviously. His control derives from his selection of character: He has chosen a conscienceless and psychologically abnormal character whose thoughts and actions are held in a groove by the quirk of his mind. (It might be argued that George Barnwell is also abnormal in his excessive naiveté and innocence, but this is not so if we are willing to admit that these traits were common in other young men of that era. In other words, he seems more typical than the central character in Knott's melodrama.) If the audience is willing to accept the mentally perverse central character of *Dial "M" for Murder,* then his actions seem plausible and convincing. The planning and scheming of this character, that is, his actions which create the plot of the play, constitute the focus. The audience becomes interested primarily in what he is going to do next and, eventually, what his wife and the others are going to do next. It becomes a delightful though suspenseful game of who will outwit whom. The main interest therefore lies in the plot. Though the audience is interested in what the characters will do, it is not interested in *what* they are and *why* they are what they are. The playwright has obviously chosen not to take the time to explain and elaborate upon character background and motive. He has given emphasis to the spinning out of the action. He seems to say, "Look, here is an amazing tale I want to tell. Don't ask me to explain or justify why this man acted in this cold and calculating way. Don't ask a lot of questions. Just look and listen. You will be fascinated, and before you know it you won't think about asking questions." The dominant dramatic value is clear.

The London Merchant and Dial "M" for Murder present comparatively simple problems in interpretation. The playwrights have not developed each element of the plays fully enough to achieve complexity, depth, and richness. Selection, emphasis, and intensification have so channeled the dramatic potentials that the dominant value and audience focal point are unmistakable. On the other hand, the great plays of dramatic literature abound in such diverse richness in values that the director may find it difficult to determine the dominance of one over another. *Hamlet, King Lear, Othello,* and *Julius Caesar,* for example, are rich in character, plot, dialogue, and theme. The wise director will try to exhaust the wealth of drama in each of these elements. Nevertheless, Shakespeare did so select, control, and emphasize his material that he gave each play sufficient organization to point up one element over the others. Even though the plot of *Hamlet* is exciting and moving and fraught with as much suspense as any melodrama, the language is sublimely beautiful and deeply touching, and the thematic patterns are rich and constantly stimulating. The character of Hamlet is undoubtedly of primary interest from the opening of the play

to its close. The master playwright, then, no less than the journeyman uses organization to give point and purpose to his work.

When the director focuses upon a dramatic value he gives a
play direction and an overruling significance for an audience, and
it is the duty of the director to provide this guidance. Confusion
of effect results when the director gives equal emphasis to all the
values of a play. Sometimes, of course, the director is unable to
bring order and emphasis to a play if the playwright has not controlled his media of expression. This is true even of a brilliant
writer like Sean O'Casey. In the discussion of unity in the structure
of a play we have seen that, though O'Casey has always had difficulty in unifying the moods of his plays, his later ones like *Cock-
a-doodle Dandy* almost defy the director to project a dominant
mood and convey clearly the central and dominant dramatic value.
The audience can come away from this play wondering whether
the playwright wishes to emphasize the comic, the serious, the
characters of the two old men who are the principal characters,
or the meaning of their struggle with youth and the liberal mind.
In order to give dominance to one of these values, the others must
be readily understood by the audience to be subsidiary. This means
that a well-constructed play clearly projects dramatic values in
their relative order of importance. It also means that plays possess
more than one dramatic value.

Though *The London Merchant* and *Dial "M" for Murder* were
written to make one element dominant, the other elements are
relatively dominant. It has already been implied that the plot of
the Lillo play and the central character of the Knott play are of
secondary importance. It is equally true that though the character
of Hamlet is the focal point of the play of that name, another
value is of secondary importance. An examination of the stage
history and critical opinion of the play will indicate the importance
of theme as the value of secondary significance. Oftentimes it is
difficult to say whether character is more important than theme
because character is used to demonstrate theme. For example,
Death of a Salesman presents Willy Loman, the central character,
whose life is the documentary evidence of a problem facing
present-day America. This problem gives the play its significance.
Willy in himself is interesting and deeply pathetic, but the revelation of his character is given dimension because it is joined to a
predicament facing modern life as we know it. Nevertheless, the
director of the play must interpret and project Willy's character
in a way that will illustrate and emphasize the theme. It can be
argued with validity that *Hamlet* also is an example of close inter-
dependence of character and theme. In rebuttal it might be said

that a single specific theme does not emerge so clearly from *Hamlet* as from *Death of a Salesman*. However, from the directorial point of view, the characters of Willy and Hamlet (if you will permit this temporary pairing) must be so interpreted and acted as to communicate their respective themes. Each word of the dialogue and all details of the plot may be clearly conveyed to every member of the audience, but failure in the acting of the principal characters will blur the meaning of the plays. If the director will utilize directorial techniques to emphasize character, then the theme will take care of itself. But let us continue with the director's problem of determining the points of focus of a script.

How To Determine Points of Focus

An author makes the dominance of a value clear by various means. One is the number and length of scenes devoted to emphasizing the particular value. The actual number of times an aspect of a play is mentioned in the dialogue or illustrated in the action is a key. The degree of completeness, complexity, and motivation of character and plot will often indicate their relative importance. The author's general aproach in terms of his attitude—satirical, fantastic, unconventional—as well as the structure and style of the play may well serve to hold in focus the significant meaning of the play. Thus proportion, emphasis, and the manner of treatment are check points for the director in determining the dominance of dramatic values and the focus of a play.

This deductive and intellectual process may appear dry, uninspiring, and academic. In fact—perish the thought—it may sound like the "formula" method of interpreting a play, which would indeed exclude individual, highly subjective, impressionistic, symbolic, and even historical interpretation. Such is not the intention here, since such aspects of interpretation can never be wholly precluded. They are, of necessity, implicit in the consideration of the dramaturgical components of a play. Symbolism, for example, is implied in all concepts of character. Each member of the audience will consciously or unconsciously apply it in its broader meanings, at least, to every personage in a dramatic work. While analyzing Willy Loman for all his foibles it is impossible to see him other than the little man of twentieth-century America, be he salesman or schoolteacher. The plot and theme of *Death of a Salesman* will carry their private, subjective, and individual symbolism. Historical implications cannot be divorced from the elements in this play. The main reference point for each is the historical period. Let the director analyzing a play use these interpretive aids in the degree

which will be most illuminating. Let him also remember that though
the emphasis in this section is dramaturgical and dramatic—the
author's treatment of his media and possible audience appeal—the
basic approach of this book is in terms of directorial imagery.

In tackling the problem it is simplest and clearest to
consider each element of a play and ask when it, rather than the
other elements, is emphasized.

1.   Mood

Seldom is mood the most dominant dramatic value in a play,
though it is sometimes the second or third most dominant. The
relative dominance of mood concerns the director only in the case
of very special plays. If mood is thought of in terms of the heavy,
strange, atmospheric, supernatural, and mystical, the plays of
Maeterlinck come to mind: *Pelléas and Mélisande, The Death of
Tintagiles, The Interior, The Intruder,* and *The Blind.* "A thin veil
separates us from the characters; a dreaming inactivity replaces
. . . action . . ."[2] In the "static theatre" of Maeterlinck the audience
peers through a mist, sees vague forms, and hears hushed voices.
This world created on the stage is beyond reality and hypnotizes
the audience into a vague, half-conscious dream state. Here mood
is very important, if not theatrically the most important aspect of
these plays, though the symbolic and thematic values are very
strong too.

The plays of Chekhov are also strong in mood values. The
silences, the yearnings, the flights of fancy, the pathetic impracti-
calities mixed with comic awkwardnesses and ineptitudes evoke
feelings of sadness mingled with humor. Chekhov presents a world
of reality, where fact is a dream to be evaded—nostalgic, sentimental, romantic. Circumscribing this world is the envelope of
feeling so characteristically Chekhovean. Yet the mood and atmosphere never prevent the audience from seeing clearly and
sharply the infinite riches of character which are always dominant
and will not take second place to any other dramatic value.

The passionate folk climate in which Garcia Lorca sets his
poetic plays is surely a significant aspect of their interpretation
and direction. The lyrical language, the hot-blooded characters,
the throbbing and plaintive music, the color of the flowers, and
the heat of the sun and the coolness of the moon play upon the
senses. The Latin flavor—earthy, flamboyant, mercurial, and fiery—
is an essential element of the world in which Lorca operates. The
director of *Blood Wedding, Yerma,* and *The House of Bernarda Alba*
must give this fact due regard.

William Saroyan and Tennessee Williams as represented by their short plays as well as their long ones are also dramatists who exploit singularly effective mood qualities. The language, the strong and pervasive nature of the emotion of their characters, and the milieu of such plays as *My Heart's in the Highlands, The Time of Your Life, The Beautiful People, The Glass Menagerie, A Streetcar Named Desire,* and *The Rose Tattoo* are particularly appealing to the sensibilities. However, such appeal, though important to recognize in the interpretation of their plays, is secondary to other values.

Maeterlinck, Chekhov, Lorca, Saroyan, and Williams are examples of dramatists who strongly emphasize feeling. Of a different kind are those who stress fancy. The emotional character of Barrie's *Peter Pan, Mary Rose,* and *Dear Brutus* is almost as important as the people, their actions, and the significance of the plays as a whole. Unless the director can project and stress the special atmosphere and spell of these plays he will miss what is essentially Barrie. Another Barry named Philip also created fanciful realms, but of a different sort. *Hotel Universe* and *Here Come the Clowns* are mystical in intention but murky in accomplishment. Yet they do establish an atmosphere which is necessary to the characters and the action. Jean Giraudoux's *The Madwoman of Chaillot, The Enchanted,* and *Ondine* represent him at his most fanciful, and their prevailing tone is significant. In fantasies of all kinds, whether by Barrie, James, or by Barry, Philip, or by Giraudoux, mood must be strongly stressed if the audience is to be induced to accept the truth of their unreality.

Plays of feeling and fancy are not the only ones in which mood plays a prominent part. On the other end of the scale of emotions lie those plays of comic tone which also project mood values. Satiric plays, especially, are tinged with shades of feeling, though founded on the hardness of thought. Holding man up to ridicule, the dramatists of such plays sharpen and aim their barbs of criticism in an atmosphere which must be tellingly felt if significance is to be comprehended. Molière's *Tartuffe, The Would-Be Gentleman, The Affected Ladies,* and *The Doctor in Spite of Himself* are comic with a purpose. And before Molière, Aristophanes clearly established a climate of satiric reference for *The Birds* and *The Frogs.* Shakespeare's *Love's Labor's Lost,* Shaw's *The Doctor's Dilemma,* Romains' *Dr. Knock,* the Spewacks' *Boy Meets Girl* and Anouilh's *The Waltz of the Toreadors* create a frame of mind for the audience in order for the playwrights to jest at the foibles and follies of people and institutions.

Lying between the two extremes of feeling and biting satire are those plays in which the dramatists mix sensibility and sense.

The romantic comedies of Shakespeare, *A Midsummer Night's Dream, Twelfth Night, Much Ado about Nothing,* and *As You Like It,* are plays in which the sharp edge of wit and satire is softened by the gentle emotion of love. "The laughter is subdued into a kind of feeling of contentment, a happines of spirt rather than an ebullition of outward merriment. Wherever the laughter is called forth it is immediately stilled or crushed out of existence by some other appeal."[3] Eugene O'Neill's *Ah, Wilderness* and Lindsay's and Crouse's *Life with Father* and *Life with Mother* possess this same mixture of the comic with the gentle sympathy of the authors. Here too nostalgia adds a further note of warmth. Mood values are necessarily emphatic in all these plays too and are secondary only to the dramatic value of character. The director must be sensitive to the presence of the affective values and must exercise great care and imagination to make the audience feel them. Their relative dominance is as important as those of character, dialogue, plot, and theme.

2. *Character*

When is *character* most important in a play? To answer the question it is helpful to ask whether the chief interest of the play is in:

a. The revelation and demonstration of character

b. What the character is rather than, and in spite of, what he does

c. The expression of the will of the characters resulting in the events and crises of the play

d. The mental struggle of a character or characters

e. The chronological or biographical study of a life

f. The development, enlightenment, or change in a character

These questions are not mutually exclusive. They tend to overlap. However, they may serve as keys and may make up a check list though they may not be absolutely conclusive. They can be of service only as they are clarified through illustration.

The revelation and demonstration of character is surely the ruling purpose of Tennessee Williams' *Cat on a Hot Tin Roof.* The play is given over to the characters' dissecting one another. They spend all their time baring their own souls or forcing others to bare theirs. They delve into the past and they prophesy the future to unveil and clarify the present. They are in search of the truth about one another, or at least what they consider the truth. They seem possessed with the unrelenting desire to stand mentally and emotionally naked before one another. As a result they stand similarly revealed to the audience: every facet, every nerve, every impulse of character clearly on view. Instead of waiting breathlessly to see what will happen next, the audience waits to see what it will learn next about the characters. Events appear unimportant in contrast to personalities. In actual fact very little happens in the sense of plot and plot complication. The childless and loveless daughter-in-law, Big Daddy's favorite son, Big Daddy, and Big Mama claw one another like the little foxes they are and tear off the last shreds of their outer coverings of flesh and pretenses to reveal their bloody, palpitating hearts and dissembling minds. The audience sits engulfed in awed suspense and terror before the X-ray pictures moving before its eyes.

If we think for a moment of the characters in Chekhov's *The Sea Gull*, we realize that they do almost nothing and their few actions could not hold our attention for long. Yet we are interested in them for what they *are*. They do not reveal one another but unravel and unveil themselves. Each one dances a sad, melancholy dance. Each is an expert dancer who turns slowly and deliberately to show every step making up the choreography of his life. We sit not only fascinated but involved emotionally and mentally. Little happens outwardly, but inwardly there is unlimited action. We learn with complete thoroughness who and what the characters are.

What better example of expression of will than Oedipus? Though Teiresias, Creon, Jocasta, the Shepherd, the messenger, and the chorus try in vain to divert him from his avowed purpose, he will know the awful truth. His pride in self-reliance and power drive him ineluctably to his journey's end of knowledge. Antigone, Electra, Medea, and Prometheus are equally nothing daunted in the grips of their unyielding wills. Macbeth, Faust, and Richard the Crookback carry us headlong on their downward course. Hedda Gabler cannot be deterred from her wayward path. Each one of these characters dominates the play and rivets our attention to him.

The mental struggles of Hamlet, Lear, and Willy Loman make them tower over all other aspects of their worlds.

Victoria and Abraham Lincoln are the center of interest in the dramatized biographies of *Victoria Regina* and *Abe Lincoln in Illinois*. Each scene of these plays is but another chronological, albeit emotional and intellectual, phase in their lives. The leaves drop from the calendar and the audience moves through the years with these giants among men. They hold center stage from the opening to the closing of their dramatic lives. Plot, language, and theme are but accessories to the facts of their existence.

When mental struggle is paramount or prominent in the creation of central characters, as it is in Hamlet, Lear, and Macbeth, these characters assure themselves of dominance of the play when they develop and move from ignorance to enlightenment.

Among modern plays, Blanche DuBois in A Streetcar Named Desire exemplifies a character whose anguish is revealed outwardly more gradually than that of the Shakespearean characters who indulge in soliloquies. She never finds enlightenment but changes from a state of mental disturbance to complete mental breakdown. Lear has a mental breakdown but recovers his sanity and gains enlightenment prior to his death.

Othello is a double-headed play until the moment of Othello's awakening, when the depth of his agony and the cleansing of his soul lift him to tragic heights. The cunning and perverse mind of Iago and the nobility of Othello hold the audience to the sticking point of interest in these disparate characters.The clear manifestation of Othello's growth in stature points up Shakespeare's chief purpose in writing the play.

These are only a few examples of plays whose dominant value is character. Someone has said that the plays of enduring value are those in which character is of paramount and universal interest: Think of the world's great plays and you simultaneously think of the great appeal of their central characters. Neither time nor custom can stale their infinite variety. Certainly members of the modern audience, even though their strong interest in a tale well told begins in childhood and will persist to old age, show an ever-increasing desire to learn about human nature. In fact, there is a progressively deeper interest in character as age and experience in playgoing increase. The history of American drama, and even world drama, shows a parallel growth in appeal of character to both the audience and the playwright. The audience of today demands greater depth of character in modern plays, the comic as well as the serious, than it did in the eighteenth and nineteenth centuries. We are no longer satisfied with cliché behavior from stock or type characters. The playwright must draw characters with a difference. This is true of characters even in melodrama and farce. Both these kinds of plays in the last twenty years in this country have been peopled with more completely drawn characters. Because of this fact they have moved toward drama on the one hand and comedy on the other. They have lost the purity of form which characterized them for so many years. In the face of public demand for greater depth and less conventionality of character and the consequent change in the forms of drama, the director will find character the primary or secondary focal point of the majority of modern plays.

3. *Plot*

We know that the first playwright was the first storyteller who showed a sense of the dramatic by reordering the sequence of the actual happening of events to increase suspense for his listeners. He soon learned that complication of situation, delaying the progression of the narrative, and painting descriptive details heightened the suspense and over-all emotional effect. Thus folklore eventually turned into plays. The works of the dramatists of every era were the natural and glorious fruition of these germinal sources. Audiences down the ages have always responded forcefully to the narration of episodes dramatized from their native myths, legends, and folklore. Though the stories of their gods and heroes came down to them by mouth from generation to generation and were a part of their everyday conversation, their enactment in dramatic performance heightened their emotional power. The sharing of a national heritage by an assembled audience enriched the experience. Thus Sophocles, Aeschylus, Euripides, and Shakespeare fashioned *Oedipus Rex, Agamemnon, Electra,* and the chronicles of the Henrys, King John, and the Richards out of materials close at hand for eager, waiting audiences ever ready to live vicariously in their common glory.

Audiences for these plays yielded themselves primarily to the mere narration. They either increased their knowledge of the past or learned for the first time by sitting before history as it unrolled before their very eyes. The sequence of events, new to them or familiar, charged with suspense and reality, was made the more vivid because it all actually happened or could have happened. The magic of "once upon a time" created its wondrous spell.

This spell falls very easily over an audience even today. Though the modern audience rebels at a high rate of coincidence and demands a certain degree of motivation and logic in events, it nevertheless succumbs to the emotional and intellectual delights of a good story. The craft of the "well-made" play, which is conventional today, makes heavy demands upon the selection, complication, and marshaling of events to create a compelling plot. (The journeyman playwright through lack of technical ability and imagination sacrifices all other values for plot. Only the master dramatist is able to bring character and dialogue alive and simultaneously fabricate a dramatic plot.)

Though the modern playwright eschews the complications of plot so characteristic of the nineteenth-century melodrama, he selects and arranges his plot ingredients with consummate care. The popular audience demands plot interest, and the commercial playwright usually obliges. Though character is the main concern of the experienced playgoer and its importance has increased for modern audiences in general, plot is its handmaiden. In certain kinds of plays—melodrama, comedy, farce, and fantasy—plot is usually of paramount importance. Let us turn next to the process of determining its dominance.

Plot as a dramatic value is dominant when:

a. The audience's chief interest is in the outcome of the story
b. The dialogue is used primarily to tell the story
c. Suspense is the primary emotional value of the play
d. Conflict and crisis in terms of situation are most important
e. Complication of situation is of great interest in itself
f. Plot moves character rather than vice versa
g. Physical action and violence are emphasized
h. Mood and atmosphere are used to fortify and point up story

Dial "M" for Murder is certainly an example of a play in which the audience is primarily interested in the outcome. Suspense as the chief emotional value and conflict and crisis in terms of situation further emphasize the plot value. These very same characteristics plus the use of dialogue for narrational rather than character or theme purposes, the heightened interest resulting from plot complications, and the effect of situation on character all give plot dominance in Agatha Christie's *Witness for the Prosecution*. The importance of situation complication, its effect on character, its exploitation of conflict and crisis, and the use of dialogue to further these values instead of character or theme values make plot emphatic in Holm's and Abbott's *Three Men on a Horse*. *The Man Who Came to Dinner* illustrates the use of these already mentioned values to underscore the plot of that play. The wise-cracking and barbed dialogue of Sheridan Whiteside is a subsidiary value. (It will be noted that suspense is important in farce and comedy no less than in melodrama.)

Angel Street may, after a cursory analysis, appear to emphasize character because of the mental state of Mrs. Manningham and the attempts of her husband to drive her into insanity. However, when we consider the importance of the outcome of the plot, the power of the suspense, the emphasis on complication of situation, and conflict and crisis in terms of situation, it will be clear that what the characters do and what happens are of paramount interest. What Jack Manningham is and what his wife Bella becomes simply serve to make the play a tale of chilling horror and suspense. They possess no complexities or depth beyond their simple neuroses, which present only a one-sided view of their characters.

The Desperate Hours, by Joseph Hayes, will serve to illustrate the importance of physical action and violence to underscore plot. The three escaped convicts suddenly break the peace of a law-abiding and loving family and through their threats of action and the action itself they create a shocking and terrifying chain of events. Brutal violence is the lifeblood of this play. What is going to happen next is the supreme question, though the theme of human fortitude accompanies it.

Mood and atmosphere play not inconsiderable parts in *Witness for the Prosecution* and *Angel Street* in strengthening the pattern of events and intensifying the emotional power of these plays. In the first the ritualistic details of the courtroom and the reflection of that locale in the barrister's room, as cross examinations and depositions dramatize the mental tactics of lawyer, defendant, and witness, charge the atmosphere and shroud the audience in suspense. The second play relies appreciably upon shadowy rooms spotted with undependable gas light which dims off and on at moments calculated to be the most spine tingling. The heavy, fussy, and elaborate gentility of the furnishings so characteristic of the proper Victorians suggests a way of life which, by contrast, makes the improper and diabolic behavior of Jack Manningham more horrendous.

Plays of fancy, stretching plausibility as they do, utilize mood and atmosphere to enhance the credibility of events. The witching hours of the day—early morning, dusk, and nighttime—together with stormy or foggy weather, are favorite aids for the creation of unusual atmosphere in which the impossible becomes possible. Such an event as the appearance of Henrik Hudson's little men in *High Tor* takes place when day is merging into night. Foreshadowed by references to the lost ship and strange noises in the mountains, it is readily believable that the imaginative Van Horn not only might think he sees or even actually see these little Dutchmen but might make love to a lovely Dutch lass. Though this play has a strong theme, the main audience appeal comes from plot —the strange happenings on High Tor. Inasmuch as the strange is mixed with the comic by juxtaposing the present with the past (the real estate men and the Dutchmen), the happenings provoke the fancy of the audience and nudge them into laughter. Of course, the poetic speech of the characters helps to weave a spell of beauty and magic over a kind of never-never land between the sky and earth. Thus an emotional climate is created to fortify the capricious events of the play and serves to give them primacy over the other dramatic values.

4. Dialogue

It has already been pointed out that the other elements of a
play owe their existence to dialogue. Can this procreative element
appeal to audiences as strongly as the others? The plays of Shakespeare, those of the Restoration and their modern descendants,
poetic plays, and plays of wisecracks and witty dialogue strongly
focus the audience's attention on dialogue or language. Granville-
Barker, writing in his *Prefaces to Shakespeare*, says, "Shakespeare
. . . intent more and more upon plucking out the heart of the human
mystery, stimulated his actors to a poignancy and intimacy of
emotional expression . . ."[4] The beauty and emotional power of
Shakespeare's language are more pervasive in some plays than in
others. They are not a strong value in *King John, Titus Andronicus,*
or *Measure for Measure,* whereas they are in *Hamlet, King Lear,
Macbeth, Othello,* and *Antony and Cleopatra.* In these plays they
are second only to character and theme. The rhythm, individual
sounds, and imaginative qualities of the dialogue give the audience a special pleasure and spiritual value separate and above
other dramatic values. The witty and epigrammatic dialogue of
the plays of the Restoration afforded their audiences their chief
delight. In these plays the important thing was not what the
characters were or did but what they said. Wilde, Shaw, Behrman,
Kaufman, and Hart use dialogue as a source of delight in many
of their plays. Dialogue cannot make a play a success, but its
sheer virtuosity can give it considerable appeal. When does it
assume importance? When it is:

    a. In verse
    b. Comic
    c. Epigrammatic
    d. Imagistic
    e. Quaint or unusual
    f. Typical of a historical period, in itself a dramatic value
    g. In dialect and expressive of a folk
    h. Recognizably typical of a social or professional group

Obviously, more than one of these characteristics will often
be found in the same play. Wilde's *The Importance of Being
Earnest* and Shaw's *The Doctor's Dilemma* are comic, epigrammatic, and possessed of period values. The importance of dialogue
in these plays is apparent, but situation and plot in the first and
theme in the latter are also very important. Fry's *The Lady's Not
for Burning* is comic and imagistic in language, and for many
people the language is its main appeal. The quaintness of the speech

of *Everyman* is associated with the period and appeals delightfully to the ear. Of course, it is secondary to the dramatic values of character and theme. The quaint dialect of the Pennsylvania Dutch in *Papa Is All* is also comic and possesses these three distinguishing dramatic assets. Again the importance of plot and character makes dialogue subsidiary. The folk dialect, along with the folkways, of Brendan Behan's plays comprises special values, though not primary ones. The naiveté and beauty of the folk speech of *The Green Pastures* constitute the play's chief and strongest appeal to a large number of the audience. Its allegoric value takes a back seat when audiences in general are concerned. Dialogue characteristic of a social or professional group may seldom assume first importance in a play, but it can be a strong supporting value. *Mister Roberts, At War with the Army, No Time for Sergeants,* and other national service plays use a language which has a strong recognition value and appeal. *The Fifth Season* and *Light Up the Sky* capitalize on the jargon of the dress and show business. Social and professional argot has been the source of satirical humor and of a particular dramatic value from Plautus to Molière, to Shakespeare, to Kaufman and Hart.

The dramatic potential of dialogue is possibly mainly stylistic and therefore esoteric to many in a general audience. It is a value which resembles background music unless it is obviously comic or poetic. Nevertheless it must not be overlooked by the director, who cannot afford to undersell this rare commodity in the modern theatre. The advent of naturalism in the nineteenth century gave conversational and colloquial dialogue a dramatic value by the simple virtue of its verisimilitude to life. Today audiences expect lifelike plays to have lifelike talk and find no particular interest in that aspect of dialogue. It has become conventional and has no surprises or stimulating values. However, Tennessee Williams, Arthur Miller, and Wiliam Inge are bringing to our realistic theatre beauty, freshness, vitality, and deep emotional power in the realistic dialogue of their plays; such qualities contribute heavily to their over-all emotional impact. The language of Giraudoux and Anouilh in translation or adaptation possesses stylistic beauty which strongly affects the emotional quality of their plays.

5.   *Theme*

If words or dialogue are the seeds of drama, theme is its flower, as we have pointed out earlier. The other play elements nourish it and bring it to florescence. When a playwright wishes to give ultimate meaning to his play he will marshal his media to demonstrate and express it. The greater the dramatist, the less obvious will be his manipulation. The master technician of the drama is Ibsen. At his best he manages to draw full-bodied characters who speak conversationally, create situations, and project a meaning. Lesser technicians transparently manipulate their will-less, fettered puppet characters into the crises which pattern a plot to point a moral or idea.

In the minds of many, plays of theme or idea mean the modern well-made play freighted with social significance—plays that have something to say. They are commonly thought to be propagandistic, urging some kind of specific reform in modern society. Actually the first playwright of the western world whose works have come down to us made it clear that he was interested in saying something of significance to his audience. Allardyce Nicoll reminds us that Aeschylus in his second play, *The Persians*, introduces "his basic tragic concept: the disaster fallen upon Persia has been wrought by *hubris,* overweening pride and ambition . . ."[5] This too was propagandistic and showed the tragedy which befell a people when their leader became a victim to these twin evils in man. Nicoll goes on to say, "In Aeschylus' thought the relation of God to man was ever paramount. It was, indeed, through this preoccupation that he succeeded with such power in establishing the tragic form of drama, for tragedy is in essence the theatrical representation of theme wherein man is set in relation to the universe."[6]

His plays of theme illuminated the minds of his audience not by the dim light of the transiency of social significance but by the brilliance of timeless moral significance. Of course the plays of the middle ages were designed primarily to teach a lesson and thus were called morality plays. Surely the plays of Shakespeare were meaningful in great variety to the Elizabethans. Molière, Corneille, and Racine made their audiences ever mindful of their thoughts about life in contemporary as well as historical France. The sentimental plays of the nineteenth century were morality plays no less than those of the thirteenth, fourteenth, and fifteenth centuries. Ibsen, having mastered the craftsmanship of Scribe and Sardou, did not remain, like them, a carpenter of plays but became an architect of great dramatic structures because he furnished them with ideas. His "problem" and "thesis" plays made the theatre a public forum for debating ethical, social, and moral questions. His were plays that "said something." The modern theatre was thus born out of forensics.

The serious-minded dramatist has, since then, sought to give his plays "a spire of meaning,"[7] and thinking members of the audience have been busy looking for it. There is no doubt that such members have increased during the last fifty years. The appeal of plays of ideas has grown accordingly. Considering the American scene alone, seldom does a Broadway season fail to furnish one or more outstanding examples, and many of these plays have proved to be notable and distinguished. Among these plays, *Yellow Jack* and *The Silver Cord,* by Sidney Howard, *Idiot's Delight,* by Robert Sherwood, *The Skin of Our Teeth,* by Thornton Wilder, *Dead End,* by Sidney Kingsley, *Golden Boy,* by Clifford Odets, *The Crucible,* by Arthur Miller, and *Waiting for Godot,* by Samuel Beckett, are exemplary. Theme is the dominant value in each and has served to advance the popular "playwright as thinker."

To formulate a check list for the director seeking to determine the dominance of theme, we can be reasonably sure of it when:

a.   The elements of dialogue, character, and plot are so manipulated that they are subordinated to the conveyance of theme

b.   The theme is directly presented rather than indirectly

c.   The title of the play indicates the theme

d.   The play is written in some form of stylization

Kingsley's *Dead End* exemplifies the first three points. Throughout most of his career Kingsley has sought to document his plays by a period of on-the-spot study of the environment, habits, and customs of his characters. He thus prepared himself for the writing not only of *Dead End* but of the earlier *Men in White* and the later *Detective Story.* These plays are as reportorial as they are dramatic. They are journalistic essays written with skill, theatricality, and passion to hammer home a theme. They are social studies of "the world we make." Like all good debater-researchers, Kingsley has marshaled his material in order to make specific deductions. *Dead End* is written "to prove that criminals are made, not born."[8] He selects characters and incidents, controls and manipulates them, in order to serve his side of the question. Certainly he wins the debate on points. The characters speak and behave convincingly if you are caught up sufficiently in the drive of the action to forget to question coincidence and fortuitous juxtaposition of social and economic forces. Though much of his dialogue was copied down exactly as it was spoken by real-life dead-end kids and grown-ups, it is edited purposefully. The conversations between Gimpy and the girl he loves present the author's point of view quite directly to the audience. In case anyone in the audience watching this play fails to realize the meaning of its impact, he merely has to think about the title. It is not called *Dead End* without a reason.

John Howard Lawson's *Marching Song* is another example

of journalistic writing for the purpose of trumpeting a social message. Here all other elements of the play are patently exploited to hit the audience over the head with its theme. The craftsmanship is blatantly inferior to Kingsley's; yet the play possessed, at the time of its original production during the depression of the 'thirties in the United States, considerable theatrical power for its emotionally and politically preconditioned audiences. The direct presentation of the theme of the play and the suggestiveness of its title made its author's thinking crystal clear.

Ernst Toller's *Masses and Man*, Kaiser's *From Morn to Midnight*, and Rice's *The Adding Machine* use the medium of expressionism to tailor the various play elements to suit the needs of the authors' themes. The machine-made symbolic characters, the rat-a-tat rhythm of their dialogue, and the assembly-line chain of events manufacture their central ideas with machine precision. These plays are angry shouts to a world shackled to war and machines. A director approaching these plays for interpretation would have to be totally deaf not to hear them.

Thornton Wilder uses some of the characteristics of expressionism, vaudeville, and allegory to clothe the philosophy of *The Skin of Our Teeth*. His symbolic characters, chosen from the pages of the Bible, are propelled through the Stone Age, the flood, and the first world war to give the play meaning to a modern audience. Comic, tragic, and imaginative, it is a work of deeply affective artistry. Directly presentational and nonrealistic, it may baffle the audience accustomed only to the conventional theatre, but it cannot fail to jar it simultaneously into profound thought.

SPECIAL DRAMATIC VALUES

The audience appeal of values other than mood, dialogue, character, plot, and theme derives from some aspect of a play or its production which is special, novel, or unique to it. Most of these special dramatic values emanate from the kind or type of play and its style.

The producer in the Broadway theatre usually seeks a play that has some one or more special dramatic values or a combination of aspects appealing to audiences. The producer's cry today is for something new, fresh, and unusual. It must definitely not be unconventional, experimental, or *avant-garde*. This is not for Broadway. Actually, the average Broadway producer wants new versions of the same old subjects presented in the conventional and accepted styles of production. Yet he wants what is called a "gimmick": an angle or device that gives the writing individuality and novelty.

The gimmick may also serve as a springboard for an unusual way of staging the play, particularly in terms of the use of scenery, lighting, and sound. The acting must remain conventionally realistic, though. The gimmick is a special dramatic value which may result from the play's particular emotional climate or mood and the author's unusual attitude toward his subject. *Arsenic and Old Lace* has a special dramatic value with great audience appeal because its serious subject is given a light treatment. We should be deeply shocked at murder, but instead we laugh at it in this play. We shake with laughter while our spines tingle with delightful suspense. *Harvey* is another popular play with an unusual angle: Its central character is a drunk living in a world of charming fancy and always accompanied by a rabbit six feet tall. The play continually teeters between the comic climate of the fanciful and whimsical and the serious mood of the factual and clinical. Here again the author's attitude toward her subject is novel and unexpected. Mary Chase, the author, charms and amuses the audience with a subject which in everyday life is a very serious matter. Furthermore, she does not portray the traditional stage drunk who so often is a good-natured, well-liked, and amusing character, exemplified by the principal character of *The Old Soak*, by Don Marquis. She gives a twist to that character by equipping him with a whimsical and capricious imagination. As a result she writes a farcical fantasy which evokes guffaws of laughter mingled with a kind of wonder and childish delight.

The special dramatic value based on a gimmick may come from the author's up-dating an old story, legend, or myth. This is essentially what Garson Kanin did when he used the Pygmalion myth as a basis for *Born Yesterday* in which Billie Dawn was transformed from an apparently ignorant, dumb, dizzy, and dependent mistress of a big-time junk dealer into an educated, intelligent, and independent young lady with a brand-new set of moral and ethical values. Here comedy clothes a theme revolving around human dignity and personal integrity. In *Pygmalion*, Shaw, of course, handled the same subject with a higher degree of artistry. T. S. Eliot's *Family Reunion* and Jean Anouilh's *Legend of Lovers* are modernizations of the ancient stories, which are enhanced in dramatic value because of their derivation. O'Neill's *Mourning Becomes Electra*, written in modern Freudian terms, also gains dramatically because of its classical references. These are just a few examples of new angles and twists in writing which acquire special dramatic values. And so a new way of looking at old subjects earns dramatic dividends for the playwright, producer, director, and audience investors.

It must be apparent from the discussion of these plays that new ways and means employed by the modern playwright have resulted in new molds as well as new dramatic values. Modern drama has made it increasingly clear that it is no longer easy to use academic classifications to pigeonhole a play according to the traditional categories of tragedy, comedy, melodrama, and farce. In this uncertain age the dramatist sings medleys of doubt and uncertainty. He will not be bound by the old labels. He is seeking to create new, unique, more potent elixirs which will burst old bottles and tear off old labels. Frank Hurburt O'Hara, writing in 1939 of *Today in American Drama*, makes these points with perceptive insight and wit when he discusses "Tragedies without Finality," "Comedies without a Laugh," "Melodrama with a Meaning," "Farce with a Purpose." Yet he says, ". . . unimportant though the classifying terms may be to the playwright while he is creating, they are convenient words for the rest of us when we are talking about plays. Like all classifying words, they are short cuts. They tell us at least what not to look for."[9] He exemplifies these chapter headings with analyses of such plays as *Anna Christie, Awake and Sing!, The Silver Cord, Craig's Wife, The Little Foxes, They Shall Not Die, Of Mice and Men, You Can't Take It with You,* and others. All defy traditional classification and labels. If they are tragedies they not only end without finality but have some of the characteristics of the happy ending associated with comedy. If they are comedies they are strangely mirthless. If they are farces they provoke thought as well as laughter. Tonally and thematically they are hybrid types of plays and refuse to be compared completely and coherently with established molds. They resemble their forebears but are children with their own individualities.

They have individuality because the playwrights have created new values and have changed the traditional molds of the plays by shifting the relative dominance of dramatic values. In a "melodrama with a meaning" like *They Shall Not Die* the emphasis is on the theme rather than on the plot. The older melodramas made plot the dominant value, and suspense and excitement were desired above all else. If *You Can't Take It with You* were a traditional farce the plot and the resultant mood necessary for laughter would be dominant, but instead its theme claims considerable attention. The playwrights to whom Mr. O'Hara refers evidently consider the emotional impact of the plot less important than that of theme. They seem to want the audience to think rather than feel.

The writing of these playwrights during and just after this country's depression and just prior to the second world war was symptomatic of the emotional and intellectual climate in which they lived. This was an era in which there was "no time for comedy." It had a scale of values different from that of the past. The traditional, whether in ethics, economics, politics, or art, no longer served. Different times called for different attitudes and different approaches. Playwriting changes with the times.

The classicists particularly find it difficult to accept this fact. For example, they refuse to believe that the Aristotelian concepts are no longer applicable to modern tragedy. Brooks Atkinson, in an article called "Tragedy to Scale," complained of those readers of his column who took issue with him and invoked classical criteria when he referred to *Death of a Salesman* and *A Streetcar Named Desire* as tragedies. He countered their arguments by saying that "If tragedy is to be written today it inevitably has a very different scale of values." He made it clear that when we compare the realism of today's drama with the poetic myths of the classics we must realize that man's relationship "to the universe was . . . much more flattering to Shakespeare, and to the Greeks, than it is to us today" and "that the world was the center of the universe, and man a more significant form of life than we know him to be today." In addition to this, both the Greek and the Shakespearean drama, unlike modern drama, selected "legendary heroes who did not have to be characterized realistically, as Willie [*sic*] and Blanche are by Arthur Miller and Tennessee Williams." Yet, says Mr. Atkinson, "Since the theory of tragedy is timeless and fundamental, logic assumes that this era, like all others, is tragic. The theory of tragedy is that man is not the master of his soul. The great decisions are made by forces beyond his control—by the gods, the fates or the consciousness of the universe . . ." He asserts that this is true today in that, in spite of our spiritual aspirations and the general advance of mankind, "evil pursues every step that good advances." And inasmuch as we are an optimistic nation we illustrate the theory of tragic irony by steadfastly believing "that the big problems can be solved and the condition of man improved . . ."[10]—that good eventually overcomes evil.

Tragedy's new look today necessarily forces the audience to adapt itself to a new orientation to the dramatic elements of a play. The tragic hero is no longer the godlike figure from mythology but John Doe, the little man from the atomic age. Shaken in religious belief by the skepticism of science, he challenges fate and the gods that may be. When catastrophe overwhelms him he does not know what hit him and is unable to relate what Mr. Atkinson calls "his bleak experience to the grim majesty of fate." He does not move from ignorance to enlightenment as Oedipus and Hamlet do. Arthur Miller, however, in his "Tragedy and the Common Man," an article on *Death of a Salesman*, asserts that from the "total questioning of what has previously been unquestioned, we learn. And such a process is not beyond the common man."[11] The modern tragedy, like its forebears, gives dominance to the dramatic values of character and theme, but the drama is reduced in size and quality. The jargon of everyday contemporary life, unlike the poetry of the classic myths, fails to lift the spirit or make the heart sing. Though it may be a time for tragedy, tragedy does not look the same any more. Because he is Arthur Miller or Tennessee Williams and not Sophocles or Shakespeare, the modern tragic dramatist must perforce create special dramatic values.

New twists to traditional characters, the modernization of old plots, and the change and shift of values to create new types or kinds of plays discussed above cannot be mentioned without citing the desire of modern dramatists to appeal to audiences through changing the conventional plot structure to produce a novel approach and treatment. Playwrights are influenced by dramatic forms of literature of the past and by radio, television, and motion pictures. The use of the prologue and epilogue, for example, has found favor with certain dramatists. Maxwell Anderson employed the prologue in *Key Largo*, Edward Chodorov the prologue and epilogue in *Kind Lady*, Arthur Miller the epilogue (though called a "requiem") for the last scene of *Death of a Salesman*. Tennessee Williams used a one-man chorus in *The Glass Menagerie* to give the audience a prologue and an epilogue. Variants of the Greek chorus have been used by such dramatists as Robert Bolt in *A Man for All Seasons,* Jean Anouilh in *Beckett,* Frances Goodrich and Albert Hackett in *The Diary of Anne Frank*, and John Van Druten in *I Am a Camera*. The device involving the use of a one-man chorus often allows the author to subjectify his approach by invoking the narrational techniques of the novel, radio, or motion pictures. The chorus sets up the narration in his prologue and then recalls the past in a series of "flash-backs" in which he may or may not participate. The epilogue then permits him to resolve the action and comment upon it. When the plot structure is handled in this manner the style of the play is affected and becomes a special dramatic value.

Plays employing dream, memory, and psychoanalytical techniques also create stylistic values. Elmer Rice's *Dream Girl,* Arthur Laurents' *Home of the Brave* and *A Clearing in the Woods,* Moss Hart's *Christopher Blake,* Tennessee Williams' *The Glass Menagerie,* Arthur Miller's *Death of a Salesman,* Maxwell Anderson's *Anne of the Thousand Days,* John Marquand's *Point of No Return,* and Sidney Kingsley's *Darkness at Noon* are examples of these techniques. Some of them remain realistic in appearance while others become expressionistically distorted, mechanized, and highly stylized. Their novelty of structure and style adds special audience appeal.

The technique of presenting a play within a play can also be especially interesting to audiences. Ferenc Molnar's *The Play's the Thing*, Luigi Pirandello's *Six Characters in Search of an Author*, and Maxwell Anderson's *Joan of Lorraine* are a few examples. This technique calls upon the audience to use its imagination on two levels and thus adds to the depth of the theatrical experience.

Clifford Odets' *Waiting for Lefty* utilizes the technique of planting characters in the audience and bringing them on stage to participate in the action. This results in making the audience involve itself so subjectively that it is swept along with the emotion of the characters and it becomes a part of fictional action which takes on complete reality. This play exploited the temper of the times by dramatizing the plight of an economically depressed and retarded section of the public. The play was a call to action. Most members of the audience of the 'thirties, emotionally and intellectually conditioned by the depression, responded readily and forcefully to the play. Diego Fabbri used a similar technique in his *Trial of Jesus (Il processo a Gesu)*. Originally produced for a predominantly Italian Roman Catholic audience, it evidently succeeded in inflaming the minds and emotions. A production of the play by students before a university audience in New England a few years ago created a considerably diminished impact. Planting actors in the audience today may be a dangerous device for serious plays because it may break the illusion rather than increase it. Olsen and Johnson employed it to excellent comic effect in *Hellzapoppin!* Orson Welles, by slightly varying the device when he used "stage" policemen to shoot at Bigger Thomas from the balcony of the theatre, created a theatrically effective moment in *Native Son*. Numerous productions have succeeded in giving the audience a feeling of actual participation in a play by having actors come down the aisles and go up onto the stage. The Broadway production of *Camino Real* utilized the technique. Several of the Shakespearean productions at Stratford, Ontario, and Stratford, Connecticut, have also used the aisles of the theatre to add considerable theatricality to the undertakings. The technique seems to give the plays the atmosphere and mood of a carnival, circus, burlesque, or musical extravaganza. It is all in the spirit of fun and entertainment, and succeeds best when it is used for comic reasons. It is a stylistic value which, under the proper circumstances, can possess great audience appeal.

The special dramatic values of style in writing and production emanate not only from modern approaches and treatments but from those of the past. Revivals of the classics in the style of the period can be highly appealing to modern audiences. The Old Vic productions of *Oedipus Rex, The Critic, Henry IV, Part One,* and *Part Two* possessed undeniable style values. The strange and the unusual deriving from the historicity of a production take on the appearance of freshness and novelty because popular audiences see so few of the classics in this country. Period plays and their productions have limited but exciting theatrical appeal.

Dramatic values which come from period flavor and manner may acquire an added piquancy when the life of a bygone era is by implication compared with modern life or is given contemporaneity by the acting, directing, settings, and costumes. Some of Shakespeare's plays have been successfully up-dated by the use of modern costumes and realistic staging. The first of the modern-dress productions was Sir Barry Jackson's *Hamlet* at the Kingsway Theatre in London in 1925. Heralded as "Hamlet in Plus Fours," ". . . the first-night audience, expecting to be amused and pleasurably shocked, soon found themselves accepting the modern costumes just as easily as eighteenth-century audiences accepted Garrick playing Macbeth in the uniform of an English general in the time of George II, or Lear in black satin knee-breeches and a velvet coat."[12] In such a production *Hamlet,* of course, had to be acted as a modern play. So acted, the characters no longer appeared to be from another era and another world but had the reality and immediacy of royal figures in any court in Europe. Moreover, Hamlet in plus fours or tweeds proved to have a kinship with modern man.

Since this production there have been others in the dress of the middle nineteenth century as well as that of the twentieth century. Other Shakespearean plays have been modernized with some degree of success. In this country the modernization of *Hamlet* and *Julius Caesar* has added to Shakespeare's popular appeal. In fact, the Shakespearean festivals at the two North American Stratfords with some of their modern productions, aided and abetted by the numerous interesting nonprofessionally acted festivals, have made William Shakespeare one of our biggest box-office draws. They have awakened audiences to the excitement, timelessness, and beauty of Shakespeare. As a result the public, like Lady Macbeth but intending to convey a meaning quite different from hers, may well ask, "Yet who would have thought the old man to have had so much blood in him?"

In effect, those aspects of Shakespeare that would seem to make him antiquated have indeed proved as transitory as time itself. Neither time nor Freud can stale his infinite understanding of human nature. In placing him in modern milieu, the themes of his plays may be changed superficially but their universal implications may become more communicable. However, in the attempt to make Shakespeare contemporaneous by changing the period of the plays with costumes and settings, the director should be cautioned against destroying the world of the plays essential for communicating illusion, credibility, and intrinsic dramatic values. Above all, up-dating Shakespeare can so call attention to the process as to cause form to dominate content and lose the essence of Shakespeare. Some examples of this will follow in the section on the "Effect of Directorial Techniques on Dramatic Values."

It can be pointed out here that in the modernization of Shakespeare his plots sometimes do not hold up well to the embarrassing light of the workaday world of causality. The characters and language of the comedies can be interpreted to skip over the plot lightly when incredibility might possibly interpose itself between the play and the audience. The comedies, by and large, rather than the tragedies have lent themselves to a change and a shift of dramatic values to create newer and fresher values for the modern audience. The disguises, surprises, coincidences, and non sequiturs of plot in plays of mixed moods like *Measure for Measure, Much Ado about Nothing,* and *All's Well That Ends Well* can jar a modern audience and destroy its belief in what it sees and hears. The outstanding modern plays and recent Broadway successes particularly are written to conform to the present-day audience's psychology and as a result the director seldom needs to fear that the audience will get out of control because of its refusal to believe. The plays of the past must be reinterpreted and directed to create the illusion of reality for a modern audience conditioned to the realistic theatre. This does not mean that these problem plays of Shakespeare's must be played realistically. No. The point is that they must be staged unrealistically but still the audience must be made to believe them. The director must give the audience a point of view which it will accept. John Houseman and Jack Landau successfully met this problem in their production of *Much Ado about Nothing* at Stratford, Connecticut. They gave the audience a point of view in their bold, unconventional interpretation of the play, and the audience accepted it and responded with audible delight. However right or wrong their interpretation of the play may be thought to be, it worked with the audience. And this does not mean that another interpretation would not work. An important cue for the director is the audience's attitude toward the characters at every given moment and incident in the play.

He must ask himself whether the audience is going to laugh at the characters because it doesn't believe in their speech, action, or thought. Laughter springs from audience superiority and objectivity to characters. If the director does not wish the audience to laugh *at* the characters he must induce the audience to laugh *with* them. If he succeeds in doing this he makes the characters and himself, importantly enough, just as smart as the audience. Oftentimes in Shakespeare the characters must take the audience into their confidence by look, gesture, or general attitude even though they have no soliliquies or "asides" to enable them to speak to the audience directly. In other words, the director in recognizing the necessity for so interpreting the play speaks to the audience and asks it to go along just for the fun of it.

In the course of this discussion of special dramatic values and their relative importance the point must be apparent and clear that play interpretation depends very strongly upon the factors of choice and emphasis made by the director. These factors determine the plan and purpose of his interpretation and production. It must be apparent too that the director can make a play convey an intention different from the one implied or made explicit by the playwright. A play is not simply written. It is interpreted and it is performed. What the audience sees may or may not be the harmonious consolidation of these three processes. Inasmuch as those elements which we have been calling dramatic values constitute the heart of play interpretation, we should consider briefly some examples of the effect of directing upon these values.

EFFECT OF DIRECTORIAL TECHNIQUES ON DRAMATIC VALUES

The analysis of a play for the dramatic potential of each value and the determination of the dominant value and the relative importance of the other values will give the director a preliminary blueprint to guide him in the direction of the play.

First of all, the knowledge of the play's dramatic values should be used to guide the director in selecting and using the appropriate kind and amount of directorial technique. Inasmuch as mood is an all-pervasive dramatic value, it can affect the other elements of a play. This means, of course, that the director's choice and establishment of mood sets the entire play in its emotional climate, gives it a particular spirit, and thereby influences the audience's reaction. For example, John Houseman's and Jack Landau's entire interpretation of *Measure for Measure* emanated from what Walter Kerr, in the July 8, 1956, edition of the *New York Herald Tribune*, calls "Mr. Houseman's breezy and bantering staging," and he goes on to say that "The vein that has been developed here is impudent and ingratiating . . ."[13] Brooks Atkinson, discussing the production in *The New York Times* on the same day, says that although "What Mr. Houseman and Mr. Landau have done with it may not precisely coincide with Shakespeare's mood when he wrote it . . . this . . . version is charming . . . and humorous . . ."[14] The mood of this production was established by jumping forward into nineteenth-century Vienna, putting the characters in period clothes to accentuate the comedy, giving the actors line readings and business which made "antic nonsense" of behavior usually interpreted seriously. Here is an example of a determination of a dramatic value and the directorial means to establish it as well as a basic change in interpretation which is untraditional, new, and individual. The play is usually interpreted in such a way as to convey the serious theme about man's natural instincts in conflict with law and society. The directors of this production apparently refused to make theme a dominant dramatic value but emphasized mood—and a mood contrary to the one most modern critics consider fundamental to the play.

A similar change from the traditional interpretation of the tone of a play is exemplified by the production of *Love's Labor's Lost* by the Brattle Players at the New York City Center. Instead of producing the play as gentle satire on the effete sixteenth-century young men who resolved to forego all feminine company and devote themselves to learning, which is obviously Shakespeare's intention, this company dressed the characters in the Edwardian period, placed them in appropriate surroundings, and made them behave in such a manner as to make the entire proceedings a chronological joke. The tone of this satire was further sounded by such brassy anachronisms as the use of the morning-glory-horned phonograph and the model-T Ford. Here is change indeed: Satire moves toward burlesque and the light touch becomes a wallop.

The 1961 production of *Troilus and Cressida*, by the American Shakespeare Festival Theatre was a similar example of an unsuccessful change of tone. By dressing the actors in Civil War uniforms and hoop skirts and placing the action before the façade of an ante-bellum mansion and pup-tents, to simulate the headquarters of the Union army, the mood of the play was quite different from that inherent in the language, characters, plot, and theme. The appearance and behavior of the actors playing Agamemnon and Priam called attention to their resemblance to Grant and Lee and encouraged the audience to look for other Civil War personages. In addition, the comic-strip portrait of Ajax and other members of the Greek army in particular diminished the seriousness of the meaning of the play. Thersites, presented as a clownish mule skinner, further detracted from the profoundly cynical commentary on the action. The siege of Troy dramatized by cannonading and rifle fire and the melodramatic destruction of the stage setting became laughable. As a result, the connotational values of production and the prevalence of the comic took precedence over the bitter satire and tragedy of this play of disillusionment. The subjects of love and war, intuition and intellect, pervading the play were thus reduced to travesty.

Deliberate changes in dramatic values occurred in Maurice Evans' G.I. production of *Hamlet* and Orson Welles' *Julius Caesar*. The first emphasized action and plot and devalued character; the second gave dominance to a timely theme and de-emphasized character. These interpretations went squarely against tradition and the critical consensus. Change of periods and costumes, the use of scenic and lighting effects, together with the establishment of melodramatic moods by a driving pace and theatricalized movement, resulted in the projection and emphasis of the desired dramatic values. Precedents for such juggling of values of the classics are, of course, to be found in the productions of Max Reinhardt and Vsevolod Meierhold.

These are willful shifts in mood values. Shifts take place very often in summer stock and amateur productions which are keyed to simple entertainment values: Comedy moves into farce, drama into melodrama, character plays become plot plays. These shifts may be equally as willful as the ones cited above, but many of them come from interpretive ineptitude, ignorance, and lack of rehearsals. For example, a recent stock production of *The Silver Whistle*, by Robert E. McEnroe, witnessed by the writer, had lost much of its charm of character and fancifulness and had deteriorated into the worst possible example of old-fashioned, hammy farce. This came about chiefly because of the caricatured characterizations of the inept company and the corny business and uncertain pace of the performance. The emphasis was on plot rather than character, and farce grew where comedy was intended. This same kind of shift in dramatic values resulted in a recent undergraduate production of Wilder's beautiful little comedy of character and theme, *The Happy Journey*. By placing the characters in costumes of the 'twenties and exaggerating their behavior, the director sacrificed the rich, warm character of the mother for caricature and turned the comedy and pathos (the last scene lost all its tenderness and was meaningless) into farce and embarrassing bathos. Whether this interpretation resulted from a failure to analyze the play correctly or from a desire to get laughs at any cost from a college prom weekend audience was not ascertained. Summer theatre productions of *A Streetcar Named Desire* and *Death of a Salesman,* plays rich in character values, no doubt have become plays of plot heavily sauced with the forced and surface hysteria which, under short-term rehearsal and production conditions, must pass for genuine emotion. Movement, pace, and business under these circumstances take the place of subtle, subjective acting which comes out of truth and life. The result is show business rather than theatre. The director of summer stock frequently is victimized by time and other factors, succumbs to the expediency of getting the show on willy-nilly, and too seldom is able to give it a point of view.

In each of the examples discussed the directors were no doubt considerably influenced by what they anticipated would be the effect on the particular audiences involved. The success of each production depended very largely on the directors' abilities in play analysis and directorial techniques.

With the unprecedented attention being devoted to the study and use of subjective acting techniques, the director strongly oriented to this training may concentrate on characterization to such an extent that he can upset the balance of dramatic values desired by the playwright. When characters are so strongly based on psychological motivations and stimuli, regardless of the type and style of play being performed, the entire spirit of a play can change —usually from comedy into the heavily serious and naturalistic.

The director who always sees a play only in terms of character and the psychology of behavior runs the risk of either innocently misinterpreting or deliberately changing the relative importance of the play elements. He fails to see that a dramatist in writing any play is creating a dramaturgic design, selecting, ordering, and relating the various parts to a predetermined whole for the purpose of making an observation about and not a duplication of human behavior and life.

It can be seen, then, that a study of the parts of a play leads to a consideration of the integrating and unifying plan of interpretive procedure to be pursued.

UNIFYING FACTORS OF TYPE AND STYLE

The study of the play elements of mood, dialogue, character, plot, and theme has led us to a consideration of the dramatic potentials and the relative dominance of each—an analysis of the play and what is to be emphasized in order to communicate the purpose and meaning. The study of these parts of a play has revealed their relationship to the whole. They foreshadow the type and style of the play and, like mood, unify the whole. We have already referred to the special dramatic values which derive from them. Our purpose now is to discuss the director's problems in determining type and style and his use of type and style to achieve unity in his interpretation and direction. No attempt will be made to trace the history or discuss the critical theories of the various classifications of type and style of plays. This is a subject too big in scope to be undertaken here. However, a knowledge of the historical and the critical must be acquired elsewhere by the director if he is to have a complete understanding of this aspect of interpretation. Let us look first at the problem of determining the *type* of play.

In our previous references to the type of play under consideration it was shown that certain dominant emotional characteristics made it unique. Every playwright has purposefully evoked this mood by the selection and treatment of his subject matter. The mood represents his own pervading feeling and attitude, and he wants the play to instill this same mood in the audience. He is dependent, of course, upon the director to translate what he has written into a theatrical production that will communicate and arouse this mood.

The classical doctrine of the unities of drama is probably responsible for the insistence upon the rigid classification of drama according to its emotional character into types distinct from each other. Tragedy and comedy are the two main types. Melodrama and farce sprang up to denote other types. The admission of melodrama and farce as distinct types implied the recognition that there is a gradation of moods between the extreme poles of the serious (tragedy) and the humorous (comedy). Over the years critics have perceived further gradations. These gradations have resulted from admixtures of emotional qualities which nevertheless seemed to have unity. The classification of plays has become an interpretive problem difficult if not impossible to solve. And this is not a modern problem. Shakespeare recognized it when he gave Polonius the speech in which he says the players who came to Elsinore were

> The best actors in the world, either for tragedy, comedy, history, pastoral, pastoral-comical, historical-pastoral, tragical-historical, tragical-comical-historical-pastoral, scene individable, or poem unlimited . . .

Classification is not an end in itself for the director as it might very well be for the critic, but the director must seek a classification to pinpoint the exact emotional characteristics of the play and to define their kind, quality, intensity, depth, and range. He must make up his mind as to what kind or type of play he is about to direct in order to decide upon the kind and amount of emotional response he desires from the audience. When he decides this he will also determine an overruling and unifying point of view toward his interpretation and production. This decision will bring purpose and order to his directorial approach and technique. Moreover, it brings discipline to his creativity.

The effect of the whole play upon the audience is indeed important to the director. Allardyce Nicoll maintains that "in drama the one essential unity is unity of impression."[15] By unity of impression he means not monotony of emotion but a variety of emotions subordinated to, controlled by, and blended with the essential quality of the all-pervading emotion. ". . . every great drama shows a subordination of the particular elements of which it is composed to some central spirit by which it is inspired, and . . . any drama which admits emotion not so in subordination to the main spirit of the play will thereby be blemished,"[16] he says. This theory of unity of impression, he points out, was anticipated by the ancient writers on Sanscrit drama. Using as his source S. M. Tagore's *The Eight Principal Rasas of the Hindus,* he says, "there were eight principal *rasas,* or impressions, which might be aroused by a dramatic poem . . ."[17] They were the emotions of love, heroism, pathos or tender grief, anger, laughter, fear or terror, disgust, and wonder or admiration. Each of these had many subdivisions, and many various rasas were employed in each work. The types of drama were determined by reference to that rasa which was most important, although every rasa was in agreement with some rasas and hostile to others. This is historical authority for determining the type of play from its all-pervading emotional impression or mood. Actual practice among professional directors brings added authority for thus determining the type of play.

The over-all mood or emotional climate, as we have called it, is felt by the director, and he hopes that the audience in turn will feel as he did. The all-pervasive mood of the play tells him whether the audience should respond to it by laughing aloud, chuckling, twinkling, being moved seriously or lightly, or alternately being aroused and touched, etc. The creative director relies very heavily upon his own emotions and his knowledge of those of the audience to tell him what type of play he is dealing with. Inasmuch as plays are evocative of a wide range of moods, from the most passionate and primitive serious emotions to the gentlest and most subtle, the director must be sensitive to and aware of the various emotional subdivisions and gradations. He must be capable of recognizing the distinction between tragedy and drama, drama and melodrama, tragi-comedy and comedy-drama, comedy and farce—high and low—fantasy and sentimentality, etc. The recognition of these distinctions is important to him in reading the play for interpretation and in directing it. Some directors are not capable of making fine emotional distinctions. A successful director of fast, slick farces may not be able to direct fantasy of a gentle sort. The director successful with hard-hitting plays of social import or dramas of Freudian frustrations may not be able to handle deep tragedy. Many directors seem to be sensitive to the extremes of emotion but not to the many gradations between the two. They are the directors who are most perceptive and responsive to the black and white emotions but do not recognize or understand the pastel shades.

Playwrights with a culture different from that of the director write plays difficult for him to interpret and stage. Saroyan's *My Heart's in the Highlands* and a number of his other plays possess a spirit elusive for many directors. Barrie's *Mary Rose, Dear Brutus,* and *Peter Pan* are "caviar to the general" (or treacle to the factually minded). Cultural differences sometimes present problems to both the director and the audience. The modern French playwrights Giraudoux, Anouilh, Cocteau, Aymé, Salacrou, Genêt, Ionesco, and Claudel often write with an attitude toward life which makes interpretation for the popular American audience a genuine problem for the director. Their plays of fantasy, satire, and irony, which mix the serious with the comic or treat lightly what audiences consider the serious and moral, are confusing and disconcerting. Usually neither the American director nor the audience knows quite how to react to them. However, it is possible that with more time and experience both audience and directors can learn to perceive their unusual emotional and intellectual qualities. Though Anouilh's *Ring round the Moon* and *Colombe* were Broadway failures, his *The Waltz of the Toreadors,* Giraudoux's *Tiger at the Gates,* and even the "far-out" Ionesco's *Rhinoceros* have achieved considerable success.

Although the director's individual subjective perception of the mood of a play will in most cases guide him in determining the type of play he is dealing with, his analysis of the relative dominance of the dramatic values in the play will tend to influence his judgment. When audience interest and appeal are centered on character, the play points to tragedy, drama, or comedy. It is to be understood that such emphasis on character derives not only from the details and facets of character in certain examples of these forms of drama but from the effect of the entire action of the play upon character. In Chekhov we will find great complexity of character whereas in Sophocles we will find simplification. Yet in both *The Cherry Orchard* and *Oedipus Rex*, let us say, the audience is primarily interested in the characters rather than in the plot, dialogue, or theme. The theme is of importance in these two plays, but the director needs to give most of his attention to the characters because they demonstrate the theme. (Brooks and Heilman, however, interpret the play primarily from a thematic point of view.) The audience is not so much interested in what is done or said, or in the meaning thereof, but in who the characters are and in what happens to them. Their problems and dilemmas and their solutions are of paramount interest. As a result a specific and cohering emotional climate is created. In any play this emotional climate is of particular kind, depth, and magnitude, and affects the audience in a definite manner.

The playwright's stress on plot—on what happens, how it happens, and the suspense, thrill, surprise, and humor emanating therefrom—tends to point toward melodrama or farce. The emotional depth and magnitude of these two forms is shallow, slight, and limited. Moreover, the total emotional effect is transient and easily dissipated. The other forms of drama leave a more lasting effect on the audience.

The playwright who emphasizes the theme of a play and makes the other values subservient usually views man ". . . as a social being and as little else, as a person surrounded by laws and conventions, as one whose happiness can be secured only by two things—by the imprint of too brash social regulations and of evil conditions and by the developing in himself of an adaptability to his circumstances."[18] Here the emotional impact is considerably less permanent and less deeply affective than in tragedy but more lasting and more disturbing than in melodrama. This is the type of play called a *drama*.

The dominance of dramatic values is indicative of the playwright's intention and purpose in writing the play. Naturally, the spirit and form of the drama he creates result from his main purpose to move an audience in a particular way and to a predetermined extent. This aspect of a play is thus a key to the type of play written.

Critical criteria are formulated from the practices of the past and the present, and the director is assisted in arriving at his conclusions about the conventional categories of plays from a study and understanding of such criteria. Inasmuch as criteria must change with time and usage, the practical director must be guided ultimately by his audience and the modern world in which he lives and practices his art. As we have already seen in our discussion of the special dramatic values which accrue from the unconventional attitudes toward the traditional types of drama, the director must exercise flexibility of thinking. Categories and labels are means toward the end of creative interpretation. Academicism must give way to practical creativity.

Subsequent to the understanding, perception, and determination of plays as types the director must utilize his conclusions to bring order, design, and unity to the emotional climate of the play: The type of play is his reference point for rehearsals and ultimate production. This reference point must be fixed firmly in his memory as he rehearses each scene in order to relate the parts to the whole. Though the parts are variations of the central spirit, they must nevertheless possess emotional qualities that are compatible and blend with this unifying spirit. For example, farce has no place in tragedy. It will not blend with the all-pervasive spirit of tragedy. Comedy scenes do cohere with tragedy. The Fool's scenes in *King Lear* must never be allowed by the director to degenerate into the farcical. These scenes, though humorous, are tinged with sadness and irony. After all, the Fool is an aspect of the complete man Lear should be. Hamlet's scenes with Polonius, Rosencrantz and Guildenstern, and the gravediggers also require directorial control to blend them with the over-all mood. The director who forgets and thinks solely in terms of how many laughs he can get out of these scenes will cause the play to lose some of its stature and magnitude. Even the scenes of melodrama in *Hamlet* must be controlled if the truly tragic spirit is to pervade the play. The appearance of the ghost is supernatural but it is not intended simply to thrill the audience. It must be circumscribed with the mystery of the hereafter to evoke awe and profound terror, emotions generated by tragedy and not by melodrama.

Macbeth has been successfully produced as an Elizabethan melodrama of emotion, revenge, and blood. It has also been successful as a tragedy. The director's interpretation of the play as a whole and his interpretation of the individual scenes will determine what type of play *Macbeth* is. The director's guidance and supervision of the actors and the physical elements of production will give the play its total key. The softening, romanticizing, and theatricalizing of a modern play like Miller's *A View from the Bridge* will push it toward melodrama and away from the tragic spirit aimed for by its original production. It must be pointed out that in these examples unity of mood is achieved, but when the mood is changed by directorial emphasis the play changes in type. The parts control the whole instead of the whole's controlling the parts.

The question of the right or the wrong interpretation is not the main point here. The point is that the director must make a choice of an over-all interpretation of the emotional qualities of a play and he must adhere to this interpretation to achieve consistency and unity. This choice must then be clearly communicated to the audience for whom it is made.

Closely akin to the type of play is its *style*. They are related because both are predominantly emotionalizing influences on the audience. Often types of plays are referred to in terms of style. A critic or reviewer of a play may speak of the "style of comedy," the "style of melodrama," etc. He is speaking of the special emotional qualities of these classifications. He is also speaking of the playwright's use of his materials to create the play. Both type and style involve the selection and arrangement of the play elements into a structure which will suggest, reflect, and represent life. Type and style are kinds and degrees of modification of life in terms of playwriting. Playwriting is an art and as art it creates not life but an illusion of life on the stage. The illusion of life on the stage takes many forms expressive of the author's attitude. His way or manner of creation is then an aspect of type and style. Shakespeare's *As You Like It* is the result of his attitude toward his dramatic materials and of his manner of using them. It is a comedy in type and a particular brand of romanticism in style. The critic or reviewer who speaks of it as a "style of comedy" is speaking loosely and not specifically. To be more nearly specific he should refer to it as a "romantic comedy." To be absolutely specific he should call it a "Shakespearean romantic comedy." The romantic style of Shakespeare is individual to Shakespeare and, as such, differs from the romantic style of other Elizabethans and of playwrights of other historical periods. As a product of the age in which he lives the playwright represents that age in his attitude and his way of working. He writes out of his background, training, and personality for the particular kind of theatrical conditions and audience of his time. The illusion of life created on the stage varies, then, from age to age.

For the most part the illusion of life we see on the stage today suggests a high degree of reality. This degree has become, in stylistic terms, the prevailing convention of the modern theatre. However, some plays and productions today are presented in the styles or conventions of the past. They appear as representatives of special and identifiable styles or as variants of style. The modern theatre is heir to the past and it also begets its own stylistic creations. We present Shakespeare on our own proscenium stages, on replicas of the Elizabethan stage, and on modified Elizabethan stages. The plays of Sophocles, Aeschylus, and Euripides are also produced in our modern theatres behind prosceniums, in front of prosceniums, and out in the open in amphitheatres. The other outstanding playwrights of the past are similarly adapted to our modern theatres, especially our educational theatres. In addition, modern playwrights have sometimes written in the spirit of some writer and theatre of another era for present-day theatre conditions. The styles of writing and production vary in accordance with the circumstances. Maxwell Anderson wrote of the Shakespearean world for today's theatre and audience when he wrote *Elizabeth the Queen*. Robinson Jeffers wrote of the Medea of Euripides for the modern theatre. Both these playwrights expressed the spirit but not the letter of Shakespearean romanticism or Euripidean classicism. In so doing they created particular styles and degrees of illusion of life.

Whatever the audience sees and hears on a stage is the illusion of life. It is not life itself and cannot be. Theatrical art, like all the other arts, interprets life. Irwin Edman, a distinguished philosopher, in speaking of art in man's experience, says that

> All the arts in one way or another, to some greater or lesser extent, interpret life. They may "interpret" nothing more than the way in which a bowl of fruit "appears" to the ordered imagination of a painter. They may "interpret" nothing more than sensation. Or they may interpret, as *Hamlet* does, or *War and Peace,* or *Ode on the Intimations of Immortality from Recollections of Early Childhood,* the confused intuitions of human emotion. A poem like *The Divine Comedy* or Goethe's *Faust* may be a commentary upon the whole human scene, its nature, its movement, and its destiny. . . . a statue by Michelangelo or Rodin, a piece of music by Beethoven or Debussy, is by virtue of its comprehensive and basic quality, its mood, its tempo, and its essential timbre, an interpretation of experience.[19]

In interpreting life the artist utilizes many means. He may attempt to represent life by imitating each detail without order or arrangement, or he may simply suggest life though he selects and orders each detail. He may even change and distort the details of life. In every case he both interprets life and creates a kind of artistic illusion which adumbrates life. In the theatre the illusion of verisimilitude may be so strong that the audience through its voluntary self-deception experiences vicariously the fictional thoughts, emotions, and actions of the characters of the play. Yet during this experience the audience knows consciously or unconsciously that it is all illusion. (This is so regardless of how hard the playwright may strive to represent life exactly and to make the audience think it is witnessing life itself.) It knows that it can withdraw at any moment and be merely a bystander. It need not participate. Life itself does not allow such choices. All of us must be "committed" and "engaged," as the existentialists say; we have no choice except to participate in life in varying degrees of activeness. This theatrical illusion is not reality in the sense of the actual. Nevertheless, all theatrical illusion has a reality of its own. Unless this reality is continuously maintained, the illusion will disappear. There are different levels of reality which create different illusions. The director must bear in mind the nature of theatrical illusion and the discipline it must effect in interpretation and production.

The illusion of life on the stage has been created by objectification of life or subjectification of life. Objective presentation consists of the playwright's reporting on life without prejudice or comment. On the other hand, subjective presentation means that the playwright writes in such a way as to reflect his particular individual bias, emotional and intellectual. The play he writes presents life as he sees it, though it may differ from the way others see it.

The various styles of writing and production arise from artistic theories and philosophies and the physical theatres for which the authors write. In general, playwriting styles are divided into two main groups, one favoring *representationalism* and the other *presentationalism.*

Representationalism tries to create the feeling that the audience is looking at life exactly as it takes place by removing the fourth wall of the room in which life is going on, or by showing the action through a window of the room or even through the keyhole of the door leading to the room. Under these circumstances the actors pretend to be unaware of the audience. *Presentationalism* tries to remind the audience continuously that it is in the theatre being addressed by and communicating directly with the actors. In this case the actors show, in varying degrees, their awareness of the audience and consciously try to speak and behave for their benefit. Naturalism and realism are styles which attempt to *represent* life. Classicism, romanticism, and expressionism are styles which frankly *present* life. Styles which employ a high degree of distortion, mechanization, simplification, or abstraction also frankly *present* life.

The origin and chief characteristics of the styles of historical periods and schools of writing comprise a subject too extensive to be discussed here. Most of the standard textbooks on play production present short discussions on styles and are helpful in teaching the director how to recognize their salient features. We must be concerned with methods of determining styles and their use as unifying factors of interpretation.

Inasmuch as style has a highly emotionalizing influence on the audience, its emotional character is one of its strongest determinants. If, for example, we consider Gorki's *The Lower Depths* we find that it is hard, dirty, dark, physical, direct, raw, vulgar, passionate, elemental, and utterly lifelike. These are adjectives descriptive of its emotional qualities. They point toward naturalism. Wilde's *The Importance of Being Earnest* is brilliant, brittle, artificial, mannered, controlled, and unnatural. Its style is highly selective in its degree of lifelikeness. It is stylized and strongly dependent upon its period flavor. Eliot's *Murder in the Cathedral* is formal, liturgical, ritualistic, strong, vertical, intellectual, simple, unadorned, sharp, and disciplined. It will be noticed that the descriptive adjectives used in connection with these plays refer to emotional qualities which affect the feelings of the audience without specifically denoting seriousness or humor. The serious or the comic may be implicit in these adjectives but they are not explicit. Nor is the degree of seriousness or humor specified. The adjectives come to mind because they describe the concomitant qualities of mood and type of play rather than those two aspects themselves.

The illusion of life created by the playwright as a result of his treatment of the elements of dialogue, character, plot, and theme is perhaps the best key to style. If the dialogue is in prose and sounds colloquial and conversational it will seem lifelike. Dialogue in verse tends to remove the play from realism. Characters that are purely symbolic and abstract appear unlifelike and stylized. The more the audience can learn about the characters the more realistic they appear. Plot structure can affect the degree of lifelikeness of the play. The plot that is loose and shows less control by the playwright tends to be naturalistic. (The loose structure of many of Shakespeare's plays tends to make them romantic in style.) Plausibility and causality of plot add to its credibility and realism. The wider the applicability of the theme, the more realistic the play tends to be. There are, of course, exceptions to each of these assertions. In regard to the applicability of the theme, for example, a theme can have universal applicability and still the play *may* not be realistic. If we assume that the theme of *Oedipus Rex* concerns the blindness of man about his own fallibility, we can agree that this is a universal failing. Yet the theme is demonstrated in a play which is classic in style. However, the universality of the theme alone does give *Oedipus Rex* a high degree of conviction and reality. The treatment of the elements of dialogue and plot does not belong in the realistic style of writing. The manner of drawing character is also inconsistent with realism. The use of the chorus and the over-all structure of the play are characteristic of classicism. The director, then, cannot come to a definite conclusion about the style of a play through an examination of the degree of reality of one element. He must add up the results of his analysis and come to a conclusion based upon his total impression. Even then he should consider other determinants.

The influence of the historical period may be very important in his considerations. Surely the physical theatre for which the author of *Oedipus Rex* wrote affected the style of the play. The fact that the play was presented in an amphitheatre with a permanent structure for the setting dictated certain writing techniques to Sophocles, who was also influenced by the entire religious, political, economic, and cultural life of Athens in the fifth century B.C. The modern playwright no less than those of the past is also conditioned by the physical theatre and his age. His style of writing reflects these influences.

The playwright's guiding purpose in writing a play may dictate the style of the play. Strindberg's intention to present the experience of a dream in a distorted mixture of mental images accounts for his use of expressionism in writing *The Dream Play*. O'Neill's desire to present a picture of fear influenced by superstition and race background resulted in the form given to *The Emperor Jones*.

The practical limitations of budget, time, stage facilities, and personnel may determine style. We have already pointed out that Welles' production of *Julius Caesar* stemmed at least partly from some of these practical considerations. Paul Gregory's staged reading of Shaw's *Don Juan in Hell* was similarly influenced. The educational theatre in particular pays heed to these matters. Skeleton scenery, unit sets, and highly selected elements of design are often used with highly realistic plays because of limited budgets and stage facilities. Such scenery determines the style of production rather than the play elements.

We have already pointed out that style becomes a special dramatic value when the director decides to produce a play in startling contrast with the period style in which it was written. Once the director decides to break away from the period of the play and to make scenery and costumes special values, this decision becomes a determinant of style. The physical production then affects the style of acting and directing. The scenery and costumes often dictate the style of modern plays as well as historical ones. Incidentally, the designer by his concept of the visual aspects of production may sometimes set the style for the director.

The director therefore determines the style of the play and its production from the over-all emotional character of the play; the degree of reality achieved by the playwright's treatment of the elements of dialogue, character, plot, and theme; the influence of the historical period of the play; the playwright's intention in writing the play; the practical limitations of budget, time, stage facilities, and personnel; and the settings and the costumes. The style chosen becomes a dramatic value and influences and controls the interpretation of the entire play and its production. Style is a strong unifying factor of interpretation and production. The direction, acting, scenery, costumes, lighting, and sound should be keyed to this factor. All the aspects of the play and its production will then be in harmony with one another.

Although a play and its production should usually be in one style, certain plays allow a change within the over-all style. Some plays may be realistic in general but may be expressionistic in one or more scenes. O'Neill's *The Hairy Ape* is an example: The Fifth Avenue scene is highly expressionistic, whereas the rest of the play is more nearly realistic. Kaufman's and Connelly's *Beggar on Horseback* is realistic except for Homer Cady's dream. Ibsen's *Peer Gynt* also changes style in the hall of the troll king scene, the insane asylum scene, and in the "button moulder" scene. However, each of these plays gains unity through one dominant style.

The average member of the audience has little knowledge of the aesthetic or technical aspects of style. Yet he is consciously or unconsciously aware of them. His awareness of them may consist only of his being vaguely dissatisfied with some aspect of a theatrical production, of his being momentarily jarred out of the illusion of lifelikeness the style has established. He is most often disturbed about a play or its production when the various parts have not been integrated into a whole. He has a compelling desire for unity which comes from style. His theatrical experience fails him to a serious degree when style is not established and maintained or is violated in terms of its proper logic.

The determination of style by the director and his establishment and maintenance of it in a production require a high degree of sensitivity, awareness, and perception. The style sometimes may elude definition or label, yet the director must be able to recognize it and create it for the audience. Style makes all the details and parts fall into place and creates order out of disorder. It charts the voyage of the theatrical experience for the audience. It gives the director the master blueprint for his overruling concept of interpretation and production.

Directorial Image

IN THE Introduction to this book it was pointed out that the chapters up to this point would make up the first four phases of play interpretation. Now we come to the fifth phase, which consists of synthesizing the previous phases into an interpretive pattern which will ultimately be based upon an over-all directorial image.

Although the general sequence of procedure is established by these five phases, it is useful to outline a specific procedural check-list and sequence. This, of course, cannot be everlastingly fixed but must be flexible. Each play demands its own particular approach. Individual directors differ in training, background, and temperament. Each must work out his own procedure for the task at hand. Nevertheless, in the interest of organized method, a sequence of procedure with some degree of universal applicability is proposed here. It is based primarily on the belief that creative interpretation depends upon great subjectivity on the part of the director in the first stages. Critical objectification should follow slowly and deliberately in the later stages. In other words, meaning and purpose should gradually evolve from the total emotional and intellectual impact of the play.

It is suggested, then, that the following should be considered interpretive points or cornerstones of approach, and this order should constitute the director's working procedure.

1. Creative preparation
   a. Receptivity to and evocation of images
   b. Response to world of playwright
2. Audience appeal
   a. Theatrical credibility
   b. Degree of audience involvement
   c. Compulsion
   d. Audience gratification
   e. Structural characteristics
3. Potential dramatic values
   a. Mood
   b. Mood variations

      c. Theme
      d. Character
      e. Plot
      f. Dialogue
  4. Focus and configuration of the play
      a. Relative dominance of dramatic values
      b. Type of play
      c. Style of play
  5. Over-all image

We will now make some brief remarks about these cornerstones of approach.

1. *Creative preparation*

a. Receptivity to and evocation of images

The impulse for creativity must be coupled with the director's positive, free, and willing responsiveness to images. He must, at this time, remain in a state of open and uninhibited sensitivity to stimuli flowing from the play as he reads it and imagines it in performance. His mind and emotions must be allowed to respond spontaneously and intuitively in order to accept all images, and he must make no rational effort to order them into a pattern. A pattern may be sensed and a tentative over-all image of the play may emerge. The director must remember that this larger image will later be subjected to critical analysis and his emotional responses will then be objectified (see pp. 10-17).

b. Response to world of playwright

After the director responds to the initial flow of images from the world of the play, he must seek to identify himself with the creative vision possessed by the playwright when he wrote the play. He may first become a part of this vision and later reconstruct it through the study and understanding of those social, political, cultural, and psychological stimuli which affected the play's origination. The discovery of the world of the playwright is a necessary and viable source of imagery for the director's preparation for the creative process (see pp. 14-15).

In the next three phases of interpretation—audience appeal, potential dramatic values, focus and configuration of the play— the director must try to put himself in the place of the audience and analyze its emotional and intellectual responses to the play.

2. *Audience appeal*

The first question about appeal involves the *theatrical credibility* of the play in terms of the level of illusion desired by the playwright. The director must ask himself whether he and, in turn, the audience can believe in the conceptual and plot premise and the accumulative fictional reality of the total play. Here the director's emotional response is checked with knowledge and experience. He compares everyday life around him with the theatrical illusion created by the playwright. The director is concerned with his own belief in the degree of verisimilitude of the play, but he is more concerned with the possible belief of the audience. He must ask whether it will believe and whether he can make it believe the play.

Next he must ask whether the audience will identify itself with the characters and will be sympathetic enough with them to care what their problems are, what they do, and how they adjust themselves. If a central character dominates the play, the question may relate almost entirely to this character. The audience must "root" for the hero and heroine or it must show some degree of partisanship and some depth of concern about the principal characters (see pp. 32-35, 117-18). This emotional adherence to characters and their cause is what we might simply call *audience involvement*. It is closely connected with the theatrical credibility of a play. If the audience believes the play, it is also sympathetic in some degree with the characters. It does not have to approve of the characters' desires, actions, states of mind, or physical conditions, but it must care enough about them to be actively interested in them.

Audience credibility and involvement predict *audience compulsion* (see pp. 57-60). The director must analyze his own and the audience's probable emotional response in terms of the play's pull, suspense, and holding power. Will the audience feel compelled emotionally to such an extent that it will desire in pleasant or thrilling anticipation to see and hear scene after scene and act after act of the play?

The next interpretive step is the director's consideration of the play's resolution. How satisfied will the audience be with the solution or lack of solution of the dramatic problem? Is the resolution dramatically logical and inevitable? If the audience has been persuaded to believe in the theatrical illusion created by the play, has been involved in it, and has felt its compulsion, then it must be gratified by the resolution. The audience must not be frustrated by dramatic illogicality. Certain emotional and intellectual expectations created by the play must be fulfilled. If, for example, Pirandello's *Right You Are* is directed and produced in a completely realistic style, the audience will feel tricked by the ending. If, however, the play is presented in some degree of nonrealism and the audience can be persuaded to believe it on the level of an allegory, the ending is satisfactory (see pp. 120-2). The director's determination of style or the level of theatrical illusion is a basis for belief and a ground rule for the entire game of make-believe which the audience must play if its expectations are to be guided and controlled. Such guidance and control lead to *audience gratification.*

From now on in the interpretive procedure the director becomes even more objectively analytical, critical, and technical. He next should analyze the play for its *structural characteristics* (see pp. 44-56). These characteristics include the *curve of intensity, inciting action, dramatic problem, climax, resolution, action in depth, unity,* and *texture.*

3. *Potential dramatic values*

The early readings for the imagistic responses will already have aroused a general feeling and sense of *mood.* Now, in this procedural step, the director will be able to refine the general into the particular in order to pinpoint more exactly the individual mood of the play. Objective analysis will take the place of free intuition and subjectivity. The director will learn the specific emotional nature of the play from the playwright's use of dialogue, character, plot, theme, and temporal and atmospheric elements.

In addition to an analysis for *mood variations,* the director will determine the function of mood in pervading the entire play and establishing a unity of impression. He will also understand the structural contribution of mood and its effect upon the design of the play.

The discovery of the dramatic potentials of *theme, character, plot,* and *dialogue* makes great demands upon the imaginative powers of the director. These parts of the play making up the totality can bring variety, freshness, and richness of dramatic appeal. The dramatic realization of these potentials will depend upon the director's personal originality, sensitivity, and depth of perception. The director's constant desire should be to find the richest possible tapestry of responses for the audience, designed and modified by the purpose of the play. His discovery of dramatic values places upon him the burden of selecting some values and rejecting others.

4. Focus and configuration of the play

The choice of values and the intention to emphasize certain ones, as we have already seen, result from the determination of the *relative dominance of dramatic values*, the focal points of the play. The determination of *type* and *style* of play will indicate its configuration.

The type of play, as we have seen, is strongly influenced by the play's prevailing mood. (As a matter of fact, the type of play often emerges simultaneously with the analysis for mood.) It is an aspect of the totality of the play and is emotional in nature. The degree of objectivity emanates from the critical evaluation involved in the director's analysis for the dominant dramatic value, the author's intention, and his application of critical criteria.

Like mood and type of play, style is strongly emotional and helps give the play shape. Like type of play, it may be influenced by mood. Its determination requires greater objective consideration than does type of play. The playwright's desire for a particular level of illusion, critical and historical influences, and the physical conditions of production are important.

5. Over-all image

The over-all image of a play is the director's highly subjective creative vision modified by his response to the world of the playwright and his critical analysis of the various elements of the play. This large image should be fragmented into smaller images for the various parts of the play. The director will find much of his free and early imagery usable if he will return to his first responses. The selection and modification of this imagery and a search for new imagery will furnish him with creative sources. He must never end his search for images and should establish a continuous flow of images which will maintain him in a creative state.

PRACTICE

In order to exemplify and test the director's procedure for creative interpretation, i.e., to find the directorial image of a play, let us select in the interest of brevity John Millington Synge's one-act play *Riders to the Sea*, a classic universally known and admired. Inasmuch as this short play embodies the general structure of the full-length play, it will serve to illustrate theory and practice.

1. *Creative preparation*

    a.   Receptivity to and evocation of images

The moment one reads the words "riders to the sea," a vivid literal image may spring to the mind: two or more figures on horseback riding toward the sea. At once it seems strange for them to ride to the sea, and the thought occurs that the image evoked by the title has a metaphoric meaning instead of a literal one. (All the way through the play the memory of the title will rise up in the mind of the reader and serve as a reference point.) The reader-director will respond imagistically in accordance with his knowledge and experience when he reads that the setting for the play is a cottage kitchen on "an Island off the west of Ireland," with nets, oilskins, some boards standing by the wall, a spinning wheel, a pot-oven, and a fireplace. Afterward he will probably have in mind a fairly definite picture of the setting. Then he will imagine the comings and goings of the characters throughout the play as the playwright indicates them in the stage directions. If he is capable of a double sort of imagination he will read and hear the dialogue and at the same time will see the behavior of the characters. He may have a sequence of definite and literal images of characters doing things and of their visual relationships to one another and the cottage. The ability to see the performance of the play in his mind's eye will depend upon his capacity for visualization.

Of course a director must have the ability to hear the dialogue of the play in his mind. The ideal director should be equally aware of and sensitive to the visual and the oral aspects of a play. (Most directors tend to be deficient in one of these aspects; they are either "deaf" or "blind.") Images are suggested by these aspects. The dialogue of *Riders to the Sea* is full of imagery, and the director will soon be conscious of it. Whereas the setting and the actions of the characters may be visualized literally, the sight of the words on the printed page and the imagined sound of them imply more than the literal and evoke the metaphoric and symbolic. Phrases like "There's a great roaring in the west" and "when the tide turns" (repeated several times in the opening speeches), "she holding him from the sea," "the pig with the black feet," and "a star up against the moon" quicken the imagination and take on meaning beyond literal images. One is struck by the frequent mention of the words "black," "white," "gray," and "red." "Black" in particular takes on significance. The phrases "the pig with the black feet," "the black night," "the dark night," "the dark word," "the black cliffs," "a black knot," and "the black hags" run throughout the play and hang in the air like so many yards of black crepe betokening death. The repeated description of Bartley's riding the red mare with the gray pony behind him soon turns into the picture of death following Bartley. The dripping red sail mentioned by Maurya, recalling the people bringing home the body of the drowned Patch, and the dripping sail in which Bartley's body is wrapped symbolize the loss of blood and life. And everywhere the sea, the tide, and the wind pervade the play like evil marauders and assume tragic significance.

Thus the director is surrounded by images—some vague and merely felt and others definitely perceived in the mind's eye as literal pictures or in the emotions and thoughts as metaphors and symbols. Soon they form themselves into a definite pattern, and meaning emerges. Images from words and phrases, the actions of the characters, the characters themselves, and the development of the story begin to suggest metaphorically the presence of death and life in conflict. If the director merges with the play, he will intuit meanings from it, and metaphoric and symbolic images will flood his mind and imagination.

A definite large image of the play will ultimately rise to his consciousness. It might very well be "a craggy rock with the sea lapping at it and wearing it away." Of course the rock symbolizes human life being destroyed little by little by the sea (Maurya's husband and her husband's father and all her sons, drowned one after another). The wearing away of the rock may be symbolized in *time* by the turning of the spinning wheel and symbolized in *life* by the stocking and shirt being woven by the spinning wheel for Michael and Bartley who are drowned. Developing further the imagery called to mind by the sea or tide, the rock, and the spinning wheel into a larger frame of reference, we see time and nature in tragic conflict with man (the rock), who is gradually but inevitably destroyed. And thus *Riders to the Sea* becomes a universally applicable symbolization of man's suffering and death.

b.   Response to world of playwright

An understanding of the world of the playwright and his creative vision must be derived from a knowledge of life on the islands west of Ireland, the three Aran Islands which belong to the county of Galway. They form a kind of natural breakwater lying across Galway Bay. The northernmost island is called Inishmore, the Great Island; the Middle Island is Inishman; and Inisheer is the Eastern Island. "Their formation is carboniferous limestone." These islands, with elevations of two hundred to over three hundred

and fifty feet, are cut off from the mainland and have a total area
of 11,579 acres. High, barren, and secluded, they could provide a
living only to stoics. One of the islands, Inishmore, called Aran,
became famous as an island resort for ascetics and teachers of
theology.[1] Here we find life as hard and barren as the rocks that
rise out of the sea and make the islands. There is little vegetation
here because there is little soil in which it can grow. However,
scrubby bushes, grass, flowers, and moss spring up from any soil
washed into the crevices between the rocks. But the sea is the
main source of life—and death. The people are seafaring, and have
been for generations. The wind, the sea, the tide, and the rocks
are constant reminders of their battle with nature.

Synge went to the Aran Islands in 1898 and in 1904 chose one
of them as the setting for his play *Riders to the Sea*. Synge's book
The Aran Islands is an account of his three years of experience with
the people of the islands. He absorbed their idiom and the minutiae
of their everyday living. He saw the women cooking in the fireplace where "turf" (peat) is used for fuel and he saw the women
spinning wool shorn from sheep who just barely managed to eke out
a living nibbling the green stuff between the rocks. And he saw the
menfolk soaked to the skin by the life-destroying salt water of the
sea when the waves beat against the sides of their fishing boats.
Through these routine events he saw the epic and tragic struggle for
life. Here in the Aran Islands he could see the magnificent spirit of
man. The film *Man of Aran,* a beautiful documentary of life on the
islands, corroborates Synge's earlier view and provides the director
of *Riders to the Sea* with knowledge essential to understanding the
world of the play.

It is said that John Millington Synge's forebear "sang so
sweetly in the royal chapel (England's Henry VIII) that Henry,
in amiable mood, bade him take the name of Synge or Sing, to
differentiate him, no doubt from the Millingtons who couldn't."[2]
The Synge of County Wicklow, Ireland, not only continued to use
the name bestowed by Henry but became the sweetest singer of
all. He was discovered in Paris in 1897 by William Butler Yeats,
one of the founders of Ireland's national theatre, the Abbey. Yeats
persuaded him to return to his native land to study the people of
the Aran Islands and write plays for the Irish Literary Society. The
dividends from the three-year period of study of the Aran Islands
were in the form of some of the greatest plays ever to come out of
Ireland. *Riders to the Sea* is one of them.

"Like the romanticist Yeats he recognized the importance of
instilling poetry into the modern drama which realism was threaten-
ing to make flat and pallid, but like a true realist, he shaped his

poetry out of colloquial speech."[3] In making imagination prevail, he created a poetic prose which elevated his plays to heights above mere realism and made himself unique among the great writers of modern drama. After writing the one-act *In the Shadow of the Glen,* produced in 1903 by the Abbey, he created *Riders to the Sea,* which the same theatre staged in 1904. This was followed by *The Well of the Saints. The Playboy of the Western World,* his best-known long play, opened at the Abbey on January 26, 1907, and created pandemonium in the audience. Though he was accused of satirizing the men and women of Ireland and was considered a traitor to his country, he refused to limit his imagination or humor and wrote *The Tinker's Wedding.* Afraid of being thought guilty of "satirizing the clergy and condoning immorality,"[4] the Abbey refused to produce it.

The unfinished *Deirdre* was his last play. He died when he was 39 years old, March 24, 1909. Though William Butler Yeats clamored for a national theatre and helped to found the Irish Literary Society, Synge's ten-year career as a playwright made Ireland's national theatre significant. No Irish dramatist other than Sean O'Casey has achieved such magnificent drama.

It is interesting to note that another great dramatist in the eastern part of the world was responsible for creating a similar kind of poetic realism out of his country's poverty, ignorance, and unrest. This was Anton Chekhov, who wrote his masterpieces *The Sea Gull, The Three Sisters,* and *The Cherry Orchard* during the same period in which Synge was productive. Both were objective while mingling poetry with reality.

Synge must be viewed in the light of the Irish Renaissance, which stemmed from a resurgence of nationalism inspired by Parnell, who was urging home rule in the British Parliament and an awakened interest in Ireland's Gaelic heritage. Scholars like Douglas Hyde and George W. Russell called loudly for a native literature. William Butler Yeats, Edward Martyn, and Lady Gregory specifically demanded an Irish national theatre and founded it in Dublin on May 8, 1899, with the premiere of Yeats' *The Countess Cathleen.* This was a stormy beginning but it was also a clarion call to other incipient Irish playwrights. By 1902 the National Dramatic Society was formed and a national theatre was a reality. Moreover, the theatre gained wide recognition as one of the foremost in the world. In 1904 Miss A. E. F. Horniman provided the means for building the Abbey Theatre, whose name to this day signifies the Irish theatre.

The Abbey took its place with those leading European theatres which also had begun new movements: the Théâtre Libre in Paris, the Freie Bühne in Germany, the Independent Theatre in London, and the Moscow Art Theatre of Stanislavski and Dantchenko. The awakening of native American theatrical talent came only a few years later.

Riders to the Sea, created out of an intense personal feeling for the people and the national dramatic impulse, because of its universal theme transcends its special environment and folkways to appeal to audiences all over the world.

2. *Audience appeal*

a. Theatrical credibility

The high degree of lifelikeness of this play will ensure audience belief in it. The simple sea folk, so like all people who live close to nature, are easily recognizable and sympathetic. Their speech and actions are completely believable. Motivation and causality operate strongly underneath all that happens. All the little actions like spinning, baking a cake in the fireplace, stirring the fire, getting the turf from the loft, taking the halter from the peg, sitting huddled around the fire, and keening are typical of the people and their environment. It is all appropriate, expected, and natural behavior which persuades the audience that it is looking at life. In fact, the audience watching this play will think that it is not only possible and credible but that there is no other way of presenting it. The level of illusion is that of high verisimilitude.

b. Degree of audience involvement

If the audience believes without question, as it does in this play, its involvement can be taken for granted. The degree of its emotional and intellectual participation will depend upon its actual acquaintance with these Irish people and its general knowledge of them. Most American audiences will not know these particular Irish fisher folk from actual association and observation but will recognize their similarity to the New England people who live near the sea and make their living from it. Even those members of the audience who are unfamiliar with sea folk anywhere will recognize the simple, unaffected way of life of a people close to nature: the taciturnity and determination of Bartley, the anguished but controlled feelings of Cathleen, Nora, and Maurya; the philosophical resignation and calm in the face of death and sorrow; the victimization of man by his environment and the forces of nature; the sympathy, understanding, and goodness of a people in a time of misfortune and unhappiness. Regardless of an audience's lack of familiarity with these particular characters, it will sympathize with and be moved by the sufferings of other fellow creatures. The humanitarian instinct will express itself and deeply involve the feelings and thoughts of the audience. In varying degrees all of us, regardless of our means of livelihood or environment, are subject to the whims and laws of nature. Audiences everywhere recognize and respond to this fact. The universal application and relevance of the meaning of the play are inescapable.

c. Compulsion

Audience involvement is often strongly based on the compelling power of the suspense generated by the sequence of actions and events. In *Riders to the Sea*, however, this compulsion takes the form of a suspense that comes from waiting to find out not what will happen next but how the characters will react to it. The outcome of the plot of this play is strongly foreshadowed by Maurya. Inevitability is inherent in the structure. Audience interest and compulsion stem from empathy with the characters and their behavior under stress rather than from the course of events.

Empathy with the characters is so strong that the audience will struggle against the inevitability of events and will hope that the characters will happily solve their dilemma and win the fight against man's common enemy, nature. Certainly partisanship works strongly in audience feeling and adds to the compulsion of the play.

d. Audience gratification

Though the resolution of the play may not bring happiness to an audience, it must be convincing in its dramatic logic. The audience's emotional and intellectual expectations must be fulfilled with a sense of aesthetic satisfaction and gratification. In addition, the resolution of the play must conform to the author's design and sense of artistic unity.

e. Structural characteristics

The architecture of the play springs from the subject matter and the author's intention. This classic and tragic subject, treating of man's struggle with the gods or forces of his universe, demands an appropriate and characteristic simplicity, economy, order, and arrangement of design and structure. Having selected the life of the Aran islanders for his subject, Synge elected to dramatize the elemental problem of their existence and to communicate a universal meaning in the Greek classic mold. Therefore, the structure of the play must be compact. This means that the elements of character, dialogue, plot, and theme must be organized in a tight interrelationship to create an easily felt arching *curve of intensity*. Nora's and Cathleen's exposition about the drowning of their brother in the sea and the grief of their mother clearly sets forth the facts of character, plot, and theme. The entrance of Maurya and the expression of her desire to keep Bartley from going to Connemara foreshadow a conflict with Bartley, who is determined to go that day. The *inciting action* propelling the play into motion is furnished by Bartley, the catalytic agent, when he refuses to accede to his mother's wishes and goes out the door to take his horse to the waiting boat. A temporary balance in the lives of the characters has been changed into a state of imbalance. The *dramatic problem* is then established and communicated. It is the springboard for the simple action of the play. Dramatic complications are Maurya's complaint that Bartley won't listen to her and the subsequent bitterness created between them. Her going out to take him his bit of bread as a peace offering is the result. This action is contrasted with that of Cathleen and Nora, who take the clothes down from the attic and confirm that they belonged to Michael. A further complication is the re-entrance of Maurya and her telling of having seen "the fearfulest thing." The highest emotional peak (the *climax*) of the play comes with the entrance of the mourning women and the men carrying the body, and the revelation of Bartley's drowning. The *resolution* comes with the preparation for Bartley's funeral, Maurya's blessing of the dead, and her resignation to the fate of man.

This play's *action in depth* is simple but rich. As the plot moves forward the characters progress from sorrow to conflict to a bigger sorrow and finally to enlightenment and peace. Here are outward and inward action in simultaneous and causal progression. The theme suggested in the opening scene of the play comes to full expression in Maurya's last speech.

The structure of the play possesses *unity* by virtue of its theme, action, time, place, and mood. The theme utilizes and integrates the other play elements in a controlled relationship to illustrate and communicate its meaning. The action is simple and straightforward without deviating from its straight line of concentrated cause and effect. Time is compressed and ties together the elements of a spare plot. The play occurs in one locale. The mood and atmosphere are single in their emotional tone and effect. The consistent seriousness, tension, sadness, and depth of feeling evoked underline and circumscribe all aspects of the play. The lyricism of the language tinges the entire play with poetry and a spiritual aura. In addition to these unifying elements, the centrality of Maurya's character focuses events and ideas.

The *texture* of *Riders to the Sea* is richly and evocatively emotional in its unity of style, mood, and kind of play, and interrelated structural elements. The absolute credibility of the entire play and the classic spirit pervading it create an aesthetic quality which is individual and beautiful. The layers of feeling created by the mood and the quality and quantity of emotion resulting from its tragic mold contribute to the audience's joy and satisfaction in a rich and rewarding theatrical experience. The choice, control, and ordering of the dialogue, characters, events, and theme weave a design of emotion and thought which has theatrical color, line, and form. The selection of particular words, their musical rhythm and imaginative qualities, their economy, directness, and clarity of communication are probably the chief textural features of the play. The theme adds weight and depth to the texture. The characters and their actions are strong in outline and deep in meaning. Here are depth, width, height, length, color, mass, and form—connotative and evocative—creating a theatrical experience of lasting and enriching value.

3. *Potential dramatic values*

a. Mood

In the preceding discussion of the subject of mood, that of *Riders to the Sea* was analyzed in general terms. Now, in approaching the play for direction, it is necessary to examine each mood determinant in detail in order to arrive at the over-all mood.

Certainly one of the strongest determinants is the dialogue. The melody of the Irish speech creates a rhythmic pattern which strongly affects the audience's emotions. The ebb and flow of it beats against our ears like the waves of the sea itself. The word order helps give the speeches their pulse. For example, taking a speech at random, let's listen to Cathleen as she speaks to Maurya: "Let you go down now to the spring well and give him this and he passing. You'll see him then and the dark word will be broken and you can say, 'God speed you,' the way he'll be easy in his mind."

The beat is definite and strong in its rise at the beginning of the sentences and in the fall at the end. The words "Let you go down now" are almost biblical in sound and suggest imagistically

Maurya's kneeling down in front of Bartley, "and he passing." This last phrase can conjure up the picture of a king riding by on his horse. The phrase "the dark word will be broken" suggests something portentous. Connotations and images leap to the mind and imagination throughout the dialogue. Surely the dialogue evokes feelings of sadness tinged with beauty.

The characters have their special tone. They are simply and sharply outlined. They are close to the earth and seem almost elemental. Their poverty, frugality, cleanness, and stoicism give them strength. They are uncomplicated and classic in outline. They are without the polish of education but have nobility of spirit. They are creatures of their environment, a way of life, and their heritage. They warm themselves with turf and use it for cooking food, ". . . it's only a bit of wet flour we do have to eat, and maybe a fish that would be stinking." Simple clothes and shelter and simple pleasures are their lot. They are patient, philosophical, and long suffering, wanting little except to live, love, and be loved. They are resigned to the omnipotence of the sea which symbolizes their fate. They are like the craggy rocks alternately resisting and yielding to the waves of the sea, which rise and fall against them with seductive caresses and brutal fury. Cathleen, Nora, Maurya, and Bartley are but children of sorrow who demand our respect and deep sympathy. They touch the heart.

The plot of the play is equally touching in its simplicity, revelations, and inevitability. It moves in an ever rising arc of pity and sadness.

The theme concerning man versus nature is serious and affecting. Here the fateful sea is implacable and man is the victim: "May the Almighty God have mercy on Bartley's soul, and on Michael's soul, and on the souls of Sheamus and Patch, and Stephen and Shawn; and may He have mercy on my soul, Nora, and on the soul of every one is left living in the world." Such a thought provokes pity and terror.

Contributing to the tone and mood are the locale and the house: "An island off the west of Ireland. A cottage kitchen, with nets, oilskins, spinning wheel, and some new boards standing by the wall, etc." A sense of isolation, bareness, loneliness, wind, and sea pervades the scene of action. It is cold and windy, "the wind rising from the South and West." The nets connote not only the sea but a trap for men and women no less than for fish. The spinning wheel symbolizes the wheel of time to which man is lashed. When the play begins, the wheel begins to turn and comes to full circle at the end.

Thus the play spins and weaves a mood pattern of somber

and moving pity and sadness which stirs the heart and leaves an indelible imprint on the mind.

b.   Mood variations

The variations of mood divide the play into units. As we have already seen in the explanation of mood units in Chapter 3, the first unit conveys a mood of uncertainty and suspense induced by whisperings and furtive actions; the second unit is short but serious and portentous in tone. We can continue with the third, which begins at Bartley's exit. Maurya cries out in protest and sorrow. Cathleen and Nora lighten the tension as they blame Maurya and urge her to go to the spring and give Bartley "God speed" as he passes by. The fourth unit creates yet another mood variation. As Cathleen and Nora hurry to bring down the bundle of clothes from the loft, suspenseful tension mounts and reaches a crescendo when they discover that the clothes do indeed belong to Michael and establish his death. Nora's weeping breaks the tension and evokes our pity. On hearing Maurya's footstep on the path outside the door, Cathleen and Nora hide the clothes against discovery by Maurya, and once more the audience is gripped in watchful waiting. The fifth mood unit begins with Maurya's slow and quiet entrance. This is followed by her keening, which further tightens the elastic of suspense. Synge stretches it as Maurya speaks in a frightened voice of the "fearfulest thing any person has seen . . ." When she says she has seen Michael, Cathleen's soft revelation that Michael's body was found does not shake Maurya's conviction that Michael rode by her on the gray pony which followed Bartley's red mare. Cathleen begins to keen, and a wail of sorrow mounts as Maurya intones her premonition of Bartley's death. The sixth variation of mood is marked by the girls' reaction to a noise they hear through the half-open door. The tension mounts through Maurya's recountal of the loss of her husband, of his father, and of Sheamus and Patch. The opening of the door and the entrance of the old women who cross themselves begins the seventh unit. This unit of quiet questioning and mourning leads into the entrance of the young women and the subsequent entrance of the men carrying the body of Bartley. This eighth unit builds to the revelation of Bartley's manner of dying. The soft keening of the women drops the tension into the quiet ninth variation, which is a requiem for the dead. When Maurya rises from her prayers, the tenth and last mood unit becomes a benediction for the dead and the living as the curtain slowly descends. The graph of these mood units shows a rising curve of intensity which slowly descends in a short line of relaxation.

We have already seen how the elements of theme, character, plot, and dialogue of *Riders to the Sea* create mood. Now it is necessary to find the special *emotionalizing and intellectualizing potentials within each element*. Some of these potentials have been pointed out above and will not be dwelt upon in this particular phase of our analysis. It must be remembered that up until now we have been concerned with the dramatic qualities of the totality of the play. We are now concerned with the qualities of the parts making up the total.

c. Theme

Let us analyze the theme values first. If the theme of a play sums up the principal characters' conflict and action and is the total emotional and intellectual significance of the play, that of *Riders to the Sea* might be expressed specifically by the statement that man is everlastingly locked in a mortal struggle with his environment and nature and must reconcile himself to his fate. The theme stems from the characters, who represent a class and kind and order of people—the people everywhere who live by the sea and die by it. These people also symbolize mankind in general in conflict with fate. From the beginning of time and to the end of time man is controlled by fate. In a sense all men are "riders to the sea." Here is a picture of man's fate in the little world of the Aran Islands. In the title *Riders to the Sea* there is an implication of the theme.

The theme is presented indirectly through the development of the plot and the words of Maurya, who as the chorus presents the theme by implication. The universal application and timeliness of the theme are readily apparent.

The director must determine his general concept of the play from its theme. The theme will guide the director and the actors in determining each moment of behavior of the characters and will hold the actors to their through-line of action. Moreover, the theme integrates the characters by giving them a point of reference.

d. Character

The characters and their relationships are clearly established in the first scene of the play. The audience learns who they are and what their problem is. The director must take care that voice and movement project those facts. Although Synge introduces Cathleen and Nora first, they are only supporting characters to Maurya, who is the principal character. The women and men who come in near the end of the play are merely subsidiary characters. At the outset the sea is established as the antagonist when Nora refers to the bundle of clothes "off a drowned man in Dunegal." We have already learned from their identifiable traits and pitiful plight that the characters are recognizable and sympathetic. The degree of audience familiarity has also been discussed. The expression of character will is apparent in Maurya's plea to Bartley not to go to the fair and in Bartley's determination to go. These are strong-willed people, and the audience admires such strength. They are not inactive. They challenge and fight against the antagonist, knowing full well that their fate is predestined.

The main relationship consists of Maurya and the sea. This is established at the outset and continues throughout. The playwright maintains it continuously, and it is the job of the director to emphasize it. He can point up the presence of the sea by means of the fishing nets and other fishing equipment. Placing the door and window on the upstage wall calls attention to the outside. The sound of the wind and waves and the characters' reaction to them will further emphasize the presence of the sea. The outside must be brought on stage at every opportunity.

The secondary relationship is that of Nora and Cathleen to one another. This stems, of course, from their mutual relationship to Maurya and to the sea. Cathleen is contrasted with Nora by her greater age and her calm management of the house. Cathleen gives the orders in the house, telling Nora to give her the ladder to the loft, telling Nora to give Bartley the "bit of new rope," urging Maurya to go down to the spring to give Bartley the bread, asking Nora to give Maurya the walking stick, and asking the men to make a coffin for Bartley. Nora, the youngest in the household, is like the classic messenger who brings in needful information about what has taken place outside and what takes place during the course of the action. Nora is the one who weeps and is the more excitable of the two girls. Age and simple traits give the characters contrast.

The greatest apparent growth of character takes place in Maurya. She moves from anguished struggle against the sea to a calm resignation and understanding of the meaning of life for man. Cathleen and Nora show a recognition of the irony of the transformation of a "great rower and fisher" into a thing symbolized by "a bit of an old shirt and a plain stocking."

Nora and Cathleen are not limned in detail. They are merely outlined by Synge, and yet they give the appearance of full dimensionality. We have seen that they have their simple individualizing and recognizable traits, and function in accordance with the purpose of the play. We find them in crisis, and they behave consistently with their natures, background, and environment. Bartley is drawn in sharp outline—quiet but determined. Maurya is an old woman, broken by grief and care. However, she still fights to preserve her sons and her home. Hers is a strong, asserting will, finally crushed. She looks forward to inevitable death and has provided for it by buying clean white boards for a coffin. She is determined that the dead will be buried with dignity and respect. She possesses the wisdom of life and is clairvoyant of death. She prophesies the approach of death and is visited with the fantastic picture of it. She has lost her place as active head of the family and is obedient to the urgings of her older daughter and helpless against the determination of her son. She is guided by a sense of fate but rebels against it. She is physically weak and spends a great deal of time in bed. And "It's hard set [she is] to walk" and might "slip on the big stones" outside. She seeks warmth at the fire.

Each of the characters expresses an individual objective in the common effort to preserve the family. This objective is divided into units which are accomplished by specific tasks. Each character adjusts to actions and events in order to obtain each unit and the overruling objective. Cathleen's objective might be said to be a desire to run the house by preparing food, making clothing, and keeping the fire going. She nourishes the family. She is the mother of the family now that Maurya is old. Nora's objective is to help Cathleen. Bartley's objective is to provide for the family's livelihood. Maurya's objective is to fight against a force predestined to destroy the men of her family. Physically Cathleen is sturdy, slow, and controlled in her movements. Her activity is devoted to household tasks. Synge indicates that she is about twenty years old. Nora is quick and light in movement. We can guess that she is about fifteen years old and in the innocent wonder of youth. Both girls have gone to school to life and have had little formal education. Both have the strength of character of their mother. Bartley is older than Nora and Cathleen. He moves slowly, with purpose and strength. He has worked hard and has struggled against stone and sea. He lives among other men like him and cares for his horses. He has the confidence that grows out of physical labor and strength. And he has the daring of a man who has fought nature and animals. His education has been provided by work and by the wisdom of his father and mother. There are three old women, who are contrasted in appearance and age, as are the two younger women. Two middle-aged men, followed by an old man and two boys, bring in the body. They too differ in appearance. Yet both women and men belong to the same stock and background. They are widows, wives, sisters, husbands, and brothers—all Irish sea folk.

All show the scars of a hard life. No one is fat. All are old for their age. All move without waste of motion. There is something of the rhythm of rowing boats in their individual and collective simultaneous rhythm. They tend to act as a group. They are the mourning chorus.

The actors for this play must possess the appearance and tonality of the characters they represent. They must be actors who look wiry and strong and have stable dispositions. There is nothing neurotic about the characters. The actors must possess rich, sonorous, and musical voices controlled by good ears for dialect. Nora's soprano voice, Cathleen's contralto, the deeper contralto of Maurya, the baritone voice of Bartley, and the voices of the other women and men comprise a choir which can sing as soloists in counterpoint and as a group in keening unison.

Each character possesses warmth and hardness. None of them is soft or weak. Each has innate seriousness and heaviness born of the grim necessity of making a livelihood and battling his environment. All the characters are close to the earth and the sea and are tough fibered and possessed of a simple dignity. Their tonality is easily recognizable and felt by the audience. The men and women mourners are rugged, strong, and simple, too.

e.   Plot

The basic situation of the play is made quickly apparent to the audience, and the director persuades the audience to accept it. It results from the conflict of the characters with the sea and presages dramatic action. Past events unfold and act upon the present when the clothes of a drowned man are thought to be Michael's and are hidden in the loft by Nora and Cathleen in an attempt to prevent Maurya's seeing them. Cause and effect are immediately operative. The director must carefully underscore all dialogue revealing and forwarding plot and must control the voices and movements of the actors to clarify and emphasize each plot unit. The mood units already indicated can be used to mark plot units in this play. Entrances and exits seem to divide the play into such units. We notice that the first unit is a "twosome scene," the second a "threesome scene," the next a "foursome scene," then a twosome scene, threesome again, and a group scene which enlarges with each entrance.

The plot premise is complete when Bartley exits. The rest of the play develops out of the material comprising the premise. The action springs out of conflict. The first implication of conflict is indicated by Nora's and Cathleen's hiding the clothes from Maurya.

Overt conflict builds into crisis in the scene between Maurya and Bartley. This is followed by the conflict between Cathleen and Maurya. The scene in which Nora and Cathleen examine the bundle of clothes and find evidence of their being Michael's is a scene of implied conflict with the sea. Maurya's entrance and mournful references to her vision are a scene of internal conflict which becomes an outer one when Cathleen urges her to tell what she has seen. This, of course, builds to the climactic revelation of Bartley's death and the resolution which comes in Maurya's prayer for the dead and recognition of man's fate.

The plot is simple and consists of only a few carefully chosen situations. Overt action is brief and limited. Internal action is simple and telescoped. The spare action is unified and does not wander from its straight line.

The director's job in projecting plot values consists of clearly revealing and emphasizing them by words and action and intensifying them by the directorial techniques necessary to establish, change, and maintain the rhythm of the performance. As the action rises to a climax the intensity increases accordingly.

f.   Dialogue

The dialogue of the play reveals the past and forwards character, plot, and theme. It is used very little for exposition. Actions and events charge it with deeply affective emotion. It comes appropriately and naturally from the characters and, moreover, individualizes each one. It is both credible and heightened by the poetic qualities which have been referred to previously. The phraseology and choice of words bring richness and surprise to character utterance. Such expressions as "and there was a star up against the moon" and "you can tell herself he's got a clean burial by the grace of God" and "who would listen to an old woman with one thing and she saying it over" have music and the surprise of utterance in them. The play is filled with emotional and thought-provoking words, a strong rhythm and melody, and images arising out of active, colorful characters and the sad events of their lives. The dialogue must be protected and savored by the actors to communicate all its rich, poetic beauty and dramatic power.

4.   *Focus and configuration of play*

a.   Relative dominance of dramatic values

The reading and study of Synge's play make theme, character, and mood dominant dramatic values. It is not an easy matter to determine their order of importance. However, as we put the play down and consider the aspect which remains in our consciousness and memory, the theme of the play stands out. The character of Maurya, however, is not easily forgotten. The mood and language are also potent and affective. The plot is so thin that what happens seems accessory rather than principal. Surely character, language, mood, and plot are selected and ordered to subserve the theme. And this is indicative of the author's intention and purpose. The director and actors will not need to look for many facets of character or psychological complexities. Simple, definite, and restrained strokes will suffice to project the characters. Yet everything is based on truth. The directorial burden is the theme of the play illustrated by character and plot, suggested by dialogue, and strongly abetted by mood. The director must exercise care and imagination to find the methods to communicate the significance of the total emotional and intellectual impact of the play.

b.   Type of play

The mood of *Riders to the Sea* is of such gravity and magnitude, and so deeply stirring of pity and evocative of terror at man's helplessness against fate that the play surely seems to be a classic tragedy. The last scene may not achieve a true catharsis in the Aristotelian sense but the emotional effect is akin to one. The dominant dramatic values are utilized and shaped to the demands of tragedy. Here the craggy, granite-like Maurya certainly possesses the stature of a tragic figure as she accepts with dignity her fate and that of all mankind. Her towering strength in adversity can only claim universal admiration. Maurya symbolizes her kind, the fisher folk everywhere who go down to the sea in ships. The "general atmosphere or spirit of the play enwraps the whole development of the 'fable'" and is appropriate for tragedy. The subject and theme are of sufficient seriousness and magnitude. The somber but lyrical mood circumscribing the play raises it to the level of tragedy, "tinges the characters with a peculiar predominating hue,"[5] and achieves a universality necessary for tragedy. Tragic irony is manifest here in Maurya's attempts to dissuade Bartley from going to the fair on a day when the "wind is raising the sea" and in Bartley's decision to go to the fair because "the fair will be a good fair for horses" and he must "go now quickly" because "This is the one boat going for two weeks or beyond it . . ." Here is a warping of good intentions by the gods. The imaginative qualities of the dialogue elevate the characters and their actions. Without a doubt the play possesses the recognizable critical criteria for tragedy. Allardyce Nicoll, a well-known English historian and critic, calls it a "short tragic essay, unrelieved in its tension . . . with an atmosphere . . . [which] comes close to the true spirit of the tragic."[6] John Gassner, an American critic, refers to it as "This tragedy of an Aran mother . . . [which] lives most fully as music and might well be defined as a tone-poem."[7] And tragedy it is by the author's intention. Man's conflict with nature is its tragic source, and the nobility of mankind in the face of suffering and defeat is expressed in the indomitable spirit of the characters. The music of Synge's language charges the play with an emotion which transcends the prosaic lower forms of drama. The simple and spare classic action grips the attention without respite as it moves to its predestined climax and resolution with a unity of emotional effect.

c.   Style of play

The pervading emotional nature of Synge's play, with its stern, hard, and majestic qualities, lifts the spirit notwithstanding its power to cause suffering and points toward a kind of modern frame of reference, though inherently classic in feeling. An examination of the elements of dialogue, character, theme, and plot results in an impression of realism, selected, motivated, appropriate, recognizable, and wholly credible. The dialogue captures the music and possesses the conviction and reality of the native Irish speech of the Aran Islands. It is conversational, yet transformed by the alchemy of art. Its word economy and imagery and strongly felt rhythm give it a simple grandeur characteristic of Greek classicism. The characters have the simplicity and strength of outline created by Sophocles. They have a basic psychology needed for reality but without the complexity of the naturalistic. They are representative and individualistic, though heightened and intensified. They are both functional and credible. The theme possesses the universality typical of classical writing. The straight development of the unrelieved tension of the plot gives it classic tightness of structure. Maurya is not unlike a Greek chorus commenting on the action, and yet she is also a classic protagonist. The playwright's over-all treatment of the play elements results in a realistic style suffused with classic qualities of selectivity, formality, "size," and the ritualistic. The play has the complete illusion of life, representational but implicitly classic in spirit. The play was written for the modern picture-frame stage and demands an audience-actor relationship typical of the realistic theatre; yet the level of illusion created by the play is raised above that of conventional realism. Modern classicism is a hybrid term which seems to contain the style of the writing.

As a representative of the Irish literary and theatrical renaissance, *Riders to the Sea* is the agony of the common man. Though the characters are specifically Irish in speech, thought, and tradition, they are universal in significance. This play, like all those produced by the Abbey Players, focuses on some part of the national scene. It is folk drama elevated to the highest pinnacle of art. Synge was a keen observer of and a sensitive listener to life in the Aran Islands. Yet he was not merely a reporter of folkways but an artist who could transmute all he saw and heard into art. The particular possessed for him beauty and universality.

This play is based in reality by its environment, but it is enveloped in a mood of somber beauty which lifts it to tragedy not unlike that of the Greeks. Like all great work, it exists on the level of allegory as well as on that of reality. The symbolic nature of the action and of the characters connotes the destiny of mankind. Its meaning is universally recognized.

5.   Over-all image

After the director's creative preparation for the interpretation of the play and a close critical analysis of its structure and dramatic values comes the over-all interpretive image. In his progress to this image the director has become more and more critical, rational, and objective. He has lost much of his initial uninhibited, spontaneous emotional response. In order to recapture this feeling and to formulate a clear creative vision of interpretation and production, he must return to that very first phase of creative preparation made just after his first readings of the play. He must recall his imagistic responses, select them, modify them, and make them conform to his study and analysis of the play. He must discipline his images without destroying their creative stimuli.

The intuitive over-all image of *Riders to the Sea* as a "craggy rock with the sea lapping at it and wearing it away" will be found a valid source of creativity. The smaller images of the parts of the play will be equally usable. First of all the director can communicate the large image in the production scheme. Then he can break down the play and find an image for each scene, each character, and each unit of behavior. Any image, large or small, used by the director is a directorial image.

Starting off with the setting, the director can think of it as an ancient sea wall, made of stone, concrete, and wood. It is gray, water stained, and crumbling. It is a place of refuge and comfort from wind and sea. When this is translated into the cottage kitchen of the play, the director and designer can visualize cracks in the walls and gray-green corners. The rough-hewn wood in the door and window frames is bleached, knotty, and gnarled like driftwood. The table, the simple, open china cabinet, the benches, stools, and ladder should also have a gray and rough-hewn look—home made. The irregularly cut beams overhead, once gray, are smoked and warped. The nets, coils of rope, oilskins, boat oars, and a wooden bucket speak of fishing and the sea. The lines of the walls, doors, and windows are not true and look as though the wind and water had changed them and made them slightly misshapen. The cottage too has been the victim of the implacable wind and sea.

The light is gray like fog. It becomes progressively darker, with shadows crouching in the corners, and the light from the fire throws gray shadows on the walls when the old keening women enter. When the men bring in Bartley's body the shadows become more black and festoon the room with sorrow.

In seeking an image for each scene of the play the director should select one which will be stimulating for him and the actors of the scene. For example, the opening scene of the play, which is between Cathleen and Nora, might be identified with the image of *secrecy*. Verbalized, the image suggests the action *to hide*. This keys the scene for both actresses: They must *hide* their voices by whispering and their movements by walking and doing things noiselessly. At the same time both must be alert to possible noises from the other room which would signal the entrance of Maurya. This does not mean that Cathleen and Nora behave exactly the same in this scene. The image *to hide* would be adjusted to the individual and distinguishing psychology of each, conceptualized by each actress' image of her character.

Cathleen might be seen as the foster mother. She cooks for the family. (It is symbolic that she is the one who thinks of sending Bartley the bread.) She also provides clothing for the family and is seen at the spinning wheel at the beginning of the play. As mother of the family she tells Nora and Maurya what to do. And Bartley gives her instructions to be carried out in his absence. He recognizes her as head of the family when he is away. She asks an old man and Eamon to make the coffin for Bartley. Nora might be seen as Cathleen's contact with the outside world. She is a receiver and a reactor. She is an alert, quick, and sensitive human instrument. She is a tender, growing plant. Therefore the image of secrecy will be reflected differently in Cathleen and Nora. Cathleen is more controlled and subtle in expressing the image. For example, Cathleen does not get up immediately from the spinning wheel when Nora tells her that they are to find out whether the bundle of clothes is Michael's but waits until Nora moves to the table to open the bundle. Her secrecy and apprehension may be seen only in looks, a slight gesture, or movement. Her voice is controlled and she speaks low without apparent tension. Nora is more open in her expression of the secrecy. Her whispering is louder; her actions are quicker and tenser than Cathleen's; she may at times use her whole body in response to an emotion.

An image can be used in visualizing the characters who come in with Bartley. Each old woman, young woman, old man, and boy can be cast and interpreted in terms of the director's particular image of him. The rocks, seaweed, sea shells, and other natural phenomena may suggest images of people, whose behavior and especially whose keening must be evoked and controlled by the image of the group as a mass and varied by the images of the individuals. By helping the actors find images to stimulate their emotions the director will bring reality and truthfulness to the scene. The sound of wind and waves can be suggestive to the director and the actors for the orchestration of the keening. The more formal and classical the director's concept of the keening, the more will the mourners suggest visually and orally a Greek chorus.

Imagery, then, can be used in interpretation, direction, and production. It is the director's creative stimulant. However, once the director establishes a definite over-all image of the play, he should sink it into his subconscious and keep it there to monitor and stimulate further creativity. Finally, the image should be transformed into the means of communicating the play to the audience. In the words of Stark Young, that rare critic who understands both the philosophical and creative aspects of theatre, "The director . . . tries to translate as closely as possible into the theatrical medium the idea or characteristic quality of the play he directs. He reads and responds to the play; in him the experience that the dramatist created is re-created, he lives it again, he decides what its quality is to be, and with the means at hand sets out to express this quality."[8]

Illustrations

The following scenes from plays directed by Frank McMullan represent various uses of the directorial image in interpretation and production.

1. Actor's Image: "Earth and Heaven Spin In Wild Discord"

Frontispiece

OTHELLO: Shakespeare

Costumes by Robert Abel; lighting by Max Stormes

Produced at the Shakespeare Festival, Old Globe Theatre, San Diego, California

This is a moment in Act III, scene 3, just after Othello's soliloquy praising Iago's honesty and knowledge of human beings and questioning Desdemona's faithfulness. Othello's agony is intensified as he contemplates the globe, compares the big world with his private world, unconsciously holds his hands as though he would choke Desdemona, and says, "If she be false . . ."

2. Scene Image: "A Wall of Men Dominated"

CORIOLANUS: Shakespeare

Scenery by Keith Cuerden; costumes by Zelma Weisfeld; lighting by Sumner Pecker

Produced at the Yale University Theatre

The image of the scene is dramatically pictorialized by the lines of the setting and the composition of the actors. The two strong vertical lines in the center of the stage, representing the gates to Corioli, sharply contrast with the horizontal lines of the steps. The latter strengthen the longer line of the Roman soldiers stretched across the stage. But the Volscian senators and their guards, raised to a level higher than the Romans, and backed by the vertical lines of the gates together with the vertical lines of the massed pikes and standards, tend to give the Volscians an appearance of dominating strength.

3. Creative Boldness: "A Quixotic Dream"

THE TAMING OF THE SHREW: Shakespeare

Scenery by Jackie Beymer; costumes by Frank Poole Bevan; lighting by Pete Howard

Produced at the Yale University Theatre

The play was interpreted as Christopher Sly's dream, in which Sly turns into Petruchio and becomes a part of the play-within-a-play presented by a group of strolling actors at a lord's castle. At the end of the play, Sly-Petruchio returns to his bed and, as he snores, the actors steal away.

The director and the designer used the form of the Elizabethan stage, with forestage and inner and upper stages. In the spirit of both Elizabethan and *commedia dell'arte* performances, the action took place in the various stage areas and also in the aisles of the theatre. The color scheme of yellow and green, together with the two-dimensional cut-out decorative elements frankly painted, emphasized the theatricalism of the production.

Here Sly is seen interrupting the performance by prompting the actors.

4. The *World of the Playwright: "Awakening and Rebellion"*

LOOK HOMEWARD, ANGEL: Adapted by Ketti Frings from the novel by Thomas Wolfe

Scenery and costumes by Clarence Salzer; lighting by Bernardo Trumper

Produced at the Teatro de Ensayo, Santiago, Chile

In this autobiographical play of Thomas Wolfe's remembrance of his youth, the past is seen as a warm, lethargic summer evening hiding adolescent rebellion. Here Eugene (Wolfe) sits alone with his dreams, hardly aware of the guests in his mother's boarding-house, which is made of gauze and designed in a stylized manner to help dramatize filmy thoughts and memories.

5. Mood: *"Summertime Storm and Autumnal Peace"*

AH, WILDERNESS: O'Neill

Scenery, costumes, and lighting by Charles Rogers

Produced at the Wellesley Summer Theatre

The all-pervading mood created by these three different groups is one of sadness somewhat objectified by the perspective of time. Yet this late summer evening scene of middle-class American family life of the first decade of the twentieth century moves the audience to a feeling of nostalgia for the past and warm sympathy for the Millers, who have problems exactly like those of families today.

The period furniture, decorative detail, gas lights, and the clothes, body positions, and spatial relationships of the actors are the technical means of communicating the mood.

6. Points of Focus, Character and Theme: "Ascent from Darkness to Light"

FAUST, PART I: Goethe

Production designed by Frank Poole Bevan; lighting by Stanley McCandless

Produced at the Yale University Theatre

The world of Faust is a ladder; each rung marks a turning point in his life. Here he has climbed the steps upward out of the darkness of the suicidal thoughts he had when he was in his study below. He now searches for the light of truth, understanding, and happiness. Line, space, area, mass, and light focus audience attention upon the dramatic values of the inner struggles of character and the meaning of the play.

7. Style: "Comic-Strip Circus"

THE MERCHANT: Adapted by Arthur Wilmurt from Plautus

Scenery by Donald Oenslager; costumes by Frank Poole Bevan; lighting by Stanley McCandless

Produced at the Yale University Theatre

This Roman comedy was presented with comic-strip characters who, in the spirit of vaudeville, maintained a free and frequent contact with the audience. The use of a permanent portal and a backdrop with two doorways (one with a saloon-like set of swinging doors), all frankly cartooned and painted accordingly, permitted a degree of stylization in movement and stage groupings which was characterized by simultaneity and automatism.

8. Style: "Heightened Reality of a Parable"

MEASURE FOR MEASURE: Shakespeare

Scenery by Otis Riggs; costumes by Barbara Curtis

Produced at the Shakespeare Memorial Theatre, Stratford-on- Avon, England

The nonrealistic scenery, consisting of a permanent portal with a traverse curtain to separate forestage from inner stage suggested a symbolic locale. The decorative detail, the street scene painted on the traverse curtain, and the set pieces for use on the inner stage, which was backed by a silk cyclorama, created a scenic environment appropriate for a romantic morality play with thematic implications for a modern audience.

9. Style: *"Romantic Fancy Revealing Reality"*

THE TEMPEST: Shakespeare

Scenery by Gordon Micunis; costumes by Joy Pranulis; lighting by Steven Arnold

Produced at the Yale University Theatre

The play was interpreted as an image of the world represented by an enchanted island upon which wrecked lives are cast in order to purge them of delusions through suffering which leads to ultimate salvation. Prospero, a deluded victim of misplaced faith and shocking betrayal, undergoes a spiritual tempest before conjuring up a storm to bring his shipwrecked enemies to the island for punishment and the discovery of each one's proper place in a new "commonwealth." Ariel, Caliban, and Miranda, aspects of Prospero himself, are seen in ritualistic progression in the symbolical pattern of spiritual awakening.

The setting, made of various shades of green transparencies, fanciful shapes, and solid masses, reflected the nature-world of the sea and island vegetation, and also the illusions, ordeals, visions, and revelations of the world of the play.

In this photograph of the production Prospero, through the agency of the creative spirit of Ariel, has called forth the masque in celebration of the forthcoming marriage of Ferdinand and Miranda.

10. Directorial Image: "A Forum for Truth"

RIGHT YOU ARE: Pirandello

Scenery by Alvin Schecter; costumes by Richard Bianchi; lighting by Bernardo Trumper

Produced at the Yale University Theatre

This production was imagined as the representation of an improvised theatrical performance of a drama, the enactment of which was forced upon the innocent neighbors of the people of a provincial Italian town: the doorway up center opened onto the stage for the principal characters of the melodrama to be acted out by the Ponza-Frola family; the level left was used for the most part by Laudisi, the stage-manager-commentator; the large central area was the meeting place of the townspeople.

In the last scene, shown here, the command performance is coming to a close, with the townspeople characters standing with their backs to us—thus becoming a part of the theatre audience—waiting in suspense for the resolution of the play. At the exit of Signora Frola the curtain at the door falls and Laudisi, who has joined the audience in watching the performance, asks the gossipy townspeople whether they are "satisfied" and then suddenly turns to the theatre audience and asks, "Are you?" Curtain.

REFERENCES

1. Creativity and the Director (Pages 3-21)

1. "The Staging of a Play," *Esquire* (May 1959), pp. 144-53.
2. May 10, 1959.
3. Harold Clurman, *Lies Like Truth* (New York, Macmillan, 1958), pp. 60-2.
4. New York, McGraw-Hill, 1959, p. 139.
5. *The Fugitive Art, Dramatic Commentaries 1947-1951* (London, John Lehmann, 1952), p. 88.
6. *A Life in the Theatre*, p. 139.
7. *The Man Who Lived Twice* (New York, Charles Scribner's Sons, 1956), p. 48.
8. Guthrie, *A Life in the Theatre*, p. 139.
9. Samuel T. Coleridge, *Lectures and Notes on Shakespeare and Other Dramatists* (New York, Harper, 1853), p. 54.
10. John Gassner, "The Source, the Path, the Vision: A Relativistic View," *Educational Theatre Journal*, XL, 4 (December, 1959), 263.
11. *Ibid.*, p. 261.
12. *Music and Imagination* (Cambridge, Mass., Harvard University Press, 1952), p. 41.
13. *Ibid.*, p. 42.
14. *Philosophy in a New Key* (Cambridge, Mass., Harvard University Press, 1942, 1951), p. 259.
15. P. 42.
16. In John Gassner, *Producing the Play* (Rev. ed.; New York, Dryden Press, 1953), pp. 275-6.
17. "Form in Production," in Gassner, *Producing the Play*, pp. 299-300.
18. "The Use of Images" (New York, Harper, 1953), pp. 25-6.
19. 2d ed.; London, Macmillan, 1905, pp. 331-400.
20. G. Wilson Knight, *The Wheel of Fire* (London, Methuen, 1949), p. 1.
21. *Ibid.*, p. 3.
22. William Wordsworth, "Preface to Lyrical Ballads," in *Literary Criticism: Pope to Croce*, Gay W. Allen and Harry H. Clark, eds. (New York, American Book Co., 1941), p. 216.
23. Pp. 45-6.
24. *Creative Intuition in Art and Poetry* (New York, Meridian Books, 1955), p. 48.
25. P. 49.
26. Copland, p. 52.

2. Dramatic Communication and Response (Pages 22-38)

1. February 18, 1957, pp. 38-40.
2. John M. Brown, *The Art of Playgoing* (New York, W. W. Norton, 1936), p. 118.
3. Clayton Hamilton, *The Theory of the Theatre and Other Principles of Dramatic Criticism* (New York, Henry Holt, 1939), p. 20.
4. *The New York Times Magazine*, April 29, 1951.
5. Arthur Miller, *All My Sons* (New York, Reynal & Hitchcock, 1947), Act I, (New York, Meridian Books, 1960), pp. 290-1.
6. Princeton, Princeton University Press, 1949, p. 32.

7. John E. Dietrich, *Play Direction* (New York, Prentice-Hall, 1953), pp. 43-5.
8. *The Art of Playgoing*, p. 17.
9. *Ibid.*, pp. 20-1.
10. *Ibid.*, p. 24.
11. *Ibid.*, p. 22.
12. Paris, Libraire Plon, 1943, p. 220.

3. Nature and Pattern of Drama (Pages 39-68)

1. Cleanth Brooks and Robert B. Heilman, *Understanding Drama* (New York, Henry Holt, 1945), p. 25.
2. P. 17.
3. Gassner, *Producing the Play*, p. 20.
4. Dietrich, pp. 30-1.
5. Arthur Miller, *All My Sons* (New York, Reynal & Hitchcock, 1947), Act I, p. 36.
6. Frank H. O'Hara and Marguerite H. Bro, *Invitation to the Theater* (New York, Harper, 1938, 1951), p. 122.
7. John Gassner, Introduction to *Death of a Salesman*, in *Best American Plays*, Third Series—1945-1951 (New York, Crown, 1952), p. 2.
8. *Ibid.*, p. xxvii.
9. Carson McCullers, *The Member of the Wedding* (New York, New Directions, 1951), Act III, scene 2, p. 111.
10. Gassner, *Producing the Play*, p. 22.
11. Act I, p. 3.
12. *Ibid.*
13. Act I, p. 5.
14. "Tragedy and the Common Man," February 27, 1949.
15. Gassner, *Producing the Play*, p. 34.
16. New York, Harcourt, Brace, 1927, p. 130.
17. S. H. Butcher, *Aristotle's Theory of Poetry and Fine Art* (4th ed.; New York, Dover Publications, 1951), p. 290.
18. Thomas De Quincy, "On the Knocking at the Gate in 'Macbeth,'" in *Selected Writings of Thomas De Quincy*, Philip Van Doren Stern, ed. (New York, Random House, 1937), pp. 1090-5.
19. William Shakespeare, *Macbeth* (Cambridge, Cambridge University Press, 1947), Act II, scene 3, p. 29.
20. Pp. 377-8.
21. William Shakespeare, *Hamlet* (Cambridge, Cambridge University Press, 1948), Act III, scene 2, p. 68.

4. Potentials of Dramatic Values (Pages 69-147)

1. St. John Hankin, *The Constant Lover*, in *The Dramatic Works of St. John Hankin* (London, Martin Secker, 1912), II, 229.
2. Walter Kerr, *How Not To Write a Play* (New York, Simon & Schuster, 1955), pp. 51-67.
3. Pp. 100-9.
4. P. 253.
5. P. 255.
6. In Gassner, *Producing the Play*, p. 277.
7. Act I, p. 31.
8. Act II, pp. 68-9.

9. Knight, pp. 73-96.
10. Tennessee Williams, *A Streetcar Named Desire* (New York, New Directions, 1947), pp. 142-4.
11. Pp. 544-85.
12. Anton Tchekov, *The Three Sisters*, Act I, in *The Plays of Anton Tchekov*, Constance Garnett, tr. (New York, Modern Library, 1930), p. 121.
13. Act II, p. 148.
14. Act IV, p. 185.
15. Henrik Ibsen, *The Wild Duck*, Act V, in *Plays by Henrik Ibsen* (New York, Modern Library, no date), p. 118.
16. Brooks and Heilman, p. 114.
17. *Ibid.*, pp. 86-7.
18. William Shakespeare, *King Lear*, Act I, scene 1, in *The Temple Shakespeare* (London, J. M. Dent, 1917), pp. 1-5.
19. *All My Sons*, Act I, p. 4.
20. Gassner, *Producing the Play*, p. 13.
21. Worthington Minor, "Directing the Play: the Complete Procedure," in Gassner, *Producing the Play*, p. 218.
22. *All My Sons*, Act I, pp. 1-2.
23. Act I, p. 22.
24. Act I, pp. 21, 25.
25. Act I, p. 26.
26. Act I, p. 2.
27. Act I, pp. 2-3.
28. Act I, p. 29.
29. Act I, p. 34.
30. Act I, p. 11.
31. Act III, p. 78.
32. Act III, p. 80.
33. Gassner, *Producing the Play*, p. 22.
34. *All My Sons*, Act I, pp. 14, 16, 18.
35. Alan R. Thompson, *The Anatomy of Drama* (Berkeley and Los Angeles, University of California Press, 1946), p. 39.
36. Stark Young, *The Theatre* (New York, Hill & Wang, 1954), p. 20.
37. Act II, pp. 62-3.
38. Act I, pp. 3-4.
39. Scene 1, p. 31.
40. Anton Tchekov, *The Sea-Gull*, Act I, in *The Plays of Anton Tchekov*, p. 7.
41. *A Streetcar Named Desire*, scene 8, p. 127.
42. Sidney Kingsley, *Dead End*, Act II, in *Twenty Best Plays of the Modern American Theatre*, John Gassner, ed. (New York, Crown, 1939), p. 710.
43. Scene 1, p. 27.
44. Edward J. Gordon, "Teaching Students To Read Verse," *The English Journal* (March, 1950), p. 151.
45. Act II, p. 19.
46. *Everyman*, in Brooks and Heilman, p. 89.
47. George Lillo, *The London Merchant*, Act II, scene 4, in Brooks and Heilman, p. 156.
48. Richard Sheridan, *The School for Scandal*, Act I, scene 1, in Brooks and Heilman, pp. 197, 200, 204, 205, 216.
49. Oscar Wilde, *Lady Windermere's Fan*, Act I, in Brooks and Heilman, pp. 35, 36.
50. Act I, scene 1, in Brooks and Heilman, pp. 196-7.

51. Act II, in *Arthur Miller's Collected Plays* (New York, Viking, 1957), pp. 189-90.
52. Louis O. Coxe and Robert Chapman, *Billy Budd* (Princeton, N.J., Princeton University Press, 1951), Act III, scene 1, p. 47.
53. Eugene O'Neill, *The Iceman Cometh* (New York, Random House, 1946), Act I, pp. 88-90.
54. Sidney Kingsley, *Detective Story* (New York, Random House, 1949), Act I, pp. 49-52.
55. Act I, p. 51.

5. Points of Focus (Pages 148-89)

1. Henri Bergson, "Laughter," in *Comedy*, Wylie Sypher, ed. (Garden City, N.Y., Doubleday, 1956), p. 180.
2. Allardyce Nicoll, *World Drama* (London, Harrap, 1949), p. 620.
3. Allardyce Nicoll, *The Theory of Drama* (New York, Thomas Y. Crowell, 1931), pp. 216-17.
4. Harley Granville-Barker, *Prefaces to Shakespeare* (Princeton, N.J., Princeton University Press, 1946), I, 11-12.
5. *World Drama*, p. 38.
6. P. 39.
7. John Galsworthy, *The Inn of Tranquility* (New York, Charles Scribner's Sons, 1932), p. 189.
8. Nicoll, *World Drama*, p. 818.
9. Chicago, University of Chicago Press, 1937, pp. ix, 4.
10. Brooks Atkinson, *The New York Times*, August 1, 1957.
11. *The New York Times*, February 27, 1949.
12. Norman Marshall, *The Producer and the Play* (London, McDonald, 1957), pp. 174-5.
13. "Cutting a Caper with the Bard," *New York Herald Tribune* (July 8, 1956), sec. 4, p. 3.
14. "Second Chance," *The New York Times* (July 8, 1956), sec. 2, p. 1.
15. *The Theory of Drama*, p. 56.
16. *Ibid.*, p. 57.
17. *Ibid.*
18. *Ibid.*, p. 243.
19. *Arts and the Man* (New York, W. W. Norton, 1939), pp. 33-4.

6. Directorial Image (Pages 190-214)

1. *The Encyclopaedia Britannica* (11th ed.; 1910-11), II, 318.
2. Burns Mantle, Foreword to *Riders to the Sea*, in *A Treasury of the Theatre*, Burns Mantle and John Gassner, eds. (New York, Simon & Schuster, 1935), p. 441.
3. John Gassner, *Masters of the Drama* (New York, Random House, 1940), p. 553.
4. *Ibid.*, p. 561.
5. Nicoll, *The Theory of Drama*, p. 99.
6. *World Drama*, pp. 691-2.
7. *Masters of the Drama*, pp. 556-7.
8. *The Theatre*, p. 86.

SELECTED BIBLIOGRAPHY

ANDERSON, MAXWELL. *The Essence of Tragedy and Other Footnotes and Papers*. Washington, D.C., Anderson House, 1939.

ARCHER, WILLIAM. *Play-Making*. London, Chapman & Hall, 1913.

BALMFORTH, RAMSDEN. *The Problem Play*. New York, Henry Holt, 1928.

BENTLEY, ERIC. *The Playwright as Thinker*. New York, Meridian Books, 1955.

BRADLEY, A. C. *Shakespearean Tragedy*. 2d ed. London, Macmillan, 1905.

BROOKS, CLEANTH, AND HEILMAN, ROBERT B. *Understanding Drama*. New York, Henry Holt, 1945.

BROWN, JOHN M. *The Art of Playgoing*. New York, W. W. Norton, 1936.

_____. *The Modern Theatre in Revolt*. New York, W. W. Norton, 1929.

BRUNETIERE, FERDINAND. *The Law of the Drama*. New York, Dramatic Museum of Columbia University, 1914.

BUTCHER, S. H. *Aristotle's Theory of Poetry and Fine Art*. 4th ed. New York, Dover Publications, 1951.

CENTANO, AUGUSTO, ed. *The Intent of the Artist*. Princeton, N.J., Princeton University Press, 1941.

CHANDLER, FRANK W. *Modern Continental Drama*. New York, Harper, 1931.

CHEKHOV, MICHAEL. *To the Actor*. New York, Harper, 1953.

CIBBER, COLLY. *An Apology for the Life of Mr. Colly Cibber*. London, John Watts, 1740.

CLARK, BARRETT H. *European Theories of the Drama*. New York, Crown, 1947.

CLURMAN, HAROLD. *Lies Like Truth*. New York, Macmillan, 1958.

COLE, TOBY, AND CHINOY, HELEN K., eds. *Directing the Play*. New York, Bobbs-Merrill, 1953.

DEAN, ALEXANDER. *Fundamentals of Play Directing*. New York, Farrar & Rinehart, 1941.

DEWEY, JOHN. *Art as Experience*. New York, Mintor, Balch, 1934.

EASTMAN, MAX. *Enjoyment of Laughter*. New York, Simon & Schuster, 1936.

EDMAN, ERWIN. *Arts and the Man*. New York, W. W. Norton, 1939.

ELIOT, T. S. *Poetry and Drama*. Cambridge, Mass., Harvard University Press, 1951.

FERGUSSON, FRANCIS. *The Idea of a Theatre*. Princeton, N.J., Princeton University Press, 1949.

FLATTER, RICHARD. *Shakespeare's Producing Hand*. New York, W. W. Norton, 1948.

FORSTER, E.M. *Aspects of the Novel*. New York, Harcourt, Brace, 1927.

FREUD, SIGMUND. *Wit and Its Relation to the Unconscious*. New York, Moffat, Yard, 1916.

GALLAWAY, MARIAN. *Constructing a Play*. New York, Prentice-Hall, 1950.

GASSNER, JOHN. *Form and Idea in Modern Theatre*. New York, Dryden Press, 1956.

_____. *Producing the Play*. Rev. ed. New York, Dryden Press, 1953.

GORELIK, MORDECAI. *New Theatres for Old*. New York, Samuel French, 1947.

GRANVILLE-BARKER, HARLEY. *Prefaces to Shakespeare*. Princeton, N.J., Princeton University Press, 1946. 2 vols.

GUTHRIE, TYRONE. *A Life in the Theatre*. New York, McGraw-Hill, 1959.

HAZLITT, WILLIAM. *Characters of Shakespeare*. Everyman ed. New York, E. P. Dutton, no date.

HOLLINGWORTH, H. L.   *The Psychology of the Audience.* New York, American Book Co., 1935.

HOUGHTON, NORRIS.   *Moscow Rehearsals.* New York, Harcourt, Brace, 1936.

JAMES, HENRY.   *The Scenic Art: Notes on Acting and the Drama.* New Brunswick, N.J., Rutgers University Press, 1948.

JONES, ROBERT E.   *The Dramatic Imagination.* New York, Duell, Sloan & Pearce, 1941.

KERR, WALTER.   *How Not To Write a Play.* New York, Simon & Schuster, 1955.

KNIGHT, G. WILSON.   *The Wheel of Fire.* London, Methuen, 1949.

KRUTCH, JOSEPH W.   *The American Drama since 1918.* New York, Random House, 1939.

LANGER, SUSANNE K.   *Philosophy in a New Key.* Cambridge, Mass., Harvard University Press, 1942, 1951.

LAWSON, JOHN H.   *Theory and Technique of Playwriting and Screenwriting.* 2d ed. New York, G. P. Putnam's Sons, 1939.

LUCAS, F. L.   *Tragedy.* New York, Harcourt, Brace, 1928.

MARITAIN, JACQUES.   *Creative Intuition in Art and Poetry.* New York, Meridian Books, 1955.

MARSHALL, NORMAN.   *The Producer and the Play.* London, McDonald, 1957.

MILLET, FRED B., AND BENTLEY, GERALD E.   *The Art of the Drama.* New York, D. Appleton-Century, 1935.

MULLER, HERBERT J.   *The Spirit of Tragedy.* New York, Alfred A. Knopf, 1956.

MYER, LEONARD.   *Emotion and Meaning in Music.* Chicago, University of Chicago Press, 1956.

NICOLL, ALLARDYCE.   *The Theory of Drama.* New York, Thomas Y. Crowell, 1931.

_____.   *World Drama.* London, Harrap, 1949.

OGDEN, ROBERT M.   *The Psychology of Art.* New York, Charles Scribner's Sons, 1938.

O'HARA, FRANK H.   *Today in American Drama.* Chicago, University of Chicago Press, 1939.

PEPPER, STEPHEN C.   *Principles of Art Appreciation.* New York, Harcourt, Brace, 1949.

_____.   *The Basis of Criticism in the Arts.* Cambridge, Mass., Harvard, University Press, 1949.

PRALL, D. W.   *Aesthetic Judgment.* New York, Thomas Y. Crowell, 1929.

PRIOR, MOODY E.   *The Language of Tragedy.* New York, Columbia University Press, 1947.

RAPHAELSON, SAMSON.   *The Human Nature of Playwriting.* New York, Macmillan, 1949.

ROWE, KENNETH T.   *Write That Play!* New York, Funk & Wagnalls, 1939.

SANTAYANA, GEORGE.   *The Sense of Beauty.* New York, Charles Scribner's Sons, 1896.

SARTRE, JEAN P.   *The Psychology of Imagination.* New York, Philosophical Library, 1948.

SEYLER, ATHENE, AND HAGGARD, STEPHEN.   *The Craft of Comedy.* New York, Theatre Arts, 1946.

SMITH, D. NICHOL, ed.   *Shakespeare Criticism 1919-35.* London, Oxford University Press, 1936.

SMITH, WILLARD.   *The Nature of Comedy.* Boston, Gorham Press, 1930.

SYPHER, WYLIE, ed.   *Comedy.* Garden City, N.Y., Doubleday, 1956.

THOMPSON, ALAN R.   *The Anatomy of Drama*. Berkeley and Los Angeles, University of California Press, 1946.
WELLEK, RENE, AND WARREN, AUSTIN.   *Theory of Literature*. New York, Harcourt, Brace, 1949.
WHITWORTH, GEOFFREY.   *Theatre in Action*. London, The Studio, 1938.
YOUNG, STARK.   *Theatre Practice*. New York, Charles Scribner's Sons, 1926.
_____.   *The Theatre*. New York, Hill & Wang, 1954.

INDEX

This is an index of people, plays, institutions, places, and books mentioned in the text. Additional references will be found in the legends for the illustrations and in the Selected Bibliography and References.